First published in Great Britain in 1996 by Osprey, an imprint of Reed Books Ltd, Michelin House, 81 Fulham Road, London, SW3 6RB, and Auckland, Melbourne, Singapore and Toronto.

ISBN 1 85532 615 9

Designed and Produced by Kew Nim, Connahs Quay, Shire Lane, Chorleywood, Hertfordshire, England.

Film origination by Krest Graphics Ltd, Unit 29, Riverside Business Centre, Victoria Street, High Wycombe, Buckinghamshire, England.

Produced by Mandarin Offset, 20th Floor, Eight Commercial Tower, 8 Sun Yip Street, Chai Wan, Hong Kong.

Printed in Hong Kong

Contents

Dedication

"When pilots did not return, I tried not to over-react,
but I was always concerned that
their sacrifice should not be forgotten."

Michael Wetz
*Pilot,
16 Squadron*

"The Photo-Reconnaissance pilots flew alone and unarmed
deep into enemy airspace. It was seldom known what
happened to those who did not return, a fact clearly
somewhat daunting for their comrades. Mostly they flew at
extreme altitudes and, until the advent of heating systems
and pressure cabins in their aircraft, they suffered
considerable hardships.
Their contribution to the pool of Allied Intelligence, upon
which the success of our military operations depended, was
enormous and can hardly be overstated.
Many of them were happy that their contribution could be
made without drawing blood but still at great personal risk
to themselves."

Jeffrey Quill
*Chief Test Pilot,
Vickers Supermarine*

Squadron Losses, 2nd TAF Period

16 (PR) SQUADRON LOSSES, 2ND TAF PERIOD
JULY 1943 - SEPTEMBER 1945

W/O R. Lidgate – killed on operational sortie 22.02.44

F/O A.L. Pearsall – missing on operational sortie 08.03.44

F/Lt M.A. McGilligan – killed on operational sortie 08.06.44

F/Sgt N.P. Morris – missing (PoW) on operational sortie 22.07.44

S/Ldr R.W. Atkinson – killed in ground accident 14.08.44

P/O H.E.W. Colgate – missing on operational sortie 31.08.44

F/O J. Wallace – missing on operational sortie 09.09.44

F/Lt A.G. Gibb – killed on operational sortie 18.09.44

P/O J.R. Brodby – killed on operational sortie 21.09.44

F/Lt J. Bastow – missing (returned) on operational sortie 21.09.44

F/Sgt D.W. Jolliffe – missing on operational sortie 01.10.44

P/O W.C. Heath – killed on operational sortie 18.11.44

F/Lt H.J.S. Taylor – missing (PoW) on operational sortie 19.11.44

F/O W.L. Johnston – killed in flying accident 30.12.44

F/Lt J.M.C. Horsfall – missing (PoW) on operational sortie 14.01.45

F/Lt J. Wheeler – killed in flying accident 08.09.45

Author's Note

I am indebted to all the individuals and organisations listed at the end of the story, and probably to many more whom I have missed out. Thank you all. But to all those who searched their memories for me, or lent printed matter, photographs and artefacts, I owe a particular vote of thanks. It seems invidious to pick out individuals for special mention, but here are a few who made very significant contributions: Bill Anderson, Gordon Bellerby, Scotty Cadan, Lewis Deal, Fred Efford, Ken Holloway, Mike Horsfall, Ron Parnell, Edgar Quested, Jimmy Taylor, Jack Thompson, and Mike Wetz, for wartime memoirs; and Professor J Ernsting, Simon Hague, Harry van der Meer, Theo Melchers, Ian Mulelly and John Welburn, for contemporary help.

I am also grateful to Chris Horsley, the current owner of PL 965, for giving me the opportunity to investigate a fascinating and largely unchronicled area of Spitfire operations during the Second World War, and thus to talk to a group of people of my father's generation for whom I have respect and admiration.

H.R.S.

F/Lt Eric Martin DFC, FM(E) Ron Parnell (Flight Mechanic Engines) and FM(A) Ron Abrahams (Flight Mechanic Airframes) of 16 Squadron at Northolt 1944. Parnell painted the appropriate "I Spy" gremlin on Martin's Spitfire, at his request. *(Photo: R. Abrahams)*

Foreword

This book is about Spitfire PL 965, which flew with 16 Squadron, Royal Air Force, on many operational sorties during the last year of the Second World War.

You cannot serve as a member of 16 Squadron without being imbued with its sense of history and proud traditions – a history that started on a quiet field outside St Omer in France in 1915 and has gone on largely unbroken ever since then. Those traditions in turn have been forged by the aircraft associated with the Squadron and, of course, by the men that flew and serviced them. And none have added more lustre to the Squadron's history than those men and machines, PL 965 among them, that flew with 16 Squadron during the Second World War.

This book serves as a tribute to those men and to the dedication and skill of those who lovingly restored her. The Squadron motto is *"Operta Aperta"* — "Hidden Things Shall be Revealed". This stems from the Squadron's reconnaissance rôle and serves as a fitting epithet for this splendid book. The memories that PL 965 evoked when she took to the skies again need no chronicling here. Her elegance and beauty are testimony enough to her distinguished past and eventful future.

Air Vice-Marshal David Cousins CB AFC RAF

Air Officer Commanding and Commandant
Royal Air Force College Cranwell
and
President of 16 Squadron
RFC and RAF Association

Prelude

How PL 965 came to 16 Squadron

16 Squadron, Melsbroek, Belgium – in the cockpit is "F/Lt Mike Horsfall, shot down just after this taken. But safe, and PoW", according to the note on the back of the photo. The ground-crew boys are also named: Cpl "Flash" Hayward, Jock Forster, Ken Holloway, Doug Jacques, Jock Pate, Beamish, Percy Last. All were FM(A)s except Cpl Hayward, who was a Fitter IIA (Airframe) and Holloway and Last, who were FM(E)s. *(Photo: K. Holloway)*

"14th January 1945 at Melsbroek, then quite a rural airfield outside Brussels. A splendid day, not a cloud in the sky: ideal for photography – and for interception.

"The sortie: 36-inch lens photocover of suspected airfields near Rheine, a lock-gate at Dortmund from 12,000 feet, marshalling-yards at Dusseldorf, and suspected rocket-sites in the Ruhr on the way home.

"At briefing, the Met. gave the mean climbing wind to 20,000 feet and the upper wind, usually 130-160 knots and backed about 30° from the climbing wind. From these the track, compass-course and ETA (Estimated Time of Arrival) at turning-points were marked on the charts and then stuck in the right boot. Navigation was then by DR (Dead Reckoning) – nothing sophisticated.

"I did my cockpit check on the runway threshold – T M P F F G H impregnated on the brain – got a green light from the hut, and was airborne at 12.30 hours – a nervous take-off, as the runway was strewn with splinters from a recent attack despite magnetic sweeping.

"For fuel economy, a fast climb to 20,000 feet was advised, thereafter moving to economical cruise at 340 TAS (True Air-Speed) and 2,100 rpm, immediately under the contrail (condensation-trail) level, so that anyone above could be seen.

"60 miles or more before reaching Germany, noisy oscillations in my ear-phones gave warning that I was now on the German radar plot and they had a good idea of my heading – henceforth life became busy.

"Accurate navigation required flying within 2° of the course and reconciling this with frequent weaving to check no one was under the tail – jets were then able to overtake from below. Inside, the wing-tanks had to be changed-over every 12 minutes to balance the aircraft, and the engine opened-up to de-lead the plugs. Spotting the enemy first was obviously vital; a suspicious object was lined-up with a convenient oil mark on the canopy and the angle watched with profound interest. If it remained constant, we had a problem.

"Passing over Rheine airfield, one of the German jet stations, I saw aircraft below. I reported this to Group, who asked for details; so I stayed some time watching them: 40-plus single- and twin-engined machines. I then descended towards the lock-gates – my priority task.

"Photographing the lock-gates took some time, as they were small and easily missed with the narrow field of the 36-inch lens at 12,000 feet. I then climbed back on course for Dusseldorf. On the way I vividly recall jumping out of my skin from a thump which shook the aircraft – the supercharger solenoid cutting-in, which I had forgotten to override during the descent. Shortly after this a more serious event: I had climbed into a major air battle and had Focke-Wulf Fw 190s on my tail.

"Aerobatics à la RFC had no future on PR. Our sole evasion was to slam the throttle through the wired-off emergency gate (3 minutes maximum), at the same time hauling the aircraft into a tight turn until black-out, and then, providing we did not flick and spin off the turn (which I did in fright on Christmas morning), climb for dear life. With the wing-tanks empty, the Spit XI was a splendid climber. With luck, this was happening.

"But suddenly the canopy disintegrated, the engine stopped and caught fire, the flying controls went slack, and all the instruments shattered. The full blast from a '190 was spectacular. Around 20,000 feet I left the aircraft and saw the dear old girl spiralling away in a smoke trail, until I lost sight of her. The contrast of absolute silence was staggering. I was a long time coming down, to a good landing in a fir tree near a flak site.

"My probable assailant, Uffz. Günter Sill of I/JG1 flying an Fw 190D-9, was sadly killed later in the day. The 16 Squadron Line Book lists seven sorties that morning. Four had brushes with enemy fighters, and two with American Mustangs – which could be just as frightening."

Later that day the Squadron's ORB (Operations Record Book) reported: "F/Lt Michael Coldwell-

Horsfall failed to return from his sortie to Dusseldorf and Almelo. We earnestly hope that some reassuring news will soon reach us. All the Squadron feel his loss intensely, because "Mike" as "A" Flight Commander and a Squadron colleague was extremely popular with everyone." Mike Horsfall was by then a Prisoner of War.

After an interval of two weeks F/Lt Douglas Petrie was appointed Flight Commander in his stead, but Horsfall's aeroplane (by design or coincidence) was replaced the same day by 34 WSU (Wing Support Unit). The brand-new Spitfire PR Mark XI was ferried across to Belgium from England and its serial number was PL 965.

F/Lt Mike Horsfall (left), with F/Lt David Stutchbury at the controls, June 17th 1945. The photo was taken by F/Lt Jimmy Taylor from the nose compartment of a Mosquito, which he was sharing with Gairns Lord Ossulston. The four were returning from Eindhoven to Hartford Bridge. Horsfall flew with 241 Squadron (in North Africa) before his stint with 16 Squadron, had operational experience on Hurricanes, Mustangs and Spitfires, and been obliged to bale out twice. *(Photo: H.J.S. Taylor)*

F/Lt David Stutchbury began flying with the Cambridge University Air Squadron and completed a Short Course in 1941. His Elementary Flying Training School (EFTS) was in Canada at Assinaboya, and Service Flying Training School (SFTS) at North Battleford, where he was selected for multi-engine rating. Advanced flying instruction was continued at AFU (Advanced Flying Unit) Snitterfield, and photo-reconnaissance specialisation at 8 OTU (Operational Training Unit) Dyce, in Scotland. Stutchbury's first operational posting was to 140 Squadron, from which he was transferred (eventually), after his navigator was killed and Mosquitos were withdrawn from daylight operations, owing to the depredations of the Messerschmitt Me 262 jet fighter. After a short break at 34 Wing Headquarters, he was posted to 16 Squadron in March 1945 (where he was converted to Spitfires by F/Lt "Tommy" Thompson), and to 26 Squadron in October, after 16 disbanded.

Battle of Britain Connection

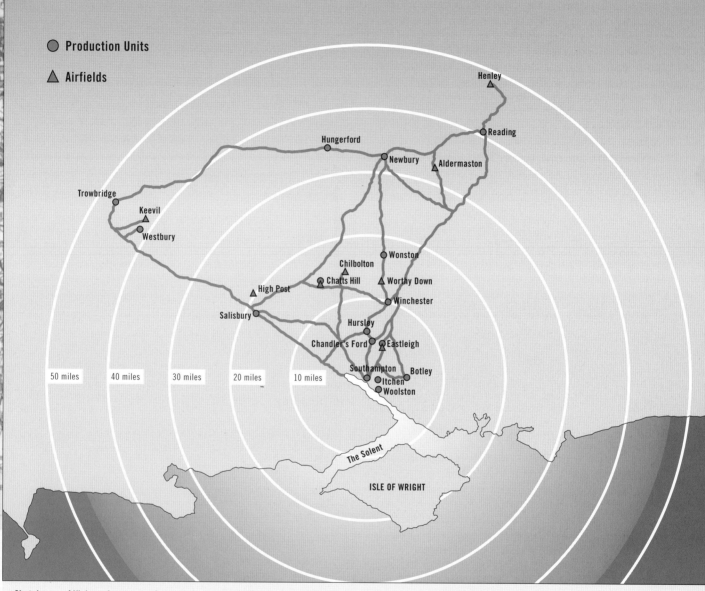

Production Units

Airfields

Henley

Reading

Hungerford

Newbury

Aldermaston

Trowbridge

Keevil

Westbury

Wonston

Chilbolton

Chatts Hill

Worthy Down

High Post

Winchester

Salisbury

Hursley

Chandler's Ford

Eastleigh

Southampton

Botley

Itchen

Woolston

50 miles 40 miles 30 miles 20 miles 10 miles

The Solent

ISLE OF WRIGHT

Sketch map of Vickers-Armstrongs Supermarine* Southern Region dispersed production centres. *See: Glossary; page 147.

PL 965, like all the production Spitfire PR (Photo-Reconnaissance) Mark XIs, was made in Vickers-Armstrongs Supermarine Southern Region, its components being made in scattered, small-scale workshops around the Thames Valley, and finally assembled at Aldermaston. The reason for this goes back to the height of the Battle of Britain.

August 23rd 1940 marked the first air raid in the Southampton area, which fortunately missed the Supermarine factories at Itchen and Woolston, which both lay alongside the Itchen River arm of Southampton Water. But on September 11th, when Eastleigh airport was dive-bombed, 49 people were killed and 92 injured – and it was there that

Spitfires built in Southampton were completed and tested. Pursuing its assault on Spitfire production, the Luftwaffe turned its attention to the Woolston works on the 15th, but though the building was damaged by blast, the bombs fell on surrounding property. The two factories were raided again on September 24th. Though Itchen did not receive a direct hit, it was damaged, and 90 people were killed and there were 40 other casualties, most of whom were aircraft workers. Another raid on Itchen the same day also hit adjacent buildings.

Two days later the bombers returned to finish the job. Despite the best efforts of the RAF fighters (which were effectively engaged by the bombers' escort) this time both the factories were completely wrecked and put out of production. There were another 92 deaths in and around the works, and a large number of injured. Once again, many of the casualties were valuable aircraft production workers.

The only consolation was, that by September 20th, Supermarine had already relocated the jig and tool department, wing production, fuselage and fuel-tank jigs and established a machine shop and tool-room at various remote locations in the city. For reasons of security and because expansion of the factories was difficult, suitable premises in the Southampton area had been requisitioned to provide what amounted to an alternative production line. Components and assemblies from this source could then be delivered to Eastleigh aerodrome for final erection and flight testing. These new production units were most often in garages, using workers who had no previous experience of aircraft manufacturing, but whose ranks were stiffened and trained by experienced Supermarine tradesmen. Others were in less likely venues: one workshop even occupied a commercial laundry.

The bombing of the two Southampton factories was a devastating blow to fighter production at a key moment in the aerial defence of Great Britain. Lord Beaverbrook (Prime Minister Winston Churchill's Minister of Aircraft Production) rushed down the same day to see for himself. He immediately applied all his autocratic power and energy to finding a means of recovery. Setting up a comprehensive but "dispersed" production system for Spitfires in the south of England began next day. Meanwhile, any existing components and the output of current sub-contractors were diverted to Vickers-Armstrongs' great "shadow factory" at Castle Bromwich, near Birmingham, to help boost the numbers of Spitfires coming from that source.

Dispersed production

Originally, the Air Ministry had made Supermarine responsible only for Spitfire fuselages, together with final assembly and flight testing. From the start, the manufacture of other components (even wings and tail assemblies) had been hived-off to various other firms. Inevitably, early production was plagued with bottle-necks and delays, as the sub-contractors struggled to get to grips with unfamiliar precision techniques and the multitude of innovations introduced with such a revolutionary new aircraft design. Although this was dispersed production of a kind, the key difference between it and the new system adopted after the bombing was that Supermarine controlled the new outstations directly, and could co-ordinate production more effectively.

Four towns with nearby aerodromes were selected as the focal points for a network of workshops. Each centre would deliver a quarter of the required number of Spitfires. These were Southampton, with Eastleigh Airport; Salisbury, with High Post and, soon after, Chattis Hill aerodromes; Trowbridge, with Keevil aerodrome; and Reading, with first Henley and later Aldermaston aerodromes.

Within six weeks, 35 of an eventual 65 units had been scouted and requisitioned, and a work-force established and set to work, 16 of them on day- and night-shifts. Luckily, machine tools and equipment had been salvaged from the wreckage in Southampton and could be installed in some places almost straightaway. Another problem was finding accommodation for experienced staff, who were distributed far and wide to supervise and train the locally-recruited work-force. It was an operation which demanded imagination, innovation and flexibility. It was made possible by the sheer hard work and dedication of the management, backed up by the sweeping powers of Beaverbrook. As a result of these measures, it has been calculated that by the end of 1940 the destruction of the factories probably cost the loss of no more than 90 new Spitfires (the equivalent of perhaps three weeks' production).

Aldermaston Spitfire

The unassuming exterior of the purpose-built works at Star Road, Caversham, Reading where Spitfire fuselages were fitted-out and engines installed – witness the low-loader truck carrying several Merlin engines which is just discernible in the main doorway behind the wire-mesh gates. A security guard is on duty in his brick-built gate-house which has defensive horizontal slit-windows. *(Photo: Vickers Collection)*

By the time that PL 965 was being built in mid-1944, the Reading centre had become specialised in the production of photo-reconnaissance marks of Spitfire. Eventually about 1,600 people (many of them women) were employed in the Reading area under manager Ken Scales, who was based at Vincent's Garage, Station Square, Reading. There it was that fuselages were built, sub-assemblies made up (such as instrument panels) and detail fitting accomplished. At a small purpose-built works in Star Road, Caversham, bare fuselages from Vincent's were fitted-out with wiring, hydraulic lines, fuel and oil plumbing, tanks, and other details. In both of these workshops engines were installed too.

Fuselage fuel tanks and other small parts like wing fairings and propeller spinners were made at Markhams, a coachbuilders in Caversham Road, while similar components came from Hawkins' in Erleigh Road, where aircraft fuel and oil tanks had been manufactured before the war.

The special leading edge torsion-box assembly of the wing was a very critical component, which had caused much grief in the pre-war phase of sub-contraction. By 1944, manufacture of this part was concentrated in Trowbridge and Salisbury, from where it was supplied to all areas. But the special leading edges for PR Spitfire wings were made exclusively in Salisbury. With no armament to worry about, the entire leading edge was sealed to provide an integral fuel tank in each wing. Complete wings were fabricated at Great Western Garage, Vastern Road, Reading. When a Spitfire was ready for final erection, engine runs and flight testing, the wings and fuselage would be loaded on to an Air Ministry Commer "Queen Mary" low-loader and transported to the aerodrome.

On the southern perimeter of the USAAF (United States Army Air Force) base at Aldermaston, and adjacent to its dispersal areas, was the Vickers compound. It was a small section surrounded by

Inside the Star Road, Caversham works. Comparison of the first two airframes (fighters) on the left with the third (PR) reveals different oil tanks and windscreens. Likewise, on the right, the second, third and fourth share those PR characteristics.There are also two tail fins visible with small PR-style fin flashes (the equal width of the red, white and blue stripes date the picture 1942 or '43). Six fuselages on the right (at the far end) also have engines installed. *(Photo: Vickers Collection)*

security fencing, which comprised a hangar with lean-to buildings, offices, stores, and a telephone exchange-cum-security building. In the hangar, the Spitfire's wings and fuselage were married; inspection panels, wing fillets and engine cowlings hand-finished and fitted; hydraulic, fuel, oil, air and electrical connections made; flying controls connected and undercarriage retraction checked. Finally, the propeller was added and (once fuelled-up) the aircraft was ready for final inspection, engine ground-running, and flight-testing.

Arthur Long has lived an easy bike ride from Aldermaston all his life. As a 16-year-old working at Thorneycrofts in Basingstoke, he answered an advertisement for tradesmen at Vickers. He started work three weeks before the first Spitfire parts arrived, which gave ample time to fit-out stores and put storage racks in place. He became specialised in hand-fitting cowlings, wing fillets and inspection covers at Aldermaston. Arthur remembers PR Spitfire '965 through a coincidence. The day he was directed to work on it he noticed its number was the same as the last three digits of his works clock number! He often wondered what became of "his" Spitfire. He recalls how every road leading to Aldermaston was guarded and all

residents and travellers needed a pass to enter the area. As Aldermaston was a USAAF base, it was not unusual to be asked "Care for a flip?" and (once airborne in a Dakota) to be invited casually to "Grab a handful of stick" by the co-pilot. These joy rides could range out over the Cotswolds or south to the Solent.

R.A. Forrester was the resident Rolls-Royce Service Engineer at Aldermaston. It was his responsibility to carry out the initial engine ground tests, adjust as necessary, rectify any snags, check the installations for leaks and effect a cure.

"The sequence of operations upon receipt of a fuselage and wings at Aldermaston," he explains "was the assembling of these items to form the aeroplane, and all inspection during these operations was undertaken by the AID (Aeronautical Inspection Directorate, who were the Air Ministry's representatives). They issued me with a Form (I think its number was 1395) which requested me to carry out the necessary ground test to prove the engine and its installation. Upon completion, this form together with a set of test results was returned to them and they then instructed the manufacturer to complete the aircraft ready for flight."

The original Rolls-Royce Merlin 70 engine installed in PL 965 was built at the Crewe works. It came from a batch of 70 (serial numbers between 184409-185331 – odd numbers only) under Air

The imposing facia of Vincent's Garage, Station Square, Reading, with its showroom windows covered with canvas and a defensive shutter with observation "letter boxes". Note the draped signboard and the air raid shelter sign on the lamp-post. *(Photo: Vickers Collection)*

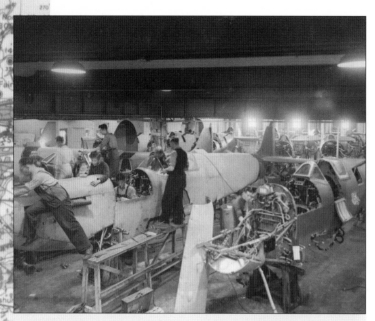

Spitfire fuselage construction at Vincent's Garage. In the centre, two workers are fitting the upper engine cowling (note the rubber mallet), another works in the fuel tank bay and three more work on the cockpit interior. The three exhaust stubs, slim fighter-style lower nose cowling and wrap-around windscreen denote a Spitfire PR Mark IV with a Merlin 40 series engine, the predecessor of the PR Mark XI. *(Photo: Vickers Collection)*

Making Spitfire wing leading edges at Anna Valley Motors, Salisbury. The four men on the left are working on a "bowser" wing for a PR Spitfire, which is identifiable by the two bulkheads, one showing a fuel feed connection and the other a "clack" valve. The completed leading-edge on the bench on the right also has a bulkhead just discernible inside it. About 15% of the workers are women. *(Photo: Vickers Collection)*

Ministry Contract SB23303/C28/A. Usually about 30 or 40 engines were tested each week and it is recorded that this one passed testing in the week ending August 26th 1944. It was dispatched ex-works on September 15th (the records also show that the engine was returned to Rolls-Royce for servicing or repair the following year and it was sent to 7 MU (Maintenance Unit), Quedgeley on December 12th 1945).

"...I carried out its first engine ground test on September 27th 1944 at the Vickers Supermarine dispersal unit at Aldermaston," remembers Bob Forrester. "Aldermaston Aerodrome was occupied by the USAAF and Vickers had an enclosed compound on the aerodrome and used the main runways. At the time of the ground test the engine was a Merlin 70 numbered Rolls-Royce 184489 and Air Ministry A482082. The propeller serial number appears to have been 6575, but I am not sure whether it was a Rotol or de Havilland Hydromatic unit.

"The following were the results obtained:
3000 rpm at 12 lbs boost
2900 rpm at 9 lbs boost
2875 rpm running on inlet magneto at 9 lbs
2850 rpm running on exhaust magneto at 9 lbs
2750 rpm at 7 lbs boost
2600 rpm at 4 lbs boost
Oil pressure 85 psi at 50°C
Coolant temperature 120°C
Fuel pressure 14 psi
Vacuum (for blind flying instruments) set to
   4½" Hg

"Incidentally, of the known survivors of the PR Mark XI, PL 965, PL 979 and PL 983 passed through my hands."

Before running-up the engine, the Spitfire was securely attached to the ground. A band was passed around the rear fuselage, which was secured to a ring in the concrete apron outside the hangar. A rope tied down the tail-wheel and the main wheels were chocked with angle-iron and strained back to the ring. It was also standard practice to drape three workers over the tail to help prevent it lifting as engine 'revs' were steadily increased from +7 boost (when the magnetos were checked) through +8 to +12. For some reason, more 'revs' were possible with the Rotol than with the de Havilland propeller. For the initial ground test, the vacuum line to the instruments of the "blind-flying" panel was "broken" and a "slave" vacuum gauge added. This enabled the vacuum to be ascertained and set to the necessary figure.

With ground-running checks completed to the satisfaction of Rolls-Royce's representative Bob Forrester (and again by the AID inspectors) PL 965 was moved to a nearby "pan handle" dispersal area which was marked out for compass-swinging. Others nearby were occupied by resident American aircraft. Here, alongside Douglas C-47s, Waco Hadrian gliders, Lockheed P-38 Lightnings or Republic P-47 Thunderbolts, it would await the arrival of a flight-test pilot.

There were about ten or twelve test pilots (concerned with both production and development), who were all based at High Post under Vickers Supermarine Chief Test Pilot Jeffrey Quill. Every day they were ferried around by light aeroplane to at least four dispersal airfields to fly Spitfires as they came off the production line. The more senior pilots were company men, but others were drawn at various times from the Fleet Air Arm, the RAF, the Belgian Air Force and the Norwegian Air Force and were often operational pilots on rest or, later, graduates of the Empire Test Pilots' School at nearby Boscombe Down. One day between September 27th and October 2nd, PL 965 was taxied out across the Reading road to

the Americans' hard runway, from which it made its first flight.

A standard production test flight schedule took about 40 minutes, and had to include at least three take-offs and landings. It covered not only a list of

The Spitfire hangar at Aldermaston in 1944. A Spitfire Mark VIII stands outside awaiting engine ground-running tests. *(Photo: Vickers Collection)*

Spitfire Mark VIIIs being completed in the final assembly hangar at Aldermaston in 1944. On either side of the rear door are racks for finished parts, tools and stores, inside lockable wire cages. There were also wire compounds for electricians, painters, carpenters, embodiment loan items (parts supplied by the Air Ministry such as radio and guns), Vickers' time-keepers, AID inspectors, Vickers' inspectors, log books, the site foreman, the chief engineer, and the Rolls-Royce representative. Several women are present (about 15% of the workers), an inspector in a white coat and at least one man who is smoking! *(Photo: Vickers Collection)*

Bob Forrester when he was at Supermarine at Eastleigh airport in 1940-41, at which time he was working on Mark I Spitfires. (Photo: R.A. Forrester)

essential functions of the aeroplane, but also checks of performance and handling at various stages throughout its flight envelope. Usually a few short flights were necessary to adjust aileron trim and engine boost and propeller pitch settings, before the proving flight. Then, during a climb to full-throttle height of at least 18,000 feet under maximum continuous climbing power and at best climbing speed, all instrument readings were observed. To establish indicated top speed and the performance of the engine and supercharger, the Spitfire would then make a two-minute level run at maximum combat power settings. This was followed by a full-power dive to the limiting indicated airspeed of 470 mph, during which trim and control responses were checked. The system had been in operation since 1938, after being set up by Jeffrey Quill and George Pickering at Supermarine and ensured a thorough appraisal of every Spitfire before it was released for delivery. It was maintained throughout the production life of the type, though different marks did require modifications or additions to the rule. At High Post the high standard of production testing was rigorously maintained.

After its successful test flight, a ferry pilot of the civilian ATA (Air Transport Auxiliary) collected

	6540			
PL 965		184469/ 482082	27-9-44.	
RPM at 12	3000		Oil Press.	85lbs
" " 9	2900		" Temp.	50°
" on In.	2875		Glycol -	120°
" " Ex.	2850		Fuel Press.	14lbs.
" at 7.	2750		Vac.	4½"HG.
" " 4.	2600		Charge.	20-14½
	6575			

A page from the notebook of Rolls-Royce Service Engineer R.A. (Bob) Forrester with details of the engine test he carried out on Spitfire PL 965 at Aldermaston.

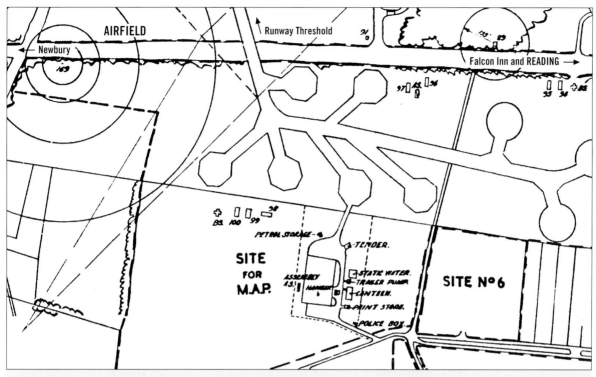

Sketch map of the southern dispersal area of Aldermaston airfield, showing the location of the Vickers hangar.

Arthur Long in 1993. He made himself the aluminium PR Spitfire as a souvenir before he left Aldermaston. *(Photo: H.R. Smallwood)*

PL 965 from Aldermaston and delivered it to the destination allotted to it by No. 41 Group, RAF Maintenance Command. This was 9 MU, Cosford, Shropshire, where it was accepted on October 2nd 1944. At this time it was the proud boast of ATA Commodore Gerard d'Erlanger that "Every machine you see in the sky has been or will be flown at some period of its life by a pilot of the ATA".

It was indeed a remarkable organisation, which was originally conceived as the National Air Communications Scheme by Sir Francis Shelmerdine (then Director General of Civil Aviation at the Air Ministry) before the opening of hostilities. It was intended to be a reserve of experienced civil pilots for civil defence, communications, or ambulance work. But in 1940 its pilots were diverted to delivering aircraft from the factories to RAF Maintenance Units (and soon from the MUs to field squadrons), which relieved operational RAF pilots of a vital, but non-combative duty. Throughout the rest of the war, ATA men and women ferried every type of aircraft from biplane trainers to four-engined bombers and flying boats. Out of a total of 1,515 aircrew, 143 lost their lives in the course of duty.

Spitfire type 365, Photo-Reconnaisance, PR Mark XI

Early photo-reconnaissance Spitfires were adaptations of Mark I and Mark V fighter airframes, originally referred to as Spitfires Types A to G. But from the summer of 1941 until the advent of the PR Mark XI in autumn 1942, the main work-horse of the PR units was the PR Mark IV. This was basically an unarmed, un-armoured Mark V fighter, with the current Rolls-Royce Merlin 45 or 46 power plant. Most were conversions (there was only a small run of true production Mark IVs) and, broadly speaking, PR status resulted from the fitting of cameras and special wings with leading edge fuel tanks (each with a capacity of 66$\frac{1}{2}$ gallons), which gave the PR Mark IV a total capacity of 218 gallons (including fuselage tanks). This

therefore gave it a greatly increased radius of operation. These wings were originally a distinguishing feature of the Spitfire Type D.

By the summer of 1942 the Spitfire Mark IX was beginning to re-equip the fighter squadrons and was welcomed for its vastly enhanced rate of climb and power at altitude. This was conferred by the Rolls-Royce Merlin series 60 engines. The spectacular improvement in performance was the result of two-speed, two-stage supercharging and came in the nick of time, because the Luftwaffe's excellent new Focke-Wulf Fw 190 fighter was very much superior to the current Spitfire Mark V. When fitted with the Merlin 70 it also benefited from a Rolls-Royce Bendix-Stromberg carburettor which

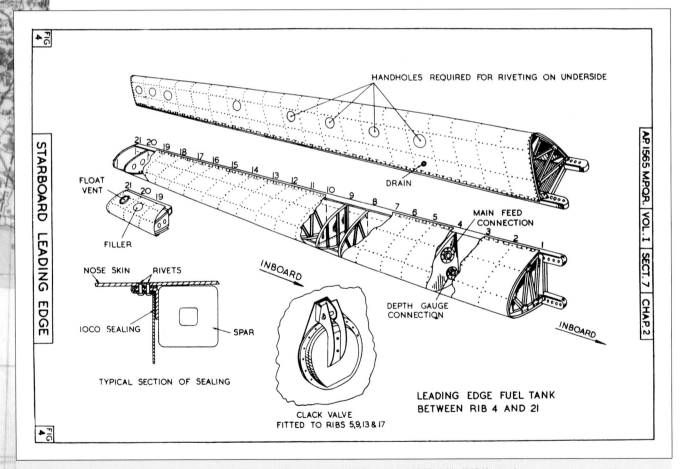

The starboard wing leading edge fuel tank (capacity 66$\frac{1}{2}$ gallons) of the Spitfire PR Mark IV and PR Mark XI. *(RAF Museum)*

| Mark number | TAKE-OFF | | COMBAT RATING | | | | | | weight (dry) |
| | boost lb/sq in | bhp | Low gear | | | High gear | | | |
			boost	bhp	altitude	boost	bhp	altitude	
45	12	1,185	one-speed, one-stage			16	1,470	9,250 ft	1,385 lb
46	12	1,100	one-speed, one-stage			16	1,415	14,000 ft	1,385 lb
61	12	1,280	15	1,560	12,000 ft	15	1,370	24,000 ft	1,640 lb
63/63A	12	1,280	18	1,710	8,500 ft	18	1,510	21,000 ft	1,645 lb
70	12	1,250	18	1,655	10,000 ft	18	1,475	22,250 ft	1,640 lb

Power increase of the two-stage, two-speed supercharged Rolls-Royce Merlin engines fitted to the Spitfire PR Mark XI, over the single-speed, single-stage supercharged Merlin of the Spitfire PR Mark IV.

injected fuel into the "eye" of the supercharger.

It is nearly impossible to find performance figures for aircraft/engine combinations which can properly be compared, because tests were carried out to provide answers to very particular questions in specific areas of development and data was not recorded in a consistent or comprehensive way. For example, figures are available for level speed at various altitudes for the PR Mark XI (Merlin 63) but there are no rate of climb figures to match. Any figures at all for the PR Mark IV are hard to find, so one must assume that the lighter Mark Va fighter with a similar engine would provide data close enough for comparative purposes. Therefore, broadly speaking, at 15,000 feet the PR Mark XI's level speed was 50 mph greater than the PR Mark IV, 60 mph greater at 20,000 feet, and 65 mph greater over 25,000 feet. Initial rate of climb was actually about 390 feet per minute lower than that of the PR Mark IV, but by 10,000 feet the PR Mark XI was climbing 1,340 more feet per minute, giving a time advantage to 20,000 feet of about 2 1/2 minutes. In terms of service ceiling, the PR Mark XI enjoyed an advantage of well over 6,000 feet.

For the purposes of long-range reconnaissance work, rate of climb is of lesser importance than speed at operational heights because, unlike the fighter which requires high rates of climb and speed for short intervals during combat, the PR aircraft climbs steadily to operational altitude after take-off, and maintains fast level flight for long periods over much greater distances. Once established above 20,000 feet, changes of altitude (which might take it above 40,000 feet) would be made with slow cruise climbs. However, without cockpit pressurisation, the pilots could not work for long at more than 7 1/2 miles above the surface of the earth, on the edge of the stratosphere.

The Spitfire PR Mark XI can be described briefly as a Mark IX fighter minus armament and some armour. It had PR Mark IV wing leading edge (Type D) tanks and an increased capacity oil tank (14.4 gallons) as originally found on the Type F. The enlarged oil tank under the engine gave its profile a distinctive "chin". Other features of the production PR Mark XI (rather than Mark IX conversions) were a drag-reducing retractable tail-wheel (characteristic of the Mark VII and VIII fighters) and one-piece wrap-around windscreen.

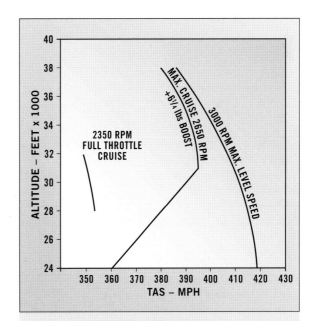

Diagram of the effect of high altitude on level speed performance of the Spitfire PR Mark XI (Merlin 63).

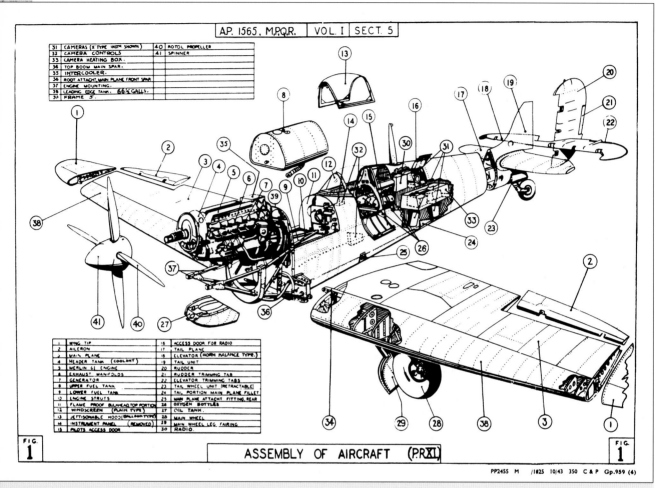

31	CAMERAS (X TYPE INSTN SHOWN)	40	ROTOL PROPELLER
32	CAMERA CONTROLS	41	SPINNER
33	CAMERA HEATING BOX.		
34	TOP BOOM MAIN SPAR.		
35	INTERCOOLER.		
36	ROOT ATTACHT. MAIN PLANE FRONT SPAR		
37	ENGINE MOUNTING.		
38	LEADING EDGE TANK. 66½ GALLS.		
39	FRAME 5.		

1	WING TIP	16	ACCESS DOOR FOR RADIO
2	AILERON	17	TAIL PLANE
3	MAIN PLANE	18	ELEVATOR (HORN BALANCE TYPE.)
4	HEADER TANK (COOLANT)	19	TAIL UNIT
5	MERLIN 61 ENGINE	20	RUDDER
6	EXHAUST MANIFOLDS	21	RUDDER TRIMMING TAB
7	GENERATOR	22	ELEVATOR TRIMMING TABS
8	UPPER FUEL TANK	23	TAIL WHEEL UNIT (RETRACTABLE)
9	LOWER FUEL TANK	24	TAIL PORTION MAIN PLANE FILLET
10	ENGINE STRUTS	25	MAIN PLANE ATTACHT FITTING, REAR
11	FLAME PROOF BULKHEAD TOP PORTION	26	OXYGEN BOTTLES
12	WINDSCREEN (PLAIN TYPE)	27	OIL TANK.
13	JETTISONABLE HOOD (BALLOON TYPE)	28	MAIN WHEEL
14	INSTRUMENT PANEL (REMOVED)	29	MAIN WHEEL LEG FAIRING
15	PILOTS ACCESS DOOR	30	RADIO

FIG. 1

ASSEMBLY OF AIRCRAFT (P.R.XI)

FIG. 1

PP2455 M /1025 10/43 350 C & P Gp.959 (4)

The main components of the Spitfire PR Mark XI. *(RAF Museum)*

Spitfire Type 365 PR Mark XI – General Information

Armament: none

Engine: Rolls-Royce Merlin 61, 63, 63A (260 aircraft produced) or 70 (211 aircraft produced)

Propeller: four-blade Rotol R3/4F5/2 or 3, R5/4F5/5, or R12/4F5/4

Carburettor: Rolls-Royce Bendix-Stromberg negative g (the PR Mark XI was the first PR Spitfire so equipped)

Dimensions: span 36 feet 10 inches; length 31 feet to 31 feet 4 1/2 inches (depending upon the engine or rudder fitted) height 12 feet 7 3/4 inches

Wing area: 242 square feet

Weight: empty 5,630 pounds; loaded 7,900 pounds; maximum permitted 8,700 pounds.

Maximum speeds with Rolls-Royce Merlin 70: 335 mph at sea level; 398 mph at 15,000 feet; 422 mph at 27,500 feet

Rate of climb: 4,350 feet per minute (initial); 4,580 feet per minute (at 10,000 feet). Time to 20,000 feet: 5 minutes

Service ceiling: 44,000 feet

Fuel capacity: 48 + 37 gallons (upper and lower fuselage tanks); 66 1/2 x2 (wing leading edge tanks); total 218 gallons

Oil capacity: 14.4 gallons in an enlarged tank under the engine

Range: 1,360 miles (maximum)

Special Equipment: air cameras; one-piece windscreen; retractable tail wheel; transmitter/receiver wireless (TR 1133 or TR 1143) with beam approach equipment; Vokes Aero-Vee filter ("tropicalised" engine air intake filter on all Merlin 70 and most 60 series engines)

The need to upgrade the first generation of PR Spitfires became so urgent that No.1 PRU produced its own 15 conversions from Mark IX fighters at Benson, the first being completed in October 1942. Initially the specialised job of fabricating and sealing the wing leading edge tanks was to be done by Heston Aircraft, but Supermarine quickly decided to do the job and converted all future airframes intended for PR aircraft on the Mark IX production lines.

In 1944 a Spitfire PR Mark XI was used for high-speed dive tests. The object of the exercise was to test handling at speeds close to the sound barrier. In one test a true airspeed of 606 mph (Mach .89) was achieved before the reduction gear failed and broke away with the propeller. S/Ldr Martindale was nevertheless able to glide back to Farnborough and land the aircraft with wheels down.

Air cameras for the Spitfre PR Mark XI

A variety of camera combinations was possible in the Spitfire PR Mark XI in a "U" (universal) installation situated between rear fuselage frames 13, 14 and 15. Two vertical cameras could be installed, with an oblique camera above. The vertical cameras were principally used for surveillance, mapping, and bomb damage assessment from medium to high level. They were normally matched and vertically fanned to port and starboard so that two overlapping photographs could be taken simultaneously. The oblique instrument was intended for medium to low level tactical work. The camera ports were covered by 1/4-inch plate glass.

Later when PR Mark XIs were needed to assist the army on the battlefield by photographing

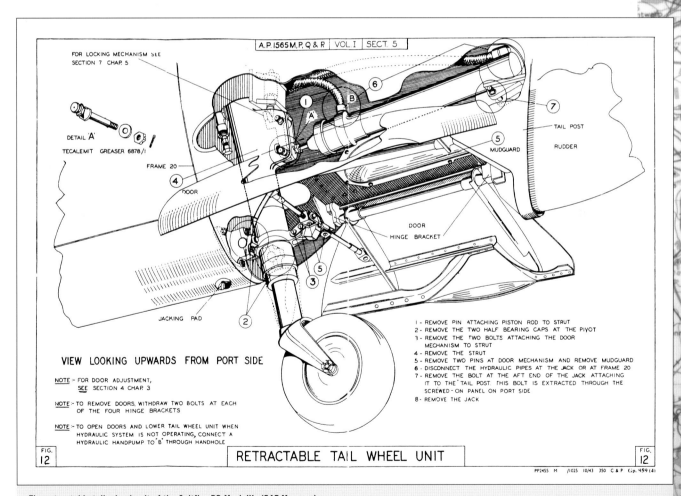

The retractable tail-wheel unit of the Spitfire PR Mark XI. *(RAF Museum)*

specific targets, an additional camera layout was devised. The standard (vertical) long focal-length lenses covered too small an area of ground if the Spitfire was forced by cloud to fly below normal operational level. A small target could be easily missed. The solution was to fit a shorter focal-length camera beneath each wing (aft of the main spar between ribs 9 and 12) in a small blister fairing. Each one was tilted slightly outward from the vertical and was protected by a glass window which was covered by a metal mud-flap during take-off.

The Spitfire PR Mark XI utilised three types of camera known as the Type F8, Type F24, and Type F52.

Type F8 camera

This fairly bulky camera was developed by the RAF in the inter-war years for standard service use.

It was the first large-format film (rather than plate) camera. Originally it was operated by a flexible drive from a small windmill fitted outside the aircraft, but this power source was later replaced by an electric motor. However, the flexible drive (which was favoured by the RAF) was retained. The camera was fully automatic with remote control to start, stop and set the time interval between exposures. Eventual picture format was $8^{1/2}$ x 7 inches.

The PR Mark XI Spitfire used the Mark 2 or 2a version of the F8 camera, with 20-inch focal-length lenses of f/6.3 or f/5.6 maximum aperture respectively, for vertical fuselage installation. The focal-plane shutter was equipped with three optional blinds with different slit widths and variable tensions, which gave a range of exposure speeds from $^1/75$ to $^1/500$ of a second. The film

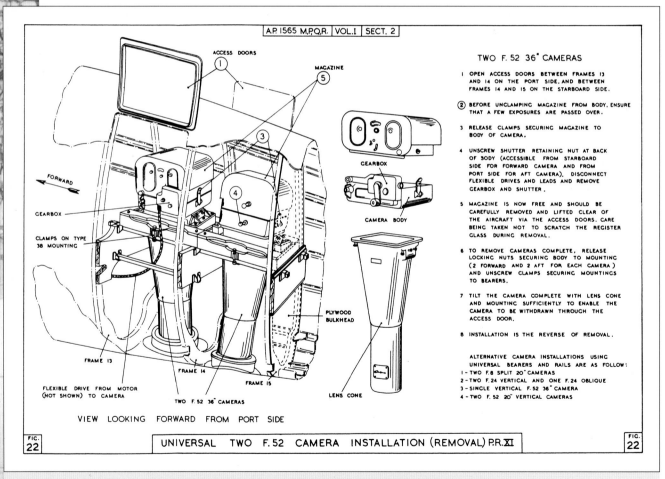

Two vertical F52 cameras in the "Universal" camera installation of the Spitfire PR Mark XI. *(RAF Museum)*

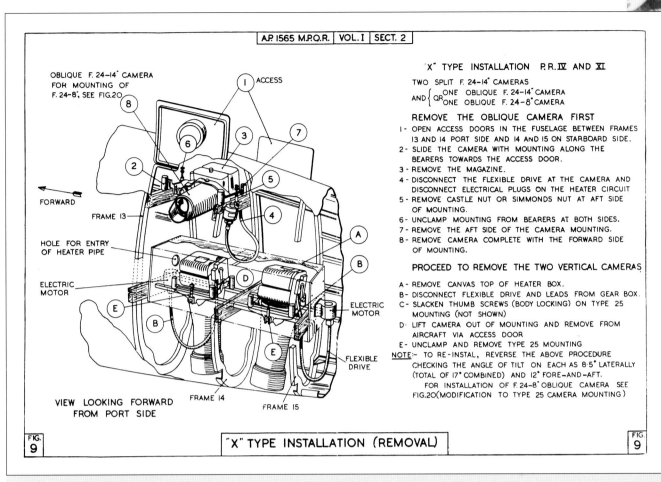

OBLIQUE F. 24-14" CAMERA
FOR MOUNTING OF
F. 24-8", SEE FIG.20

1 ACCESS

"X" TYPE INSTALLATION P.R. IV AND XI

TWO SPLIT F. 24-14" CAMERAS
AND { ONE OBLIQUE F. 24-14" CAMERA
OR ONE OBLIQUE F. 24-8" CAMERA

REMOVE THE OBLIQUE CAMERA FIRST

1 - OPEN ACCESS DOORS IN THE FUSELAGE BETWEEN FRAMES 13 AND 14 PORT SIDE AND 14 AND 15 ON STARBOARD SIDE.
2 - SLIDE THE CAMERA WITH MOUNTING ALONG THE BEARERS TOWARDS THE ACCESS DOOR.
3 - REMOVE THE MAGAZINE.
4 - DISCONNECT THE FLEXIBLE DRIVE AT THE CAMERA AND DISCONNECT ELECTRICAL PLUGS ON THE HEATER CIRCUIT
5 - REMOVE CASTLE NUT OR SIMMONDS NUT AT AFT SIDE OF MOUNTING.
6 - UNCLAMP MOUNTING FROM BEARERS AT BOTH SIDES.
7 - REMOVE THE AFT SIDE OF THE CAMERA MOUNTING.
8 - REMOVE CAMERA COMPLETE WITH THE FORWARD SIDE OF MOUNTING.

PROCEED TO REMOVE THE TWO VERTICAL CAMERAS

A - REMOVE CANVAS TOP OF HEATER BOX.
B - DISCONNECT FLEXIBLE DRIVE AND LEADS FROM GEAR BOX.
C - SLACKEN THUMB SCREWS (BODY LOCKING) ON TYPE 25 MOUNTING (NOT SHOWN)
D - LIFT CAMERA OUT OF MOUNTING AND REMOVE FROM AIRCRAFT VIA ACCESS DOOR
E - UNCLAMP AND REMOVE TYPE 25 MOUNTING

NOTE:- TO RE-INSTAL, REVERSE THE ABOVE PROCEDURE CHECKING THE ANGLE OF TILT ON EACH AS 8·5° LATERALLY (TOTAL OF 17° COMBINED) AND 12° FORE-AND-AFT.
FOR INSTALLATION OF F. 24-8" OBLIQUE CAMERA SEE FIG.20 (MODIFICATION TO TYPE 25 CAMERA MOUNTING)

FORWARD

FRAME 13

HOLE FOR ENTRY OF HEATER PIPE

ELECTRIC MOTOR

ELECTRIC MOTOR

FLEXIBLE DRIVE

VIEW LOOKING FORWARD FROM PORT SIDE

FRAME 14
FRAME 15

FIG. 9

"X" TYPE INSTALLATION (REMOVAL)

FIG. 9

An F24 camera mounted for oblique photography in the "X-type" camera installation of the Spitfire PR Mark XI. The same oblique mounting was utilised in the "Universal" camera installation. *(RAF Museum)*

magazines were interchangeable, each being fitted with a fold-over flap for protection when removed from the camera.

Type F24 camera

Also introduced between the wars, this general purpose camera was fully automated, with interchangeable magazines, and its gearbox allowed for a complete cycle of operations within 1.6 seconds. It could be fitted with a range of different focal-length lenses, those used in the Spitfire PR Mark XI were: 5-inch for wing camera installation, and 8-inch (f/2.9 or f/5.6) or 14-inch for vertical or oblique fuselage installation. There were four shutter blinds with different slit widths (plus a facility to fully cover or uncover the film for night photography) and variable tensions, which gave a range of exposure speeds from $1/60$ to $1/1000$

of a second. These features made it a very versatile camera, particularly for use in smaller reconnaissance aircraft, the picture format being 5 x 5 inches.

Type F52 camera

Designed to replace the Type F8, this camera became the RAF's main photo-reconnaissance equipment during WWII. A range of seven lenses, specially collimated to its body, was available. The Spitfire PR Mark XI utilised the 20-inch focal length f/5.6 or f/6.3 lens and the 36-inch f/6.3 or f/6 lens in vertical fuselage installations. It employed a similar gearbox to that of the Type F24 and film magazines for 250 and 500 exposures on 9-inch sprocket-driven film were available. The picture format was $8^{1/2}$ x 7 inches.

Formidable Opponents

The Spitfire PR Mark XI had three new opponents by the time that PL 965 entered service during the last five months of the Second World War, although the two least conventional turned out to be less of a practical problem than was at first feared.

After initial misgivings, the Focke-Wulf Fw 190-D9 *"Dora-9"* (or *"langnasen-Dora"*) was eventually thought by many a *Jagdflieger* to be the finest piston-engined fighter ever operated by the *Luftwaffe*. It differed from its radial-engined production predecessors in having a 12-cylinder liquid-cooled V-configuration engine – the Junkers Jumo 213A-1. Although this aircraft was hoped to be the answer to the high level daylight bomber menace, it remained most potent at flight levels up to 20,000 feet, where its rate of climb, level speeds, dive performance and manoeuvrability eclipsed all other conventional German fighters and most of the Allied types too.

The Messerschmitt Me 262A-1a *Schwalbe* was the first turbo-jet fighter to go into service anywhere in the world. As such, it provoked much apprehension among the Allies. In the autumn of 1944 they had no operational fighter that could get within 70 mph of the Me 262 at best level speed. It was that superiority (which it maintained at altitudes well in excess of 20,000 feet) which was of special significance to the fast, high-flying but unarmed PR Spitfires, which were often engaged in

Vickers Supermarine Spitfire PR Mark XI

photographing suspected jet airfields.

The Me 262 was, however, very vulnerable to attack while taking-off and landing. The two Junkers Jumo 004 turbo-jet engines could only be given full thrust after some altitude had been achieved – and were closed down for a glide approach to touch-down. Emergency attempts to restart usually failed, or resulted in sudden (disastrous) asymmetric thrust if only one re-lit. Focke-Wulf Fw D-9s were among the conventional fighters detailed to protect them at these critical times. Paradoxically, the jet was also compromised when it was attacking the bomber streams, because pilots often decelerated dramatically in order to engage the "heavies". Thus it temporarily lost its advantage over both the escorting fighters and the gunners of its intended victims.

The Messerschmitt Me 163B-1a *Komet* rocket aircraft was even more unconventional, being a tiny,

tail-less swept-wing interceptor propelled by a Walter HWK 509A-1 (or -2) rocket motor. Its fuel consisted of a pair of lethally toxic chemicals known as *T-Stoff* and *C-Stoff*, which reacted violently when mixed together to produce a maximum thrust rating of 3,748 psi (pounds per square inch). Its rate of climb to service ceiling was phenomenal, as the figures in the table on page 26 reveal, but its spectacular fuel consumption allowed it a maximum of only 12 minutes of powered flight. Its tactics were to climb high above the target and swoop down in a glide attack at an unapproachable high speed, then either zoom up for another pass (if the motor re-lit) or continue the glide back to base. Unfortunately, once the motor died the Me 163 was even more vulnerable to conventional attack than the Me 262 and its pilot still had to face a one-off, 160 mph landing (after jettisoning the explosive dregs of his fuel) on a belly-skid!

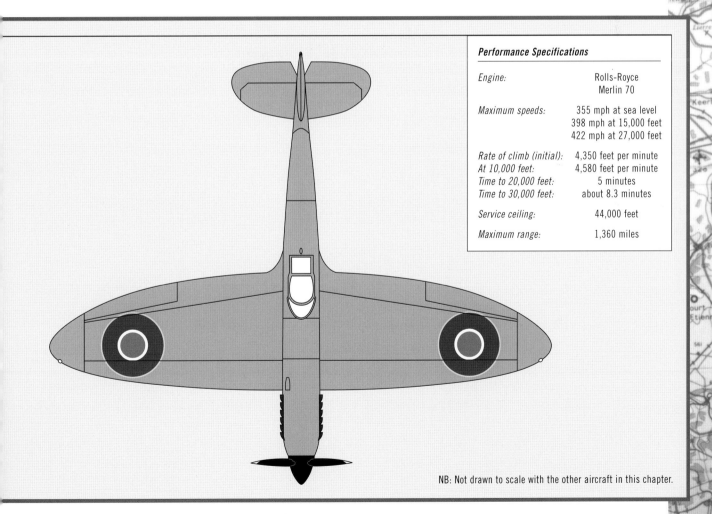

Performance Specifications

Engine:	Rolls-Royce Merlin 70
Maximum speeds:	355 mph at sea level
	398 mph at 15,000 feet
	422 mph at 27,000 feet
Rate of climb (initial):	4,350 feet per minute
At 10,000 feet:	4,580 feet per minute
Time to 20,000 feet:	5 minutes
Time to 30,000 feet:	about 8.3 minutes
Service ceiling:	44,000 feet
Maximum range:	1,360 miles

NB: Not drawn to scale with the other aircraft in this chapter.

Focke-Wulf FW 190-D9

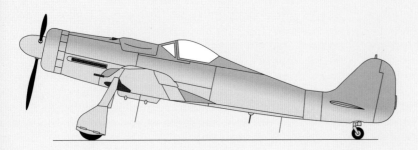

Performance Specifications

Engine:	Junkers Jumo 213A-1
Maximum speeds:	357 mph at sea level
	397 mph at 10,830 feet
	426 mph at 21,650 feet
	397 mph at 32,810 feet
Rate of climb (initial):	3,124 feet per minute
At 13,120 feet:	2,915 feet per minute
Time to 19,685 feet:	7.1 minutes
Time to 32,810 feet:	16.8 minutes
Service ceiling:	39,372 feet
Maximum range:	520 miles

NB: Not drawn to scale with the other aircraft in this chapter.

Messerschmitt Me 262A-1a

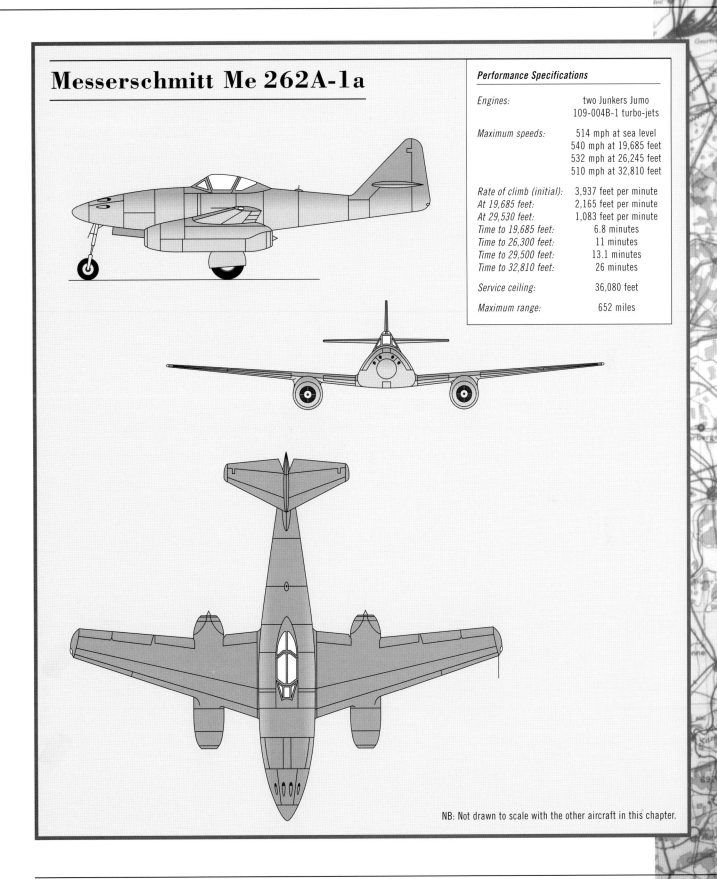

Performance Specifications

Engines:	two Junkers Jumo 109-004B-1 turbo-jets
Maximum speeds:	514 mph at sea level
	540 mph at 19,685 feet
	532 mph at 26,245 feet
	510 mph at 32,810 feet
Rate of climb (initial):	3,937 feet per minute
At 19,685 feet:	2,165 feet per minute
At 29,530 feet:	1,083 feet per minute
Time to 19,685 feet:	6.8 minutes
Time to 26,300 feet:	11 minutes
Time to 29,500 feet:	13.1 minutes
Time to 32,810 feet:	26 minutes
Service ceiling:	36,080 feet
Maximum range:	652 miles

NB: Not drawn to scale with the other aircraft in this chapter.

Messerschmitt Me 163B-1a

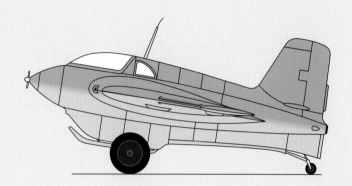

Performance Specifications

Engine:	Walter HWK 509A-1 or A-2 rocket motor
Maximum speeds:	516 mph at sea level 593 mph from 9,850 to 29,500 feet
Rate of climb (initial):	15,950 feet per minute
At 32,800 feet:	33,470 feet per minute
Time to 29,500 feet:	2.6 minutes
Time to 39,370 feet:	3.35 minutes
Service ceiling:	52,480 feet
Maximum range:	78 miles

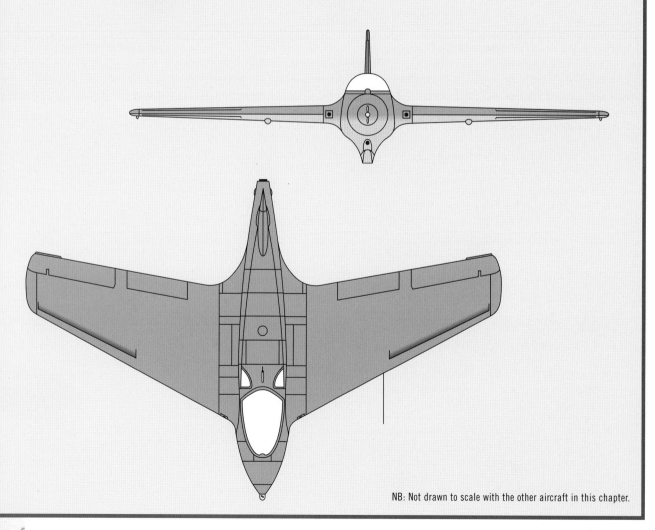

NB: Not drawn to scale with the other aircraft in this chapter.

IP & IP

PL 965 spent two months at 9 MU Cosford, Shropshire, having service equipment fitted (including radio) and awaiting allocation to an operational unit. Then, on January 5th 1945, it was moved to No.1 Photo-Reconnaissance Unit (PRU) at RAF Benson. More specifically, it went to a unit known as "IP & IP" – Initial Preparation and Installation Photographic. Once again the delivery pilot would have been ATA and, though only 15% of them were female, they are still remembered with particular appreciation by the RAF pilots.

"It was quite a sensation when Spitfires were first delivered to Benson by young lady ATA pilots – and very good they were too (the young ladies!)" recalls F.H.C. Efford DFC, then Flight Lieutenant in command of the IP & IP Flight.

"One hangar at Benson (a pre-war regular airfield) was given over to the work-force that dealt with the initial preparation work and the installation of the photographic gear. When the hangar personnel had completed their tasks the aircraft (Spitfires and Mosquitos) all came to IP & IP Flight for testing, before handing over to an operational unit."

After the fitting of photographic equipment and the incorporation of the latest engine and airframe modifications, he test-flew PL 965 twice. The first was a 15-minute sortie on January 9th when the

F/Lt F.H.C. Efford DFC (right) with a PR Mosquito at IP & IP Flight, No.1 PRU Benson. *(Photo: F.H.C. Efford)*

aircraft proved satisfactory to 2,000 feet, and the second was a 45-minute sortie on January 11th on altitude test – which was again without problems.

"My test was largely based upon experience. You developed a feeling and could usually tell if all was not right. I would walk slowly round the aircraft checking that all looked and felt correct. Sitting in the cockpit, I did the same and made certain that all the control surfaces worked freely and in their correct directions. Then there was the

YEAR 945		AIRCRAFT		PILOT, OR	2ND PILOT, PUPIL	DUTY	
MONTH	DATE	Type	No.	1ST PILOT	OR PASSENGER	(INCLUDING RESULTS AND REMARKS)	
-	-	—	—	—	—	——	TOTALS BROUGHT FORWARD
Jan.	3	SPITFIRE XI	PM125	SELF	–	TEST.	O.K TO 1,000'
Jan.	3	SPITFIRE XI	PL859	SELF	–	TEST.	O.K. " "
Jan.	9	SPITFIRE XI	PL965	SELF	–	TEST.	O.K. " 2,000
Jan.	10	SPITFIRE XI	PL970	SELF	–	ALT. TEST.	O.K.
Jan.	11	SPITFIRE XI	PL965	SELF	–	ALT. TEST.	O.K.
Jan.	14	SPITFIRE XI	PL968	SELF	–	COSFORD – BENSON.	
Jan.	14	SPITFIRE XI	PM143	SELF	–	TEST.	

Entries from the Flying Log Book of F/Lt F.H.C. Efford DFC recording his test flight sorties from Benson's IP & IP Flight in Spitfire PR Mark XI PL 965 on January 9th and 11th 1945.

engine run-up. Of course, you only used part-throttle on a Merlin (or Griffon), but you could see if the temperatures and pressures registered normal readings. Indeed, you could tell by the sound of the engine if all was well.

"Then there was the take-off – that was the danger time for any fault to show up, particularly with the Mosquitos. All being well, you continued climbing up to about 32,000 feet and en route noted: whether the engine temperature and pressures were normal; whether the airframe responded normally to control; whether the compasses (magnetic and gyro) were registering correctly; whether the radio was working properly. Incidentally, Mosquitos had two radios: a VHF like the Spitfires, but also another radio worked by the navigator which had a line aerial to lower, test and then rewind.

"At about 32,000 feet you would work the camera exposure control and counter and also test the cameras over a definite target (the film would later be processed to check all was OK). Finally, you would throw the aircraft around a bit and also do a flat-out dive with a sharp pull-out. If nothing dropped off and everything seemed well, the aeroplane had passed the test. Any defects noted would be corrected by the ground staff and the kite re-tested."

Service pilots normally took the tested Spitfires from Benson to the allotted squadrons, although F/Lt Efford very occasionally did that chore and sometimes collected them from the MU.

FLIGHT LIEUTENANT F.H.C. EFFORD DFC – PL 965 Pilot

In 1941 Fred Efford trained in Canada (Moosejaw) and Wales at 53 OTU (Llandow). Later that year he flew Spitfire fighters with 118 Squadron (Ibsley) and 41 Squadron (Merston) before joining No.1 PRU (Benson). In '41 and '42 he was on various detachments (St Eval, Gibraltar, Mount Farm) and in '43 was awarded the DFC. From July '43 to October '45 he was posted Flight Lieutenant in command of IP & IP Flight (Benson) until transfer to 540 Squadron. Total flying time on Anson, Auster, Harvard, Master, Spitfire, Mosquito: 1,035 hours (Spitfire 800, Mosquito 175).

"If you had taken off from Benson, landed at Southwold to have your fuel topped right up, flown on in daylight and alone to, say, Berlin, only to find that the weather forecast was inaccurate and the unexpected 5/10 cloud cover did not permit photography, you did quite well getting back to Benson all in one piece. We counted that as an operation. And although on that cited occasion you brought back no photographs, you had gained an immense amount of meteorological information which you had jotted down on you knee pad. I did 89 such flights."

Sorties in PL 965 (non-operational):

09.01.45: Test 15 min
11.01.45: Altitude Test 45 min
Total: 1 hr

F/Lt F.H.C. Efford DFC (left) listens to a "line-shooting" colleague on IP & IP Flight, No.1 PRU Benson. *(Photo: F.H.C. Efford)*

34 Wing, 2nd Tactical Air Force

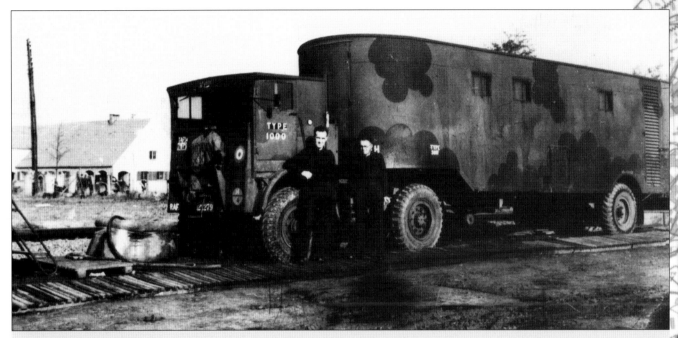

The multiprinter vehicle of No.7 Mobile Field Photographic Section, Melsbroek 1945. Note the "duck board" walkways and the large canvas water tank in front of the vehicle. *(Photo: RAF Museum)*

The same day that PL 965 was declared fit for action by F/Lt Efford, it was collected from Benson by F/Lt Douglas Petrie DFC, currently "on rest" from 16 Squadron with 34 Wing Support Unit (WSU) at Northolt, Middlesex. The trip from Benson to Northolt took 20 minutes.

Spitfire PR Mark XI PL 965 had been allocated to 34 Wing of 2nd TAF (Second Tactical Air Force) but was not immediately issued to the Wing's Spitfire squadron. Instead it was held temporarily as a reserve aircraft at its Support Unit. During the first weeks of 1945 the pool of spare aircraft was depleted, as six Spitfires had been rushed out to replace one lost in an accident at the end of December and five taken out of service as a result of enemy action on January 1st (of which more later). In January 1945, 34 Wing itself with its three photo-reconnaissance squadrons was operating from Melsbroek airfield, in Belgium.

Duties and Squadrons

The primary duty of 34 Wing was to provide the aerial strategic reconnaissance (and secondarily some additional tactical reconnaissance) required by the British forces in North-West Europe – Headquarters 21st Army Group and Second Tactical Air Force. The three squadrons of the Wing flew different types of PR aircraft: 140 Squadron (the founding member) was equipped with Mosquitos, for visual reconnaissance and day and night photography (using *Gee* and later *Rebecca H* radar systems); 69 Squadron flew Wellingtons specially modified for night visual reconnaissance and low-level photography; while 16 Squadron used the Spitfire PR Mark XI for, in the main, high altitude photography and pink Fighter Reconnaissance FR Mark IXs for low level "dicers".

The Wing at this time was commanded by Group Captain R.I.M. Bowen DFC, who had in the past commanded both 16 and 140 Squadrons and its ultimate master was Supreme Headquarters Allied Expeditionary Forces (SHAEF). "Thirty Four Wing, An Unofficial Account" records:

"One of the advantages of Melsbroek was the proximity of the Wing to 2nd T.A.F. Headquarters, which was in Brussels; apart from its parties,

FLIGHT LIEUTENANT D. PETRIE DFC – PL 965 Pilot

Douglas Petrie was seconded from the Royal Artillery in 1941 for flying duties. He trained at 7 EFTS, Desford and RAF College Cranwell, joining 169 FR Squadron (Twinwoods Farm) on the Mustang I in 1942. Posted to 16 (PR) Squadron (Hartford Bridge) later that year, he flew Mustangs until they were replaced by the Spitfire Mark XI in 1943. At the end of his first "tour" of operations in 1944, his "rest" was with 34 WSU (Northolt). He rejoined 16 Squadron in 1945 (Melsbroek), but transferred to 140 Squadron (Melsbroek and Eindhoven) for night "recce" (reconnaissance) work with Mosquitos. His DFC was awarded the same year. Late in 1945 this phase of his RAF career was rounded off in Air Dispatch Letter Service (ADLS) communications flying with Spitfire Mark XIs (Bückeburg). He retired from the RAF in 1959 with the rank of Squadron Leader.

Total flying time on Anson, Auster, Canberra, Dakota, Harvard, Hurricane, Lancaster, Magister, Master, Meteor, Mustang, Oxford, Proctor, Spitfire, Storch, Tempest, Tiger Moth, Tomahawk, Vampire, Valiant, Wellington: 3148 hours (Spitfire 564).

Sorties in PL 965
(operational and non-operational):

11.01.45: Benson – Northolt 20 min
16.02.45: Ops – 25 min (recalled from sortie)
13.01.46: ADLS Hague – Schleswig – Cuxhaven –
return 1 hr 55 min (recorded as
PM 965)
Total: 45 min (confirmed)

F/Lt "Pete" Petrie DFC in the cockpit of a Spitfire PR Mark XI. Note the curved, one-piece windscreen and the "cross-hairs" painted on the sliding canopy, which were was used in conjunction with a mark on the port aileron as a means of sighting the oblique camera. The four screws forward of the cockpit door betray the fitting of a Type 35 Camera Control. Behind his head is a padded head-rest, above which is the hood release catch. The cable running along the frame of the hood controls the hood-release gear. Visible in the rear cockpit, attached to the pilot's armoured back-protector plate, is the voltage regulator. *(Photo: D. Petrie)*

Year 1945		Aircraft		Pilot, or 1st Pilot	2nd Pilot, Pupil or Passenger	Duty (including Results and Remarks)
Month	Date	Type	No.			
				—	—	Totals Brought Forward
Jan	11	Spitfire XI	PL965	Self	-	From Benson
Jan	11	Mosquito	JJ642	Self	P/O Parrish	Local Weather Test
Jan	13	Spitfire XI	PL395	Self	-	Air Test
Jan	13	Spitfire IX	MK808	Self	-	Weather Test
Jan	14	Spitfire XI	PL	Self	-	From Benson
Jan	14	Mosquito	JJ642	Self	P/O Parrish	To Brussels

Entry in the Flying Log Book of F/Lt "Pete" Petrie DFC recording his ferry flight in PL 965 from Benson to Northolt on January 11th 1945.

which were numerous and most enjoyable, almost daily personal visits were made possible for the purpose of discussing tasks, which were always passed to the Wing by the Reconnaissance Centre. This was a joint Army and Air Force Office… where much "coffee housing" was done and where the telephone was in continual use for 20 out of every 24 hours!".

PI Sections

The wing also had two PI (Photographic Interpretation) Sections which were responsible for initial (First Phase) Air Force reports and "…could handle all the sorties taken by the Wing on any given day in time to brief the pilots for the early sorties next morning." In her book "Evidence in Camera", Constance Babington Smith explains:

" 'First Phase' meant immediate reporting of important new items: the movements of ships and aircraft, of rail traffic and canal traffic; the extent of bomb damage and the position of ammunition dumps. In cases of special urgency this information was to be available three hours after the aircraft landed. 'Second Phase' reports were to be out within twenty-four hours, and they were to give not only quite a lot of detail on general activity but also, by dealing with a day's accumulation of cover, a coordinated view of what was going on. The 'Third Phase' reports, to be issued later, were to be very detailed statements for specialist recipients, on such things as airfields, factories and military installations."

The Second and Third Phases were not normally applicable to 34 Wing since, once it was established in Europe, there was no Central Interpretation Unit (as there was at Medmenham in UK) to coordinate the PR data accumulated in the prevailing fluid tactical situation.

According to its unofficial history, on 34 Wing, both PI sections:

"…usually had to work throughout the 24 hours in order to keep in touch with which tasks were being attempted so that they could know what to expect when viewing the negatives."

One of the sections served the RAF side, which typically concerned itself with marshalling yards, airfields and bomb damage assessment, which always required an immediate report. The other was involved mainly in Army tasks, which (before moving into Europe, at any rate) were of a more long-term strategic nature. However, with the advent of the Normandy landings and also the expansion of night photography, the tactical requirements of the ground forces became just as urgent. When a pilot landed after a sortie, he reported immediately to the Intelligence Officer, who noted down objectives, operational height, en-route weather and any details if an enemy interception had occurred. He would then contact the PI Section to make them aware that pictures would soon be sent over.

While this was going on, the pilot produced a trace of his route, complete with the position of targets covered. The camera magazines had already been removed from the aircraft and rushed off for developing by No.7 Mobile Field Photographic Section. The films were processed in machines which developed, fixed, washed and dried the negatives as fast as four feet per minute. The negatives were then graded by exposure quality and handed on for printing.

Once the prints had arrived at the PI Section, had been scrutinised and a First Phase report compiled, the results were dispatched by teleprinter or telephone to the relevant Command or units, which could then take action.

The senior Air Force Photographic Interpreter of the Wing was Squadron Leader Michael Spender (brother of the poet Stephen Spender and Humphrey Spender the artist), who was one of the original civilian experts discovered in 1939 by the "Godfather" of photo-reconnaissance, the Australian adventurer Sidney Cotton. The origin of the Photographic Reconnaissance Unit reads like a spy novel, and can be discovered in "Evidence in Camera" and Cotton's own memoirs "Aviator Extraordinary". Spender was fatally injured on May 3rd 1945 in an Anson piloted by Wing Commander Gordon Hughes (himself a well-known PR pioneer) who was also badly hurt.

Met Flight

The success of PR operations was largely dependent upon weather, often some hundreds of miles from the home airfield. It was therefore a great advantage to all three constituent squadrons when No.1401 Meteorological Flight joined 34 Wing at the beginning of February 1945.

Tac R Squadrons

There were two other Reconnaissance Wings allotted to 2nd TAF and 21st (British) Army Group.

Spitfire PR Mark XI PA 888, an aircraft occasionally flown by F/Lt L.L. "Scotty" Cadan, with 34 Wing Servicing Unit (Northolt) in February 1945. *(Photo: E. Quested)*

35 and 39 Wings were attached to 2nd British and 1st Canadian Armies respectively for short-range operations within 150 miles of the front line. Both Wings fielded a pair of Fighter Reconnaissance Squadrons, which used cameras principally to confirm visual reports, and also a PR squadron apiece – 4 Squadron and 400 (Canadian) Squadron – to provide larger and better quality pictures. 34 Wing took care of all PR work of interest to the British forces beyond this radius of operation.

Benson Squadrons

In 1944 the home-based squadrons of the PRU based at Benson (dubbed 106 Wing since the formation of 34 Wing) and the Allied Central Interpretation Unit (Medmenham) were amalgamated into 106 PR Group. With the US 7th Photo Group (Mount Farm) they were responsible for all European strategic PR apart from that directed by SHAEF to 34 Wing.

No.34 Wing Support Unit

After 34 Wing was formed in July 1943, with the task of providing photo-recce services for 2nd TAF, it rapidly became obvious that the current method of supplying replacement aircraft and pilots to the PR squadrons in the field was inadequate. To paraphrase an official report, PR aircraft had to go to so many different units for various modifications before they were ready, that the time factor and difficulty of control made it essential that *34 Wing itself* should have the means of bringing up to operational standard all PR and NR (Night Reconnaissance) aircraft in 2nd TAF. Likewise, holding PR pilots and aircraft at fighter GSUs (Group Support Units) had proved unsatisfactory.

No trained personnel were available in those establishments to ensure the operational state of either pilots or aircraft. Neither were they under the immediate eye of the OC (Officer Commanding) 34 Wing who was, after all, the PR and NR expert.

As a result, it was proposed that two new units be set up in 34 Wing and based at 34 Wing's airfield. One would be 34 Wing Support Unit, which would include a training section and reserve aircraft preparation flight. The other would be an associated Servicing Echelon. The anticipated aircraft reserves needed would be six Spitfire XIs, six Wellington XIIIs and three Mosquito XVIs. In the case of Spitfires, these would be released by 41 Group to RAF Benson for camera fitting, and thence direct to 34 WSU for the remaining preparation – instead of from Benson to 84 GSU, where they would previously have been fitted with VHF radio and undergone the final acceptance check. The training section would also maintain a number of aircraft of all three types – in the case of Spitfires there would be four.

Specifically, 34 Wing Support Unit policy was:

"i. To hold, service and render operationally fit the reserves of aircraft for all Photographic Reconnaissance and Night Reconnaissance squadrons in 2nd TAF.

ii. To bring to operational standard PR and NR aircraft ex-category repair AC (ie, where repair is beyond the unit's capacity) and those received surplus from other units.

iii. To train reserve aircrews in photography by day and night; radar Gee and Rebecca; navigation and flare dropping; to maintain the standard of air gunner's training and to give operational polish to the reserve PR pilots."
(From: Public Records Office AIR 26/48, 49)

"On 23rd July (1944) authority was given for the formation of a Wing Support Unit which was to supply replacement aircraft and crews. It formed at Northolt ...and, during the rest of the war it was based in England where it trained crews, modified aircraft and carried out some very valuable work in the development of the technique of Night Photography." *(From: "Thirty Four Wing. An Unofficial Account")*

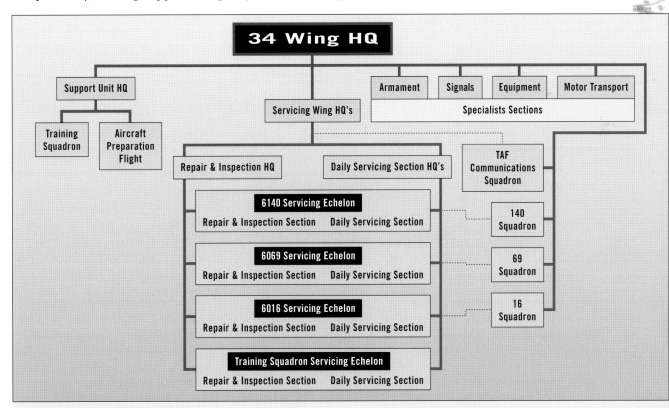

Diagram of the relationship of 34 Wing Headquarters with the Squadrons, Servicing Echelons and 34 Wing Support Unit.

Into Action with 16 Squadron

The only known wartime photograph of PL 965, taken on April 26th 1945 on 16 Squadron's dispersal area at Melsbroek. The serial number is readable on the original print, and the small "R" painted under the spinner is also discernible. The Spitfire is being marshalled into a parking position, but the lack of visibility over the nose requires the signals to be relayed to the pilot by two airmen. The pilot may be F/O Jock West AFC, who photographed railway junctions north of Hamburg in "R" 965 that day, but the length of the shadows suggest it is either early morning or late afternoon. *(Photo: Flight)*

After PL 965 arrived at 34 WSU, it did not tarry long in the reserve aircraft pool. On January 14th another replacement Spitfire was required by 34 Wing's photo-reconnaissance Spitfire squadron, particularly when F/Lt Mike Horsfall failed to return from his sortie that afternoon. PL 965 was therefore allotted to 16 Squadron and ferried to Melsbroek airfield, near Brussels, which was the operational base of 34 Wing. 16 Squadron's dispersal was in one corner of an area bounded by three hard runways, laid-out as a triangle. It was a large pre-war airfield with permanent buildings, many of which were camouflaged – a group of hangars had been disguised by its previous German owners as a village, and there was a dummy chateau – but it had been heavily bombed before the RAF arrived late in 1944.

The airfield was crowded with the machines of several 2nd TAF squadrons in addition to those of 34 Wing, including Mitchells of the medium-bomber squadrons of 2 Group. There were also a large number of "pranged" American bombers (B-17 Fortresses and B-24 Liberators) which had not been able to face a return trip over the North Sea after being shot-up on daylight missions over Germany.

The identifying code given to PL 965 was "R-for-Robert" and the single 18-inch high capital letter was painted in white on the fuselage alongside the recently ordained red-white-blue-and-yellow "C-type" British roundel, which had also replaced the long-established red-and-blue-only PR roundel on the upper surface of the wings. A 6-inch "R" was also painted on the aircraft's "chin" below the spinner. A week later PL 965 flew its first operational sortie .

16 Squadron was commanded by Squadron Leader A.N. (Tony) Davis DFC and his Spitfires were, in the winter of 1944-45, called upon mainly to provide photographs of enemy territory for bomb damage assessment, to monitor airfields suspected of harbouring jet- and rocket-propelled aircraft, and to build up photographic mosaic maps.

The blue-painted Spitfires normally operated at altitudes between 20,000-30,000 feet, cloud permitting, always flew alone and carried no guns.

The CO

"Tony was a splendid CO (Commanding Officer) with a great sense of duty and, probably owing to his army background, a concern for our ground-crew, often overlooked in the RAF in those days. Whilst he would tolerate a fair amount of fooling about, any casualness with regard to duties would be severely jumped on." *(J.M.C. Horsfall)*

"The very finest of COs, who did far more ops than he should have done." *(D. Stutchbury)*

"Tony Davis was one of the best leaders I've ever met. He was always anxious to take all the most dangerous and difficult ops and we used to try to stop this if we could." *(M.A. Wetz)*

"He was much respected for his bravery and his modesty, even shyness. He took many of the more dicey operations himself, and we only knew of them when we heard that he was the pilot of the plane that took off in low cloud, or when one of the Ops Room boys mentioned something about the sortie after his return. (As all our sorties were individual, we did not usually know what each other was doing or had done. We only started to ask questions when someone was reported as being overdue – which happened too frequently in my short time with the Squadron.) Tony himself would never tell us what he had been doing, unless it came out indirectly because it was connected with another sortie that someone else had to fly. (We often had to fill in gaps in a line-overlap or mosaic left by somebody else – a difficult job to pin-point one's position exactly over the ground in order to do so.)

"Tony was stern and, like a ship's captain, somewhat remote, even when we were living in the field in tents. But he could also be fun, although usually on his own terms. He had a big Ford station-wagon allotted to him, and would take a dozen or so of us out to a meal in a restaurant in, say, Amiens, and be a laughing cavalier; but you couldn't tease him unless you were very sure of your ground. During our early experience of meeting the vertical contrails of V-2 rockets, I reported the first one, which was labelled "Taylor's Folly". A few days later, Tony reported having almost run into a large object at 30,000 feet, which we decided was an errant Met balloon. So we got hold of a toy balloon, filled it with gas, painted V-3 on it, and tied it to the foot of Tony's bed while he was asleep. He woke up – and this time he was amused!

"On another occasion, as we were rather an ill-disciplined lot, being a collection of individuals who never flew in formation together or protected each other's tails in the air, Tony decided we were too slack in getting down to breakfast in our Mess tent – and thereby being a burden on the cooks and waiters. He therefore decreed that all officers had to be at breakfast by 8.30 am and anyone arriving after that would not be served.

Eindhoven, summer of '45 with a Spitfire PR Mark XIX. Left to right from the back: F/Lt F.C. Jones, F/Lt Johnny Wheeler, F/Lt Dicky De Mestre, F/Lt Jack Barker, F/Lt Ken Snell, F/O David Stutchbury, F/Lt "Tommy" Thompson, F/Lt Elmo Müller, Lt André Estaria. F/Lt "Scotty" Cadan, F/O "Q-for" Quested (Engineering Officer), F/Lt Norman Godfrey (OC "A" Flight), S/Ldr Tony Davis DFC (Commanding Officer), F/Lt Eric Martin DFC (OC "B" Flight), F/O Don Williams (Adjutant), F/Lt Mike Wetz. *(Photo: Norman Godfrey)*

"Next morning, all we good boys were in on time and feeling very virtuous. A few minutes after 8.30 Tony came in. Somewhat ostentatiously, I lifted my wrist and looked at my watch. All hell broke loose! Tony went red, then white in the face, screamed 'Dumb insolence!' at me, and ordered me to leave the Mess. No hard feelings thereafter, though. He didn't like my home-knitted grey polo-neck sweater, either. Being ex-Woolwich, he was offended by this 'dirty-neck sweater'!

"He had typical RAF initiative, too. When we arrived at Amiens-Glissy airfield in September 1944, we found an American Mustang on the runway, u/s (unservicable) because it had somehow got a wire cable twisted round its propeller. It was quickly smuggled out of sight and emerged a few days later without the wire or its USAAF markings, earmarked as Tony's private hack. I don't remember seeing it at our next airfield, Melsbroek, though, so some slightly higher brass-hat than Tony probably pulled his rank to win it off him.

"I was up at Cambridge in 1947 at the same time as Tony was doing a short course to learn Russian. He came to tea one day and chatted like any other friendly undergraduate. Then he looked at his watch, exclaimed 'Sorry, old boy, I've got to run to see my tutor', grabbed his gown and a pile of books, and rushed out in a way most unbecoming for the ex-CO of 16 Squadron!" (H.J.S. Taylor)

16 Squadron dispersal area at Melsbroek, late 1944. 13 Spitfires are identifiable, 6 Dakotas and a "pranged" Halifax. (Photo: M.A. Wetz)

PR Problems and Solutions

F/Lt John Wendelken (NZ), F/Lt Norman Godfrey, F/O Mike Wetz. Interesting features visible in the cockpit behind the pilots are: seen through the one-piece windscreen, the camera control unit; in front of the instrument panel; leaning at about 45° to the right is the spade-grip of the joy-stick; inside the cockpit door, the escape crow-bar; and behind the pilot's seat bulkhead, the two cylinders of the voltage regulator. *(Photo: Norman Godfrey)*

Training and Conversion

For historical reasons the PR Squadrons were administered by Coastal Command, because the Royal Navy had been their earliest serious customer for keeping tabs on movements of the German fleet. It was therefore no accident that the dedicated Operational Training Unit (No.8 OTU) for PR conversion training was based on a former operational Coastal Command airfield at Dyce, near Aberdeen, on the north-east coast of Scotland. PR pilots were traditionally (but not invariably) recruited from Coastal Command because they did both a pilot's and an "in depth" navigation course, as they could anticipate long

hours patrolling the sea lanes, out of sight of land for many hours. Such skills were also essential to the lone PR pilot deep in enemy territory.

As Michael Wetz points out, "...to fly to Berlin and back with only a knee pad and a few maps stuffed down your boots required a certain amount of mental navigation and a standard higher than that of an average pilot. As far as I was concerned, I volunteered for PR. I completed my training in the States at Pensacola (a US Navy base) on Catalinas. As a Biggles fan from youth, the prospect of flying Catalinas, where you die of boredom, was an awful prospect. When I heard that there were vacancies and was accepted on PRU Spits, I was over the moon.

"After a few days holiday we went to Dyce. I seem to remember that we alternated between one day on classroom work and one day on flying. After our day's flying we usually had a big party in Aberdeen because we had the next day to recover. It was an enjoyable time. The local girls were very pretty.

"Here we were also introduced to high level flying and photography. After flying-boats I found the runway very short and narrow and was rather clumsy at getting the aeroplane down on the deck again. You learn that after flying high for a while – say 30,000 feet or above – you tend to land too high and overshoot the runway. I did so on one occasion, leaving my mark with the propeller. It helped if, for the last ten minutes or so of your sortie, you flew low to restore your perspective; and this was I believe a custom on many squadrons."

Cheating the flak...

"When you remember that high level Spits had no guns, only petrol in the wings – you had to re-think your approach to certain problems. A number of us (mostly the younger new boys in 16 Squadron) used to have long discussions on the best way to solve almost any problem that might occur. As a new situation came up we would argue it out and try to come to a conclusion, so that when anyone was confronted by a similar situation they would know what to do, and the best way to do it so that the odds favoured them.

"For instance: when going through flak (enemy anti-aircraft fire) at, say, 30,000 feet it took 8 seconds for (gun-laying) radar to fix your height and speed, 8 seconds to work out where you would

be and to lay the gun, and another 8 seconds for the shells to arrive. Now, if you flew a "lazy eight" path through the flak, your mean line of advance on the ground was slower than your actual speed. The result was that boxes of bursts would be thrown up either side of you and in front. Provided you kept it up, the only danger was from a "rogue" shell.

"At low level it was a harder problem. If it was bursting behind, you had to gradually increase your throttle setting so that it never quite caught up with you when the gunner corrected his aim.

"If it was in front he would tend to expect you to panic, fly faster and end up being hit. The remedy was to fly slower and slower so that he stayed in front of you and you never ran into his line of fire. This took a steady nerve but did increase your chances. We got this from helpful gunners on our side."

...and the interceptors

Michael Wetz recalls how a seasoned pilot once remarked to him (while the squadron was operating from UK) that it was prudent not to begin to descend until you were crossing in over the British coastline. It wasn't long afterwards that the advantage of this was demonstrated. While following the Dutch coast on his homeward leg, he noticed a couple of minute dots far below, climbing towards him. The Germans had scrambled a couple of '109s to try to intercept him. Well above them, he nevertheless used his aircaft's superior climb performance to ascend to about 40,000 feet, where the air was so thin that even the Spitfire was wallowing around – but from where he was able to observe the German fighters claw their way up to their ceiling and fire a few vain winking bursts at him before they gave up and dived for home. Had he not maintained altitude over the enemy coast, but been already losing height and thinking only of a friendly touch-down minutes away, the '109s might have been lucky.

Another incident illustrates the benefit of keeping a constant all-round lookout. Spotting a bright condensation trail approaching him, Michael Wetz's first reaction was that an enemy aircraft was intercepting. But the initial anxiety was quickly replaced by one of amazement that the pilot (of what was by now clearly a PR Spitfire) was completely unaware of the aerial advertisement made by his snowy wake. Deciding to do something about it, he made for the Spitfire and recognised it as one from his own squadron. A brief RT (Radio-Telephone) message reminded the pilot (who was

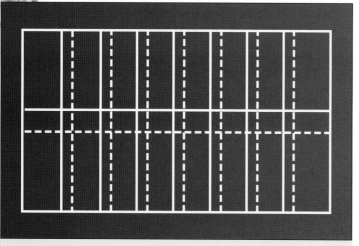
Diagram of the overlap system for vertical mosaic-mapping photography.

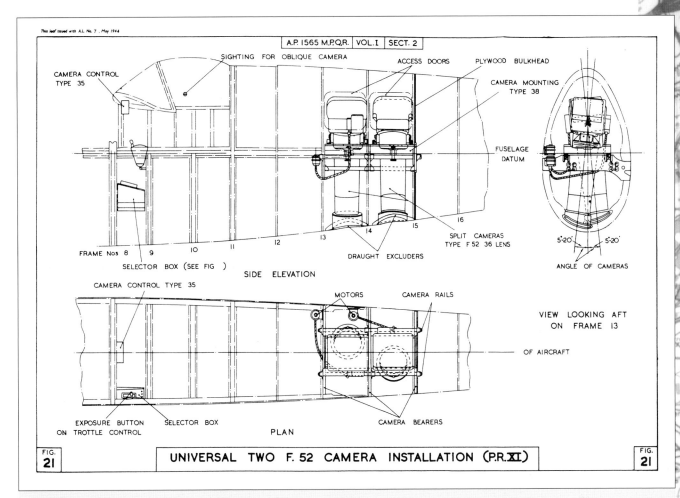

This leaf issued with A.L No. 7, May 1944

A.P. 1565 M.P.Q.R. | VOL. I | SECT. 2

CAMERA CONTROL
TYPE 35

SIGHTING FOR OBLIQUE CAMERA

ACCESS DOORS   PLYWOOD BULKHEAD

CAMERA MOUNTING
TYPE 38

FUSELAGE
DATUM

16

15   SPLIT CAMERAS
TYPE F 52 36 LENS

FRAME Nos 8   9   10   11   12   13   14

DRAUGHT EXCLUDERS

SELECTOR BOX (SEE FIG)

5°20'   5°20'

ANGLE OF CAMERAS

SIDE ELEVATION

CAMERA CONTROL TYPE 35

MOTORS   CAMERA RAILS

VIEW LOOKING AFT
ON FRAME 13

OF AIRCRAFT

EXPOSURE BUTTON   SELECTOR BOX
ON TROTTLE CONTROL

PLAN

CAMERA BEARERS

FIG.
21

UNIVERSAL TWO F. 52 CAMERA INSTALLATION (P.R. XI)

FIG.
21

The Universal Camera Installation in the Spitfire PR Mark XI (with two F52 36-inch lens cameras) showing fore-and-aft offset arrangement and lateral inclination. *(RAF Museum)*

perhaps worrying about something completely different) about the danger of flying at condensation level. The Spitfire PR Mark XI was provided with a rear-view mirror intended as much for watching for contrails as for enemy fighters on your tail.

"I can remember being jumped by two Me 163 rocket planes. We had worked out that their terrific speed and climb was in fact their weakness. So every time they came in to attack, I just throttled back and went into a tight turn as per procedure agreed. They only had fuel for about 12 minutes. So they were soon back on their way to base."

"On 16 Squadron we had regular unofficial sessions (usually in bad weather) and when new pilots joined us we did our best to brief them so that they would know what to do to improve their chances." A simple idea that was adopted by the older ones was keeping their eyes open and making

themselves discreetly available when less experienced pilots were preparing their flight-plans.

"I regret that there were some who didn't follow this approach and I feel they might have lasted longer if they had done. Most pilots were very willing to learn and listen and generally the standard of professionalism was very high."

Ops assignment

"We got our orders from Group (No.84 Group Headquarters, 2nd TAF) and these were interpreted by the 34 Wing ops room staff, who were usually pilots who had finished a "tour" and were "on rest". High-priority operations were to photograph bomb damage after a raid – typically on a marshalling yard or bridges – or special requests for large-scale pictures of a small area – often for parachute drops. A routine job was to cover marshalling yards and German aerodromes as you passed by. Tasks were given to the next person on the roster and after your op. your name was put at the bottom and worked its way up again.

"Around invasion time (June 1944) we were given rather shorter trips at low level (which were done with oblique cameras) and in addition, were asked to count trains and say which way they were going. This was a nice change and in fact, they gave us some Spits with two cannon and four machine guns. Provided we carried out our sorties we were allowed to attack suitable targets... a train was most exciting..."

These interesting Spitfires were FR IXs. Their standard "c"-type (universal) wing-armament consisted of two 20 mm cannon and four .303 inch machine guns, but they also had a single port-facing oblique camera in the fuselage. They were painted pale pink overall, with "invasion stripes" on the under-surfaces of the wings and half-way up the side of the rear fuselage. The serial number, in letters about 2 inches high, was above the small PR fin-flash, and two-colour roundels appeared on upper surfaces only.

PR piloting problems

Jimmy Taylor reveals, "PR Spitfire pilots had a host of difficulties to contend with in the air, which made it a continual surprise to me that Spitfires were able to bring back photographs as effectively as the Mosquitos. The latter had two people to handle the tasks and the headaches: navigation to and from the targets, identification of each target, operation of the cameras, and survival in a hostile environment, which included flying at both very high altitude and much lower down, coping with winter weather and strong winds at height, keeping a constant check on the instruments and listening to the beat of the engine like one's own heart, and – above all – searching the sky endlessly for the speck of an enemy aircraft or the puff of an anti-aircraft shell.

"On a clear day, Spitfire navigation was no great problem, although from 30,000 feet roads and canals looked no wider than the finest hair. But when the ground was covered with 7/10 or more clouds, it was our job to get below them and take our photographs at whatever height was possible. The snag here was that we could lose our estimated DR position (arrived at by compass course and elapsed time) during our descent through cloud from, say, 30,000 feet. If we had reached ETA over the target, we would descend in

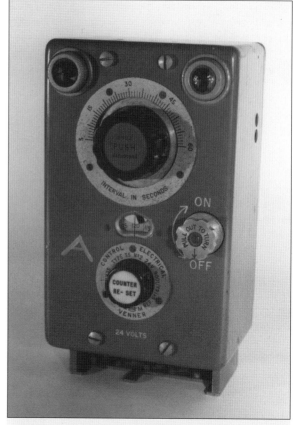

The Type 35 No.2 Camera Control Box, which was positioned just below eye-level above the flying-instrument group in the centre of the instrument panel. At the top left: red light = 4 seconds before exposure. At the top right: green light = exposure taking place. Lower: Time-interval Selector: 5-60 seconds on the scale marked "Interval in Seconds" around the knob. In the centre of the knob: Single Exposures Push. In the middle: the small kidney-shaped window is the exposure counter, "115-125" visible, going up to 500. To its right is a knurled knob for the control switch marked "Pull Out To Turn" and "On/Off". At the bottom is the " Counter Re-set" knob with details of the instrument engraved around it. *(Photo: T. Melchers)*

a circle, in the hope of emerging from cloud over the desired spot. But the wind and our airspeed would usually differ from our flight-plan during the descent, and under the cloud-base everything seemed relatively dark and it was difficult to pick out distinctive features on the ground – woods, roads, railway-lines, canals, rivers, bridges, villages, and so on – and then locate them, and therefore our position, on the map. Of course, while we were peering with some degree of urgency at the countryside passing round us, which often obstinately refused to conform to what was shown on the map, we were very much aware that we were over enemy territory, with the German radar whining away in our ears, and of our vulnerability to their alerted fighters and flak.

"Photographs suitable for stereoscopic viewing by the photo-interpreters required each picture to overlap its neighbour by 10% sideways and by 60% fore-and-aft. The first was achieved by the positioning of the two big F52 36-inch focal-length lens cameras installed behind the pilot's seat for high level work, or of the two F24 5-inch lens cameras set in the wings for low level sorties. But the second was dependent on the time interval between exposures, which was itself dependent on our ground-speed and height. The higher we flew, the stronger the winds predicted by the 'Met' (Meteorological). experts: at 30,000 feet, we usually found the prevailing wind to be 100 mph from the West. So with our normal cruising speed of 360 mph, upwind we would be doing only 260 mph, but downwind 460 mph over the ground. If we set our interval between exposures at, say, 8 seconds, upwind we would have more than 60% overlap, and downwind less. So in our pre-flight preparation, we had to work out the likely variations in exposure intervals according to the direction in which we would take our photos. Considering that 'Met' had no access to weather reports from Occupied Europe (unless Intelligence could overhear or decode German forecasts), it was astonishing how accurate their predictions were. For us, doing a mosaic of photographs over an area of, perhaps, 10 square miles meant following a course similar to a farmer's when ploughing a field: up and down in parallel lines, adjusting the exposure interval each time we flew upwind or downwind. It called for precision flying in keeping to a constant heading, speed and height for maybe 15 minutes or longer.

"There was, however, a built-in problem with vertical photography, at any height, from a Spitfire: how could we tell that we were still exactly over the target – road, railway-line, canal, or the unseen parallel lines of a mosaic – when we were unable to see directly beneath the aircraft? Apparently, no one had thought of, or succeeded in, cutting a hole in the bottom of the fuselage for the pilot's benefit (although it had been done for the cameras). So the only way of looking beneath us to check on our accurate positioning was by turning the aircraft on its side and looking down through the canopy between exposures. Fortunately, a red light came on 4 seconds before an exposure, and a green light during the exposure; so, with an 8-second

exposure interval, we had 4 seconds in which to make a quick but vital check that our compass course was proving accurate. But herein lay the snag: as soon as we upturned the aircraft, the gyro compass and the artificial-horizon both "toppled" and spun out of control until they settled down again after a minute or so, as did the magnetic compass in its bowl. So we had to return to straight and level flight and our intended heading without the aid of our instruments – and we needed to look beneath us at least every minute.

"All this we had been trained to do in about 40 hours of flying, navigating and photographing at No.8 OTU at Dyce, near Aberdeen. The real headaches occurred if things went wrong, either through our own misjudgment or through mechanical failure. The first we could try to remedy by re-taking bits we thought we had missed. The second required the skill of a

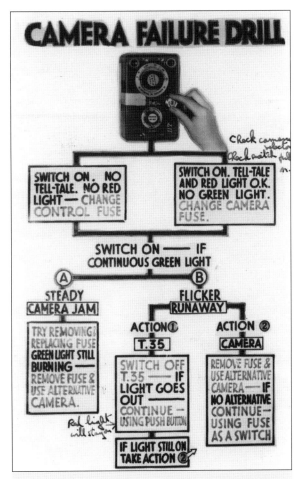

Camera control failure drill "…quite clear" (Photo: H.J.S. Taylor)

contortionist! The camera mechanisms, the control-box (see the illustration), and the warming-jackets round the lenses, were all protected by fuses, as in a motor-car. The fuse-box was down by our left foot. The instructions for clearing stoppages or jamming were quite clear (as on the illustration). All we had to do was bend down below the instrument panel, pick out a silly little fuse, and replace it with a new one – according to whether the red or green light was permanently on or off or flickering. I personally found the Spitfire cockpit comfortably warm, so I did not wear full high level kit and several layers of gloves. Even so, with just silk gloves on my hand, it was a job to pick out the right fuse from the holder and replace it. Meanwhile, at 30,000 feet, the Spitfire was beginning to lose its normal stability: a slight pitch-up of the nose would induce a stall

In a street in Brussels, October or November 1944: F/Lt A.P.G. "Bunny" Holden, F/Lt C. Leagh-Murrey, F/O D.J. (Don) Williams (Adjutant), F/O J. "Jock" West AFC and F/O H.J.S. (Jimmy) Taylor. All are wearing Service Dress uniform except Williams who is in battledress. *(Photo: J.M.C. Horsfall)*

Flying Officer H.J.S. (Jimmy) Taylor began RAF service in 1941 at 11 Initial Training Wing, going on to elementary flying at 4 EFTS. Pilot Training continued under the Arnold Scheme in the USA next year, where he gained his "wings" and became an instructor at Greenville Army Flying School, Mississippi, serving there until the summer of 1943. Spring 1944 found him back in UK at 6 AFU, Little Rissington, and June at 8 OTU, Dyce, Scotland (for PR training). He joined 16 Squadron in August and was made a PoW when he baled-out at 14,000 feet after his Spitfire's engine failed over the Dutch/German border on November 19th 1944. He spent the remaining months of the war in Stalag Luft I before being liberated by the Russians in May 1945. His only other serious problem with a Spitfire was in the rain, on the perimeter track at Melsbroek when he taxied into a Belgian steam-roller. The Belgian crew baled out. Of more than 1,300 flying hours, 101 were on Spitfires. In the '50s he gained a Private Pilot's Licence in Baghdad and a Gliding Association Certificate in 1993.

and a spin, and a slight pitch-down would quickly develop into a fast-accelerating spiral dive. So, after groping around by our left foot triumphantly or in vain, we would emerge rather breathless, sucking-in oxygen in deep pants, to discover we had tumbled off our delicately-balanced perch, had lost several thousand feet and our heading, and were a sitting-duck for any hostile aircraft that might have approached while we were fiddling with the fuses.

"Coming back from Hun-land was not too difficult if we had found our original or secondary targets and knew where we were (our pre-flight planning included our return course). But if the sortie was abortive for some reason – cloud-cover, camera malfunction, enemy interference – we could only estimate the course to fly to get home. At 10,000 feet, we could get a 'homing' from base from nearly 100 miles away; but at 2,000 feet, the distance was reduced to only 20 miles for the controller to help us down through cloud or over unfamiliar country. I remember one such occasion when I returned with the cloud-base at 400 feet and I was very glad to trust the controller; but I was more worried when several other folk began to emerge from the low cloud and we were all milling around together looking for the airfield – PRU types never liked flying near other aircraft!

"If anyone failed to return from a sortie after 5½ hours (the limit of our fuel), apart from hoping that he would surprise and relieve us by walking into the Mess one day, we could only speculate as to which of the variety of hazards which beset us in the air had brought about his downfall.

"These tragedies apart, in spite of the difficulties mentioned above, the Spitfire pilots apparently brought back a high proportion of the required pictures, although quite a lot of "gap-filing" had to be done after someone else's incomplete sortie – and these small stretches (indicated on our maps by lines of blue wax-crayon) were harder to locate and fill-in than covering the whole of the original area. No doubt, we learned by finding-out about our successes and mistakes from the photo-interpreters, and some of the more experienced pilots were always ready with advice for the newer arrivals. But for me, at least, besides the "gremlins" that usually lurked in or on the aeroplanes, Lady Luck also kept close to my side – and failed me only once." (Jimmy Taylor baled-out and was taken prisoner on November 19th 1944).

PL965 Pilots I

FLYING OFFICER W.F. BARKER

F/O "Barry" Barker had the distinction of claiming an Me 163 rocket interceptor destroyed, when it apparently failed to pull out of a diving pursuit of his Spitfire from about 25,000 feet and "went straight in" on January 14th 1945. A further outcome of the incident was a visit from Farnborough technicians to quiz him about any "shock stall" symptoms he might have experienced during the power dive. Shock stall occurs because, at very high speed, part of the airflow over the top surface of the wing reaches supersonic speeds. This causes a shock wave to form on top of the wing causing a loss of lift, ie a stall. This is accompanied by buffeting and general loss of control. Barker enlisted in the Royal Engineers on September 1st 1939 and transferred to the RAF in 1941. A P/O by 1943, F/O six months later and F/Lt within two years, he was de-mobbed in December '45. Back in '46 he retired in 1963 with the AE award. *(Photo: L.L. Cadan)*

Sorties in PL 965 (operational):

14.02.45: Ops 1 hr 30 min (no photos)
02.04.45: Ops 1 hr 25 min (no photos)
17.04.45: Ops 2 hr 40 min (photos)
Total: 5 hr 35 min

Extracts from the 16 Squadron Line Book and Operations Record Book concerning F/O "Barry" Barker's sorties on February 14th and April 2nd and 17th 1945, flying PL 965. (From: 16 Squadron archive & the Public Records Office)

43

FLYING OFFICER C.D. BURTON DFC

Don Burton joined the RAF in 1941, attained the rank of P/O and F/O in 1944, was awarded the DFC in June 1945 and de-mobbed in September.

Sorties in PL 965 (operational):

13.03.45: Ops 1 hr 30 min (no photos)
Total: 1 hr 30 min

F/O Jimmy Taylor, F/Lt "Bunny" Holden, F/Lt Derek Wales and P/O "Don" Burton in a wrecked street in Amiens, September 1944. Burton is wearing his side-arm, a .38 inch Smith & Wesson revolver on a webbing belt with an ammunition pouch, for protection of the party. An "Acme Thunderer" warning whistle hangs from his right lapel. *(Photo: J.M.C. Horsfall)*

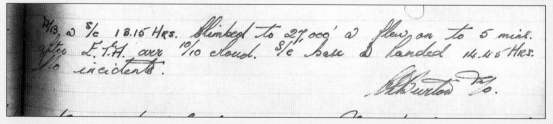

Extract from the 16 Squadron Line Book concerning F/O Burton's sortie on March 13th, flying PL 965. *(From: 16 Squadron archive)*

FLYING OFFICER W.T. MOODY

Trevor Moody joined the RAF in 1939 as an airman and was later accepted for pilot training. He was granted a temporary commission in the General Duties branch as a P/O in June 1944. At the end of the year he was promoted to the war-substantive rank of F/O. He returned to civilian life in May 1946.

Sorties in PL 965 (operational):

22.02.45: Ops 2 hr 5 min (photos)
19.04.45: Ops 2 hr 45 min (photos)
Total: 4 hr 50 min

F/O Trevor Moody with the 16 Squadron communications "hack", Auster MT 284, at Eindhoven 1945. *(Photo: L.L. Cadan)*

---

without incident.

S.20". 27,500'. Lippe Canal.
Climbed to 28,000' on course to Wesel. Photographed Lippe Canal, returned and photographed Wesel. Returned to base. Landed 12.35. No incidents.

S.20". 29,000'. Defence lines in Munster area.

Extracts from the 16 Squadron Line Book and Operations Record Book concerning F/O Trevor Moody's sorties on February 22nd and April 19th 1945, flying PL 965. *(From: 16 Squadron archive & the Public Records Office)*

Ebbett.

A/B. 16·30. climbed on course to 27,000'. Photographed HAGTE then on to PERLEBERG. Waited for PARCHIM to clear, so went on to WOODSTOK, took pictures, then back to PARCHIM & back to BASE. Landed 17.15. No incidents. Moody :-

FLIGHT LIEUTENANT E.N. GODFREY DFC Croix de Guerre

F/Lt Norman Godfrey was a member of the Territorial Army and was "called up" for duty in the Advance Party in 1939. He transferred to the RAF in April 1941 and was posted for initial training to Torquay, Devonshire. At the end of the year he "passed out" from flying training at 3 BFTS (British Flying Training School), Miami, Oklahoma, USA, with the rank of Pilot Officer. Operational training continued at the picturesque old airfield at Old Sarum, Wiltshire (41 OTU), flying Lysanders, and his first squadron posting came in March '42 when he joined 231 Squadron in Northern Ireland. Based at Maghaberry, Long Kesh, and Nutt's Corner, the Squadron was flying Lysanders and Tomahawks, patrolling the border with neutral Eire or participating in army exercises.

After a year Norman Godfrey transferred to 169 Squadron which moved airfields six times in March '43 before arriving at Andover, Hampshire. Here, for the first time he flew operationally, with Mustang Is. Duties included

F/Lt Norman Godfrey settles into the cockpit of his Spitfire PR Mark XI. He is wearing a "Mae West" (Life Jacket Mark I) and the heavy harness with its large circular quick-release catch on his chest is for his seat parachute. Behind him is the head rest, and one of the harness straps with its triangular locking-pin hangs out of the cockpit from the back of the pilot's seat. *(Photo: E.N. Godfrey)*

YEAR 1945		AIRCRAFT		PILOT, OR 1ST PILOT	2ND PILOT, PUPIL OR PASSENGER	DUTY (INCLUDING RESULTS AND REMARKS)
MONTH	DATE	Type	No.			
		—	—	—	—	TOTALS BROUGHT FORWARD
March	15	Spit XI	PL965	Self	—	Ops. Wilhelmshaven - Mapping North of Schleswig-Husum.
	18	Spit XI	PL965	Self	—	Ops - Zwolle - Gronigen area Mapping.
	20	Spit XI	N147	Self	—	Ops - Mapping Zwolle

Entry in the Flying Log Book of F/Lt Norman Godfrey recording his sorties in PL 965 during March 1945. *(E.N. Godfrey)*

"Lagoons" (shipping recces), "Populars" (photo-reconnaissance of the adjacent French coast), "Rhubarbs" (small-scale offensive sorties against targets of opportunity), and "Anti-Rhubarbs" (against German hit-and-run fighter bombers along the South Coast). In October, Godfrey left Middle Wallop and joined 16 Squadron at Hartford Bridge, Hampshire, staying on until the end of his extended tour of duty the following summer. After a rest period instructing in various OTUs, he rejoined 16 Squadron at Melsbroek, Belgium, in March 1945 as F/Lt commanding "A" Flight. In August he left the Squadron for Benson, and was promoted to Squadron Leader with a base appointment.

Norman Godfrey's Log Book records about 950 flying hours (350 on Spitfires).

Sorties in PL 965 (operational):

15.03.45: Ops 3 hr (photos)
18.03.45: Ops 2 hr 5 min (photos)
Total: 5 hr 5 min

Extracts from the 16 Squadron Line Book and Operations Record Book concerning F/Lt Norman Godfrey's sorties on March 15th and 18th 1945 flying PL 965. *(From: 16 Squadron archive & the Public Records Office)*

FLIGHT LIEUTENANT H.K. SNELL

Ken Snell, remembered as "a good and conscientious pilot" joined the RAF in March 1941 and was granted a temporary commission as a P/O in April 1942. By October he was a probationary F/O (war-substantive) and was promoted to F/Lt in April 1944. After the war, in February 1946, he was granted an extended-service commission as a F/O and regained the rank of F/Lt in July 1946. In the autumn he transferred to the Secretarial branch but relinquished his commission in November 1949 for health reasons. *(Photo: 16 Squadron archive)*

Sorties in PL 965 (operational):

21.01.45: Ops 2 hr 5 min (photos)
Total: 2 hr 5 min

Facing page: one of the photographs taken by F/Lt Ken Snell with the 20-inch focal-length vertical cameras of PL 965 from 16,000 feet at about midday on January 21st 1945. The railway sidings at the small town of Mechernich (in Westphalia, south of Köln) had just been under attack from USAF Thunderbolts. Black smoke with a patch of bright of flame at its heart rises from the vicinity of the railway yard, where long lines of trucks are visible. Snow-filled craters are evidence of earlier raids. *(Photo: Air Photo Library, Keele)*

A/B at 1045 hrs and S/C for Blankenheim. Climbed to 19000 where contrails started so let down to 18000 and flew on to target area. Targets were all covered by 10/10th strata/cu. cloud so flew around looking for clear areas. At Mechernich I saw a quantity of black oil smoke and red fire and as I photographed it I saw it came from a rail yard at that moment being dive bombed by Thunderbolts. Waited 30 minutes and photographed it again. During this time the place had been under fairly constant attack. As targets were still covered by cloud I returned to base without incident. Pancaked 1250.

Kenneth Snell
F/Lt.

Extract from the 16 Squadron Line Book concerning F/Lt Ken Snell's sortie on January 21st 1945 flying PL 965 (the aircraft's first operation). *(From: 16 Squadron archive)*

16/1613 21 JAN 45 F20" // K56

4009

FLIGHT LIEUTENANT W.J. WENDELKEN

F/Lt John Wendelken, a New Zealander, arrived in UK in the autumn of 1942 when he joined 7 (P) AFU, Peterborough, and subsequently 41 OTU, Hawarden. He was posted in April '43 to 16 Squadron at Andover, currently flying Mustangs Marks I and II, and moved with the Squadron to Hartford Bridge in July. During this period he was detached to: Middle Wallop on interdiction patrols at low level and below cloud base (disruption of road, rail and waterways in France); Benson with the Photo Reconnaissance Unit; Exeter for operations in the Cherbourg area and anti-E-boat patrols; and Wittering on interdiction over Holland. After baling out over Holyhead in May 1943 he spent four hours in a dinghy. According to Doug Sampson (Australian – who completed a second tour with 16 Squadron in June 1944), Wendelken "was the star in the drama at Wallop. He flew into me when he was number two in a dog-fight practice, and did a 'supersonic' belly scrape with half a port wing".

In 1944 he served with 15061 Mobile Radar Unit, moving up through France to Holland, returning to England and 34 WSU in January '45, with duties between Hartford Bridge and Melsbroek, Belgium. The following month F/Lt Wendelken was back with 16 Squadron, where he

Facing page: A Mustang I of 16 Squadron, Hartford Bridge 1943 or 1944. Front row: F/O Douglas Petrie, F/Lt Tony Davis (OC "A" Flight), S/Ldr Ken Mackie (CO), F/O John Wendelken (RNZAF), F/Lt Richard Pughe (OC "B" Flight), F/O Gibbons. Back row: F/Lt Douglas Sampson (RAAF), F/O Gerry Bastow (RCAF), F/O Ransley, F/O Jerry Winter, F/O "Nobby" Clark, F/Lt Norman Godfrey. (Photo: D.W. Sampson)

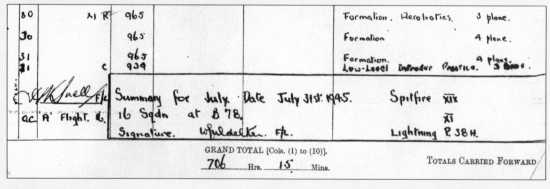

Entry in the Flying Log Book of F/Lt John Wendelken recording sorties in PL 965 during July 1945. *(From: W.J. Wendelken)*

remained operational at Melsbroek and Eindhoven until VE-Day.

In June 1945 he was detached to Bückeburg near Minden with 2nd TAF Communications Wing, flying Spitfire PR Mark XIs from 16 Squadron which had been specially converted for ADLS duties. When the Squadron disbanded in September he was posted to 268 Squadron (renumbered 16 Squadron in 35 Wing next month) for aerial photographic mapping of Holland, the Ruhr and canals. He left the RAF in 1946 with over 935 hours total flying time logged and resumed his career in forestry in New Zealand. *(Photo: W.C. Anderson)*

Sorties in PL 965
(operational and non-operational):

02.03.45: Ops 2 hr 20 min (photos)

03.07.45: Base (B78) – Manston – Croydon – Base
2 hr 55 min

04.07.45: Aerobatics/performance climb 1 hr 30 min

05.07.45: Air test 45 min (+12, 2850, empty wing tanks,
4000 ft.p.m. to 10000 ft, IAS 130-125 mph)

30.07.45: Formation/aerobatics 1 hr 20 min (3 plane)

30.07.45: Formation 50 min (4 plane)

31.07.45: Formation 1 hr (4 plane)

01.08.45: Formation 1 hr 15 min (4 plane)

Total: 11 hr 55 min

A/C 13:15. Climbed to 18000 ft Photos of Dunkerque between cloud breaks, landed 15:30. No Incidents.

Wendelken. F/L

Extract from the 16 Squadron Line Book concerning F/Lt John Wendelken's sortie on March 2nd 1945 flying PL 965. *(From: 16 Squadron archive)*

PILOT OFFICER W.J. WILLSHAW DFC

P/O "Willy" Willshaw had already done a tour in the Western Desert (North Africa) as an NCO (Non-Commissioned Officer) pilot before joining 16 Squadron. "A great chap, I liked him immensely. We put him up for a Commission several times but he took a delight in failing." He had three sayings which summed up his approach to life: "Too true – Fair enough – We had our chips", recalls Mike Wetz. Willshaw's Commission actually did come through in February 1945, back-dated to October '44. A final accolade came on June 1st – a well-deserved DFC. *(Photo: W.J. Wendelken)*

Sorties in PL 965 (operational):

06.02.45: Ops 2 hr 10 min (no photos)
21.02.45: Ops 2 hr 20 min (photos)
22.03.45: Ops 2 hr 20 min (photos)
Total: 6 hr 50 min

Facing page: one of P/O "Willy" Willshaw's photographs taken with a 20-inch focal-length vertical camera of PL 965 from 26,000 feet at about 11.00 hours on March 22nd 1945. *(Photo: Air Photo Library, Keele)*

"No incidents W. Anderson.
A/B 09.25 hrs and climbed to 23,000, later climbing to 25,000 as base of cloud rose. Flew over cloud, and set course for base after flying for 10 mins past E.T.A on targets. Returned to base with u/s R/T, flying over nearly 10/10ths cloud whole of way back. No incidents. Landed 1135 hrs.
mJWillshaw u/o.

A/B 0920 Climbed to 25,000'. S/c for target and flew over 10/10ths till E.T.A. + 7 min. Then returned to base – engine running

S.20". 25.000'. 16/1734. Mapping Area – Quakenbruck – Bremen – Niemburg.
Climbed to 25,000'. Majority of target area clear so made three runs in area. No incidents. Landed 16.25 hrs.

Extracts from the 16 Squadron Line Book and Operations Record Book concerning P/O "Willy" Willshaw's sorties on February 6th and 21st and March 22nd 1945, flying PL 965. *(From: 16 Squadron archive & the Public Records Office)*

s/c HAMM 09.15 hrs. All targets in clear areas. Made runs on all, returned to base. No incidents. Landed. 1135 hrs.
JWillshaw P/o.

16/1910 :22 MAR45:F20" KAS/26.000'

3678

FLYING OFFICER J. WEST AFC

John West enlisted as an AC2 in 1941 and was commissioned in 1943 as a Pilot Officer. War-substantive rank as Flying Officer (February '44) and Flight Lieutenant (August '45) followed, but he relinquished his General Duties commission at the end of the war. In August 1954 he became a Flight Lieutenant in the RAF's Education Branch and received a permanent commission in 1955. He was promoted to Squadron Leader in 1961, retired in 1978 and died in 1983.

Sorties in PL 965 (operational):

18.03.45: Ops 1 hr (photos)
24.03.45: Ops 2 hr (photos)
10.04.45: Ops 2 hr 25 min (photos)
26.04.45: Ops 2 hr 10 min (photos)
Total: 7 hr 35 min

F/O "Jock" West AFC at Eindhoven 1945. Note the red and white ribbon of the Air Force Cross beneath his pilot's wings. *(Photo: W.C. Anderson)*

Climbed on track to UTRECHT. Most of area covered by Sc and Cu cloud. Took photos in gaps. Went to ZWOLLE on Recce and returned to base without incident.

Challis W/O

J West. F/o.

S.20". 25,000'. Airfields - Meppel - Wilhelshaven Area.
Climbed to 25,000' - reached Meppel O.K. - saw boxes of Forts going back to England - went to Wilhelmshaven area - took photographs of airfields and returned to base without incident.

Extracts from the 16 Squadron Line Book and Operations Record Book concerning F/O Jock West's sorties on March 18th and 24th and April 10th and 26th 1945, flying PL 965. *(From: 16 Squadron archive & the Public Records Office)*

No incidents.

A/B 1430. S/C ULZEN. climbed to 26000' ... Target area over returning US Bomber formations. Returned to base and landed at 1655 without incident. J West F/o

---

S.20". Railway Junctions N. of Hamburg.
Set course Luneburg. Arrived in target area to find Eastern part of area covered with S.C. cloud and thick C.S., base 20,500'. Photographed clear targets and returned to base, landing at 12.50 hours. No incidents.

Bellerby's One Hundredth Trip

"On joining 16 Squadron in January 1945 I had done 75 sorties with 680 and 682 PR Squadrons (some 222 hours) and I had trouble convincing the Air Ministry that I was not tour expired. In the Middle East and Italy we could opt for an extended tour – 100 PR *sorties* rather than the standard 200 *hours*. It seemed a pity to miss the final war months and eventually I got a posting to 34 Wing, where I knew the Wingco, Gordon Cole, from Middle East days, and he posted me to 16 Squadron. I guarded those remaining 25 trips to see out the Hitler war.

"Brussels that winter seemed incredibly luxurious after more than two years in and around the Mediterranean: a tour on Hurricanes with Desert Air Force and then PR work with 680 and 682 Squadrons in Cyprus (Dodecanese and Crete), Italy, Corsica and southern France – before contracting jaundice and being flown out to the UK with a plane-load of US army casualties.

"We did a lot of mapping – northern Germany, Holland and Denmark. In Holland we were looking for "Crossbow" (V-weapon) sites. After the Rhine crossing of March 24th '45 there were sorties covering German jet airfields and more mapping. Most trips were at 25-26,000 feet just below the (condensation) trail height in winter in northern Europe. A typical sortie was only two hours, sometimes less, which was a nice change from four hours-plus trips in the Middle East and Italy. German fighters were more interested in bombers than PR aircraft and heavy flak was most unusual.

"When over Holland, we frequently saw V-2s being fired from around The Hague and always took bearings. With three reports you could get a nice triangulation and then Bomber Command would pay a visit. USAAF were frankly bad news and I never lingered in their neighbourhood; their fighter escorts would take off after us. P-38s were no problem but sometimes they had Spitfires, which were another matter. Aircraft recognition clearly was not a part of their training, it seemed!"

PL 965 Gets Away With It

"My log book tells me it was a mapping sortie north of Hanover in the Nienburg/Celle area. Four runs at 26,000 feet, two hours 15 minutes. No recollection of the target, of course, but I certainly recall the Fw 190 and the four Me 262s!

"The '190 came up just as I finished my runs. I went "through the gate" and climbed away to 30,000 feet and then left the area rapidly. There were lots of USAAF planes around, but I can't recall where they were bombing that day. The

F/Lt Gordon Bellerby's knee pad notes from his sortie on May 7th 1945 while flying PL 965. *(From: G. Bellerby)*

Year 1945 Month	Date	Aircraft Type	No.	Pilot, or 1st Pilot	2nd Pilot, Pupil or Passenger	Duty (Including Results and Remarks)
—	—	—	—	—	—	Totals Brought Forward
MAY	1	WELLINGTON X	NG 505	F/SGT RYDER	SELF	EINDHOVEN — BRUSSELS EVERE
		ANSON	NK 674	F/L ANON	SELF	BRUSSELS EVERE — LE BOURGET
	4	ANSON	NL 221	F/L FRIPP	SELF	COULOMMIERS — EINDHOVEN
	7	SPITFIRE XI	PL 965 R	SELF		EINDHOVEN — B. 154 (REINSEH
		SPITFIRE XI	PL 965 R		·	500' – 5,000' X P.R. DENMARK SHIPPING SURVEY
						ECKENFORDER - COPENHAGEN - FLENSBURG
	10	SPITFIRE XI	PL 970 E			LOCAL DEMAND. RHINE BRIDGES:
						WESEL - DUISBERG - DUSSELDORF - KOLN - COBLE
	12	SPITFIRE XI	PL 965 R			LOCAL DEMAND. SUB PENS AT
						IJMUIDEN (14" OBLIQUE). THE HAGUE AMS

Gordon Bellerby's Log Book entry, May 7th 1945. The sortie was his own 100th: it marked the end of his second "tour"; the same day fighting ceased on the Western Front making this PL 965's last wartime operation. (From: G. Bellerby)

'262s scared the hell out of me – after all, four are a bit much! But somehow they missed seeing me. Must have all had their heads inside the cockpit. They crossed beneath my tail at right angles and I kept on going flat out for home."

> S.20" 26.000'. 20" Mapping N. of Hannover.
> Set course for target area. Arrived to find it just clear of low cloud (St & St.Cu). Did four runs before finishing film. At end of last run saw one F.W. 190 about 2,000' below but he did not see me. Saw 8th Air Force was being attacked by Jets near Hannover. Covered Osnabruck M/Yds. on way back with few remaining exposures as visual obtained of probable V.2 train in the yards. As finished this run, four M.E. 262's passed about 200' below my tail quite close but they didn't see me amazingly. Retired at high speed seeing numerous other aircraft on way to base. No other incidents. Landed base 09.45.

Extract from the 16 Squadron Operations Record Book concerning F/Lt Gordon Bellerby's encounters with enemy aircraft on March 21st 1945 while flying PL 965. (From: The Public Records Office)

One Hundred Up with PL 965

"16 Squadron was a good one and Tony Davis a fine CO. The camaraderie of a fighter squadron was far more pronounced than in a PR one, where we were all individuals flying singly. Leave was regular (unlike the desert days) and I was in Paris for three days when I heard the news of Hitler's death. I cut my stay short to hustle back to Eindhoven and not miss that 100th trip I had been saving!

"Just got it in on May 7th and of course it had to be a 'dicer' (low level sortie) – luckily the German fleet had decided to surrender, as otherwise it's unlikely I'd be writing this rambling epistle."

Gordon Bellerby's final wartime sortie that afternoon was a shipping survey, using the 14-inch oblique camera of Spitfire "R" PL 965 in the Eckenforder, Copenhagen and Flensburg areas.

"After completing my recce I climbed up and sent an RT report 'in clear' back to B.154 (where I had refuelled on my way out) for relay to Eindhoven. Weather had improved and I then had

SINGLE-ENGINE AIRCRAFT				MULTI-ENGINE AIRCRAFT						PASS-ENGER	INSTR/CLOUD FLYING [Incl. in cols. (1) to (10)]	
DAY		NIGHT		DAY			NIGHT					
DUAL	PILOT	DUAL	PILOT	DUAL	1ST PILOT	2ND PILOT	DUAL	1ST PILOT	2ND PILOT		DUAL	PILOT
(1)	(2)	(3)	(4)	(5)	(6)	(7)	(8)	(9)	(10)	(11)	(12)	(13)
81:59	884:06	5:30	26:10							70:45	21:35	12:00
				3 day leave in PARIS						:30		
				HITLER REPORTED DEAD						1:10		
										1:40		
	:55											
	3:30			SUCCESSFUL. REFUELED B.154. 100TH P.R. OP. 1000 HRS. EXTENDED 2ND TOUR LAST DAY OF EUROPEAN WAR. COMPLETED.								
	1:45											
	1:10			B.D.A. ON BOMBER COMMAND'S RAID WITH TEN TON BOMBS ON THE SUBMARINE PENS.								

fun doing beat-ups along the beaches outside Copenhagen. Lots of enthusiastic waves from the bathers (no topless those days!). I then flew around running off film, including German sailors standing on the turret of their light cruiser but shaking their fists, I think! I was sorely tempted to land at Kastrup and capture Copenhagen single-handed – still regretting this!"

A/B 1215 and landed B 154 to refuel. A/B again 1400 hs and flew to Kiel area. Covered shipping in bays around Copenhagen island. Not much activity except amongst the Danes around Copenhagen which was covered with Danish flags. Saw about 100 Stirlings landing VI¹ A/B. Did at Copenhagen. Landed base at 1730. No incidents.

G Bellerby F/Lt.

A/B 1230 and landed B 154 to refuel. A/B again at 1355 and

Extract from the 16 Squadron Line Book concerning F/Lt Gordon Bellerby's sortie on May 7th 1945 while flying PL 965. *(From: 16 Squadron archive)*

"*The great news came over the air at 20.00 hours this evening announcing the unconditional surrender of Germany, Two days holiday was granted to all personnel. There was quite a party in the mess, and everyone was in wonderful spirits. Later, about 23.00 hours, there was quite a good fireworks display. The Prime Minister is to make the official announcement at 15.00 hours to-morrow, the 8th May, 1945 which is the official V.E. Day. Ceasefire is officially at midnight on the 8th.*" (16 Squadron Operations Record Book, May 1945)

May 7th 1945 – the day the fighting stopped. Almost certainly captured with the F28 14-inch oblique camera of PL 965 by F/Lt Gordon Bellerby, German troops waiting to surrender at a small railway station near Copenhagen. A number of the vehicles appear to be draped with white sheets. *(Photo: L.L. Cadan)*

FLIGHT LIEUTENANT G. BELLERBY DFC – PL 965 Pilot

F/Lt Gordon Bellerby at San Severo, Italy, in 1944 with a Spitfire PR Mark XI of 682 (PR) Squadron. Note the familiar red and blue PR fuselage roundel, the "KDs" (khaki drill shorts) and suede "desert" boots. *(Photo: G. Bellerby)*

F/Lt Gordon Bellerby DFC joined the RAFVR in 1940 and began flying training during 1941 at 2 BFTS, at Glendale and Lancaster, California, later embarking for UK to join 59 OTU (Crosby on Eden). From there he was posted in '42 to 94 Squadron, flying Hurricanes with the Desert Air Force in Libya. When he completed his first tour next year, he had a spell instructing at 71 OTU (Ismailia) before joining the PR course at 74 OTU (Petah Tiqua, Palestine) at the beginning of 1944. His PR postings in the Mediterranean theatre were to 680 and 682 Squadrons in Cyprus, Italy, Corsica and southern France.

Towards the end of the year he was invalided back to UK, going on from 34 Wing to complete his second tour with 16 Squadron (Melsbroek and Eindhoven) as "A" Flight Commander from March 1945. His DFC was gazetted in July and

his wartime service finished in '46 after another spell at 34 Wing and then 309 FT & ADU (Ferry Training and Aircraft Delivery Unit), Benson.

Total flying time on AT-6, Hurricane, Spitfire, Stearman, Vultee BT-13A: 1029 hours (Spitfire 416).

Sorties in PL 965
(operational and non-operational):

21.03.45: Ops 2 hr 15 min (photos)
07.05.45: Eindhoven – B154 Reinsehlen 55 min
07.05.45: Ops 3 hr 30 min (photos)
12.05.45: 14" oblique 1 hr 10 min BDA (Bomb Damage Assessment) on Bomber Command's raid with 10-ton bombs on submarine pens at Ijmuiden
28.05.45: Ardennes – Liége – Bastogne 1 hr 20 min (HQ Wing/16 Sqdn)
Total: 9 hr 10 min

Andy's Tour

F/O "Andy" Anderson (Commissioned March 1945) wearing his Irvin sheepskin flying jacket and Service Dress cap in a Spitfire LF Mark XVI, possibly in November 1945. Note the inboard .5-inch machine-gun and the outboard 20mm cannon, late-war "rear-view" or "tear-drop" canopy and "whip" radio antenna. *(Photo: W.C. Anderson)*

**Sorties in PL 965
(operational and non-operational):**

21.03.45: Ops 1 hr 25 min (photos)
31.05.45: Low level obliques 1 hr 40 min (photos)
Total: 3 hr 5 min

There were very few NCO pilots on 16 Squadron, but there, as in other operational squadrons, they undertook the same duties as their commissioned colleagues, although RAF convention of the time required them to use the Sergeants' Mess and be billeted separately from the officers. Such distinctions tended to become blurred once everyone was having to "make do" in the less-than-ideal living conditions prevalent in 2nd TAF. This suited men from the more egalitarian Commonwealth countries and those who had been trained in America, who were not always at ease with such social discrimination. "Andy" Anderson's progress illustrates how an

eighteen-year-old engineering apprentice became a twenty-year-old RAF pilot (before he had a driving licence). It reveals some of the varied tasks a quite junior pilot might be detailed to "get on with". He was expected to accept very immediate and substantial dangers and responsibilities: personally to complete allotted duties; take care of expensive bits of Air Ministry "kit"; get himself to, look after himself in, and get himself home from far-flung foreign outposts (in an age when most people never left these shores in a lifetime); and ultimately, (unarmed) to survive hostile action to bring home valuable operational intelligence. If it sounds dramatic, the spirit of the times was not heroic. Rather, these were simply jobs which had to be done, and you did your best.

Southern States and Brown Jobs

Once he had finished initial training at Scarborough in 1941, Londoner Bill Anderson was shipped to the southern states of America (mainly Georgia and Alabama) for flying training in sturdy Boeing PT-17 Stearmans, Vultee BT-13 Valiants and AT-6 Harvards. When he returned in 1943 he went on to further service and operational flying training in various units in southern England. Then as now, it took time to adjust to the problems of navigation in crowded Britain compared to well-spaced America. Over there they had radio navigation and flashing-light beacons upon which to "home"; runways and airfield approaches were illuminated at night; and ground features such as cities, railroads, lakes and mountains were widely separated and stood out clearly, invariably (so it seemed) in good weather. And there was no black-out!

The most memorable incident of this period occurred when his Lysander lost its propeller in flight, dictating a forced landing at Shoreham. His passenger was a peace-time work-mate serving on anti-aircraft (AA) duties in the area. The lucky soldier later announced that his only previous flight had been in 1917 when the aeroplane had, on that occasion, shed a wing! The propeller was recovered from a muddy stream in Shoreham harbour, and for a long time afterwards Anderson wore its DH symbol as an unofficial badge.

By December 1943 he was flying with 667 Squadron at Gosport. During this period, the army needed anti-aircraft practice and simulated low level and dive-bomb attacks to prepare the troops for the coming invasion of Europe. This unglamorous but necessary task fell to 667, flying Defiants and Hurricanes, many of which were of pre-war manufacture. Anderson soon became "browned-off" with beating up "brown jobs", mainly on the Isle of Wight and the Dorset coast and applied successfully for Photo-Reconnaissance training. In May 1944 he reported duly to 8 OTU at Dyce, in Scotland.

Highland Fling

After an hour and a half's local flying and landing checks in a Miles Master, he was introduced to flying the Spitfire PR Mark IV for the first time – and not without incident, because a main wheel tyre burst on take off! Fully aware of his predicament, but without a radio, he opted to continue with his sortie, not only because he would have to face the landing sooner or later (and why not later?), but also because he would rather tackle the inevitable after gaining some handling experience of the aircraft. So he and his "Number Two" set off for a spirited work-out of their Spitfires, including as they thought, a number of discreet, but illicit, low level beat-ups. However, there was quite "a flap on". The burst tyre had been spotted from the control tower at Dyce, and strenuous efforts were requested of the Observer Corps to keep track of the movements of the two "unsuspecting" Spitfires as they jollied around the Highlands. When the time came to land back, Anderson suddenly found himself in the circuit with another Spitfire formating on his wing tip. This unwelcome intruder turned out to be the Station Commander, who gestured forcefully and then produced a board inscribed "YOU HAVE A BURST TYRE". Although the subsequent landing ended in a "ground loop", no serious damage was sustained.

Anderson does not remember his PR course as particularly high-powered. It began with in-cockpit instruction on how to operate the oblique and vertical cameras, and went on to include high (with oxygen) and low level navigation to targets, which were then photographed and the pictures later assessed. The longest sortie lasted 5 hours 15 minutes. There was classroom work, some brushing up of navigational technique and health checks in a decompression chamber, anticipating high altitude operations. After about 45 hours flying in five weeks, it was all over.

Very Long Hops

Posted to 309 Squadron, Benson, in July his work turned out to be with 10 ADU (Air Delivery Unit). After the usual local area familiarisation sorties and a couple of air and fuel consumption tests, Anderson was allotted his first delivery, which was of a brand new Spitfire PR Mark XI, lately received from No. 6 MU at Aldermaston. Destination? Karachi!

Two more long-distance trips followed (to Blida in Algeria, and Karachi again) before Anderson was posted to 34 WSU at Hartford Bridge. He was there for five weeks, collecting new Spitfires from Benson and getting some practice in, flying non-operational photographic sorties. Eventually, on

May 31st 1945 – Low level oblique photographs taken with the F24 14-inch oblique camera of PL 965 by W/O "Andy" Anderson on a practice sortie in the Ruhr valley. *(Photos: W.C. Anderson)*

November 21st 1944 he ferried himself and Spitfire PL 976 to Belgium where they joined 16 Squadron at Melsbroek.

PR Ops and "Shaky Dos" on 16 Squadron

On arrival at Melsbroek he found 16 Squadron had recently lost two of its veterans – Clyde Heath killed on a "dicer" to the strategic Venlo bridge over the river Maas on November 17th and Jimmy Taylor missing on the 19th (later reported captured and a prisoner of war). After a few days to settle-in and a local proving flight to pin-point (friendly) targets around Bruges, Anderson's first two or three real PR operations were hampered by foul weather. Heavy cloud did not, however, prevent him spotting "a jet job" (which fortunately didn't attack) and several V-2s, and experiencing his baptism of light flak. As he was eased into Squadron routine, December presented its crop of casualties. Group Captain Ogilvie, Officer Commanding 34 Wing, went missing over the North Sea on the 11th and on the last day of 1944 F/O Johnston "spun in" while approaching to land and was killed.

Anderson was sped back across the North Sea by high-powered launch after home leave at Christmas. There was a flap on about the Germans' Ardennes offensive, so when persistent fog kept normal transport on the ground, the RAF called on its Air Sea Rescue craft to "do the honours" for its returning aircrew. This meant that he was on site to witness the "fireworks" of the New Year's Day attack on Melsbroek by the Luftwaffe. When, a few days later, F/Lt Horsfall failed to return from a sortie, it certainly looked as though even the most experienced pilots were as vulnerable as anyone in this game. Then on 20th Anderson almost "bought it" himself:

"...At approx. 20 miles south of Zwolle two aircraft appeared from behind a belt of cloud 90° to my starboard. The nearest aircraft, which I recognised as a long-nosed Fw 190, opened fire at a range of approx. 150 yards. He appeared to be using RP *(rocket projectiles)* as well as cannons or machine guns. I immediately did a climbing turn to starboard; he did likewise but remained on the other side of my turn. We continued this circular climbing to 20,000 feet, but he appeared to be able

6RACTICE: P/O ANDERSON: MAY 31. 45:

to maintain my rate of climb with ease. I then straightened out and dived towards a large cloud about 5 miles distance and at about 17,000 feet. The enemy aircraft came out of his turn to the rear and slightly starboard at about 3,000 yards range. I received the safety of the cloud and the last I saw of him, he was still about the same range and position. The second aircraft, which I did not recognise, was not seen again. I set course for base and had quite a lot of trouble dodging Americans. Two aircraft which were Mustangs were very persistent but finally sheared off..." *(From: 16 Squadron Operations Record Book)*

By comparison, February was a quieter month and the weather permitted a few successful photographic sorties. He was also able to avoid trouble by spotting five jets over the Ruhr before they spotted him. But next month provided more excitement on 21st:

"Took photos of two A/F (airfields) on way to Bremen. Arrived over Bremen and started mapping runs over ¹⁰/₁₀ths *(meaning solid as cloud)* bomber formations. Observed four a/c (aircraft) approaching in *(condensation)* trails at about

32,000 feet. They passed directly overhead and I easily recognised them as being '262s. All four suddenly did a steep diving turn and came down directly at me. I put my aircraft into a steep turn but they dived straight past, one of them being only about fifty yards distance (so close that I should have reported him for dangerous flying). It appears they were not interested in me but went straight down and had a crack at the bombers about 2,000 feet below, much to my relief..." *(From: 16 Squadron Line Book and Pilot's Log Book)*

Fortunately his second sortie that day, this time in PL 965, was quite peaceful (see illustration below).

But the jet theme continued to recur for Anderson and the next incident illustrates the dangers both of being too visible when working "in trails" (at an altitude when condensation trails form in the wake of the aircraft) and of mistaken identity. 24th March:

"S.14" *(camera)*. 30,000 feet. Wesel-Münster-Enschede. Arrived target area and started runs, but was continually chased back by Spitfires that insisted that I was a jet job. I eventually contacted Kenway *(ground control)* and had them called off.

On my sixth run I observed six possible '262s approaching and on applying throttle my engine quit. I lost 10,000 feet and was seriously thinking of becoming a PoW when she picked up again. I managed to get back to base with it continually stopping and starting. (A very shaky do)." *(From: 16 Squadron Operations Record Book and Pilot's Log Book)*

Actually, by now he was a Commissioned Pilot Officer, but as far as the ORB was concerned (perhaps because notification usually came through months after the event) he remained a Warrant Officer until June! The remainder of Anderson's 58 operational sorties presented only minor problems and the majority were completed successfully. But the war in the air continued to claim lives up to and beyond the end. On May 3rd an Anson carrying S/Ldr Spender (the Wing's senior Air Force Photographic Interpreter) crashed on take-off. He died from his injuries and the pilot was badly injured, too. A few days after VE-Day, while in transit from Copenhagen to Eindhoven, W/O Anderson came across a wandering Me 109. He instructed the German to follow him in, but unhappily the '109 crashed 15 miles short of base when its fuel ran out.

End of Tour Sight-seeing with PL 965

On the last day of May 1945, Anderson took Spitfire PL 965 on a practice sortie at low level by way of a sight-seeing tour of the Ruhr, routing via Münster and the Möhne dam. His pictures reveal tranquil villages, apparently untouched by war, in stark contrast to total devastation in both the residential and industrial areas of the cities. The dam, one of the targets of the famous "Dam Busters" raid of 1943, is fully repaired, with defensive anti-torpedo nets replaced, but below its wall are obvious signs of the deluge which burst through the 200-foot breach. A few weeks earlier such a sortie over "Happy Valley" (as Bomber Command crews wryly nicknamed the Ruhr) would have been impossible except at high altitude beyond the reach of its concentrated heavy flak.

In July there was an interesting attachment to the ADLS flight at B.151 Bückeburg, near Minden. From there specially modified Spitfire PR Mark XIs seconded from 16 Squadron couriered urgent dispatches for SHAEF. After his squadron was disbanded, Anderson returned to this unit (now called ADLS Squadron, BAFO Communications Wing) where his first sortie ended in disaster.

"In heavy haze the Hurricane (which had extra fuel tanks) suffered engine failure on take-off. A quick switch to gravity feed – no dice. At about 6-700 feet the aircraft stalled and seemed to flutter down. I remember dykes, lots of mud and slime and being helped out by Canadian soldiers." His Log Book records laconically: "Engine cut at 200 feet (1,000 yards viz) crashed at Sengwarden near Wilhelmshaven. Complete wreck but walked away. Thank God."

Despite the prang he remained on ADLS until transferred to 2 Tac R (Tactical Reconnaissance) Squadron at Celle, Germany, in January 1946. May found him an acting Flight Lieutenant with the Accident Investigation Branch of BAFO (British Air Forces of Occupation) where he finished his RAF service in mid-summer. By the time he returned to his apprenticeship in "civvy street", he had clocked-up nearly 1,000 hours flying on 17 types, a third of it shared with Spitfires.

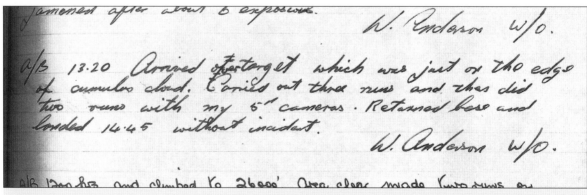

Extract from the 16 Squadron Line Book concerning W/O Andy Anderson's sortie on March 21st 1945 while flying PL 965. *(From: 16 Squadron archive)*

Officers Commanding

GROUP CAPTAIN R.I.M. BOWEN DFC – PL 965 Pilot
Officer Commanding 34 Wing (PR) 2nd TAF

G/Cpt R.I.M Bowen DFC, Officer Commanding Headquarters 34 Wing, in discussion with a pair of "Wingcos" and, between them, a Squadron Leader. Behind them are representative aircraft of 34 Wing: Spitfire PR Mark XI "L" PL 985 of 16 Squadron, used for high level, long-distance recces; a Wellington XIII used by 69 Squadron for night photography; and a Mosquito XVI of 140 Squadron, since the advent of jet and rocket fighter opposition unable to operate in daylight over Germany. *(Photo: Flight)*

G/Cpt Richard Bowen began flying training in 1938, and progressed through various Army Co-operation schools and training establishments, flying such types as the Hart trainer, Audax, Fury, Lysander and Blenheim. He joined 168 Squadron, which was forming at Snailwell in June 1942 and working up on Tomahawks. His operational experience developed flying "Rhubarbs" and "Populars" with Mustangs from Bottisham and Odiham. Moving on to 16 Squadron at Andover in May '43, he flew "Anti-Rhubarbs" against hit-and-run fighter bombers on the South Coast.

That year, as a Wing Commander, Bowen briefly commanded the Squadron, before he was posted to command 140 Squadron at Hartford Bridge when 34 Wing was formed in July. There

he presided over the gradual change from Spitfire PR Mark IVs and PR Mark XIs to Mosquitos (with experiments with other types en route). By the end of the year, work was concentrated on mapping the intended invasion area in Normandy. In April 1944 the Squadron moved to Northolt, operating both night and day up to and during the invasion period. September found 140 Squadron in France at A.12 Balleroy and almost immediately, B.48 Amiens/Glissy, when Bowen left for Staff College.

He returned to command 34 Wing at B.58 Melsbroek on Christmas Eve 1944, replacing G/Cpt Pat Ogilvie, who was missing over the North Sea. G/Cpt Richard Bowen remained with the Wing until July 1945, when he was posted to 106 Group Headquarters. He remained in the

Continued overleaf >

RAF as a senior Staff Officer, and retired in 1959 from his appointment as Air and Naval Attaché in Caracas. His wartime service was recognised with the award of the DFC, American Silver Star and Belgian Croix de Guerre. His Log Book records 60 types flown from single to four engines, ranging from the Hart, Audax and Fury biplanes to Meteor and Vampire jets.

Sorties in PL 965 (operational):

23.03.45: Ops 3 hr (photos)
Total: 3 hr

Facing page: high-level photograph taken by G/Cpt Richard Bowen in PL 965 on a sortie covering seven airfields in the Rheine-Hopsten-Achmer-Hesepe area on March 23rd 1945. *(Photo: Air Photo Library)*

This photograph and the one on page 65 were taken at Melesbroek on April 26th 1945. Here flight mechanics are at work on a PR Mosquito XVI of 140 Squadron. A Spitfire PR Mark XI of 16 Squadron is in the background. *(Photo: Flight)*

Entry in the Flying Log Book of G/Cpt Richard Bowen DFC recording his sortie in PL 965 on March 23rd 1945. The notes say: "Airborne 09.35 hrs. Climbed out over Arnhem. Photos 24000' of 7 A/F's (airfields) Rheine area. Also photos Rheine town just after Fortress raid. Photos A/F & mapping Meppel area. Chased by Mustangs. Bombers & fighters everywhere". *(From: P. Bowen)*

> Continued
from overleaf

4035   16/1920:23MAR45:720"//K45:25,000'

SQUADRON LEADER A.N. DAVIS DFC – PL 965 Pilot
Officer Commanding 16 Squadron

W/Cdr Tony Davis and his French bride, Dominique in 1951.
(Photo: H.J.S. Taylor)

S/Ldr Tony Davis DSO DFC came from a military family, attended the Royal Military Academy, Woolwich, and graduated in the Engineering Tripos at Magdalen College, Oxford. As a regular soldier he was evacuated from France via Dunkirk in 1940 and was seconded to

the RAF the following year, joining 16 Army Co-operation Squadron, flying Lysanders and later Mustangs. When S/Ldr R.W. Atkinson was killed in a ground accident on his first day as CO of the Squadron, Davis (who had been on "rest" since completing his first tour of duty) was appointed to replace him. He remained with the Squadron until June 1945, when he was offered a permanent commission in the RAF and was promoted to Wing Commander. His DSO was gazetted In July 1945. After a sojourn at Cambridge, where he read Russian, he became Air Attaché Budapest. In 1952 a spell at Joint Services Staff College was followed by a refresher course on jets and night fighters before he served as CO at RAF Stations Leeming and then Coltishall. During the '60s he was Station Commander at Leuchars, Defence Attaché Moscow (as Honorary Air Commodore), and OC RAF Staff College Andover (as Group Captain), and retired from the RAF in 1969 as Honorary Air Commodore once more. He died at his home in France in August 1988.

Sorties in PL 965 (operational):

04.04.45: Ops 2 hr 15 min (photos)
Total: 2 hr 15 min

NB: At first sight of the 16 Squadron Line Book, it seemed that F/O David Stutchbury flew PL 965 on April 4th 1945. However, further investigation proved that his alleged sortie times clashed with those of S/Ldr Davis' (detailed and precise) entry for the same day, and that the aircraft's serial number had been pencilled-in afterwards. The mistake was carried over when, subsequently, the Operations Record Book was typed-up. This time no Spitfire was identified for Davis' sortie, but "PL 965" again appears as a hand-written addition to Stutchbury's report. Actually, Stutchbury's Flying Log Book identifies PM 125 for the sortie.

NB 0735. Climbed through 1/10 medium St.Cu. to 29,000. Some gaps in Bremen area. 3 Airfields photographed. 2 e/a seen taking off from Bremen. Landed 0950. No incidents.
A. Davis S/L.

Extract from the 16 Squadron Line Book concerning S/Ldr Tony Davis' sortie on April 4th 1945 flying PL 965. *(From: 16 Squadron archive)*

Tommy and the '262s

"I guess one's memory is better when it comes to relating the few bad experiences," explains "Tommy" Thompson, the Canadian ex-16 Squadron pilot. "I cannot say I had a lot of them, but I will admit I was scared shitless every time I took off. I think part of it was my age (the oldest one on the Squadron) and my many more hours of flying experience. I hate to think what would have happened if I had gone straight from SFTS to an active squadron. We barely knew how to fly when we graduated. We were supposed to have 50 hours but, with only four or five active Oxfords, we shared (four of us) 15 to 20 minutes each at the controls. I actually had 37 hours of solo time. Of the 83 odd students at 34 SFTS, Medicine Hat, I heard only ten survived the war. Three of us were made Instructors and the balance went on bombers.

PL 965 Sees 'em Off

"On the flight in question (5th April 1945) I show in my log book that I was flying at 30,000 feet. I was returning from Bremen area to Melsbroek, Belgium. Off my starboard wing I could see the two Me 262s headed towards me. I do not recall whether I contacted "Penman" – our Wing station – but we had had a brief outline of their performance, speed, etc, and were told we could not outrun them.

"Our best method was to attack, as the German pilots were young and inexperienced; and while they had been told the blue Spits had no guns, they were not prepared to accept or believe the information received from their Intelligence. With my heart in my mouth I turned into them for the semblance of an attack!

"They might have been 2,000 feet below when I saw them and at 1,500 feet away I turned on them. They both broke, with the one on my right turning south and diving. I had the advantage and got within three to four hundred feet – on his tail. I was very excited and following him for perhaps a minute, I broke off when I saw good cloud cover at somewhere near 20,000 feet. I do not know what happened to the other '262 – if I did, I have forgotten now. I know I could have shot him down if I had had guns!"

F/Lt "Tommy" Thompson dressed for a high altitude sortie in the autumn of 1944. From the top, his visible clothing consists of a Type-C leather flying-helmet, with Mark VIII split-lens goggles and a Type-G moulded rubber oxygen mask with integral microphone. The Mark 1 life-jacket (Mae West), which was made of yellow fabric and inflatable by means of a small CO_2 bottle, was personal issue (as was his parachute) and went with him wherever he was posted. Beneath his serge battledress blouse and extending well below his bottom is a heavy-weight, knitted navy pullover (which superseded the earlier polo-neck "Frock White" submariner-style sweater). Over his battledress trousers he has long white socks pulled above the knee. His black fleece-lined "escape boots" (marked with his initials) have uppers which can be easily separated from the calf-pieces to give the appearance of civilian shoes. Stuck in the top of the right boot is his map and in his right hand he carries his leather flying gloves or gauntlets and the pad containing his flight-plan. *(Photo: J.M.C. Horsfall)*

Extract from the 16 Squadron Line Book recording F/Lt "Tommy" Thompson's encounter with German jet fighters while flying PL 965 on April 5th 1945. *(From: 16 Squadron archive)*

More Jet Trouble

"I had one other run in with Me 262s and this was the worst one. On May 3rd 1945, flying Spit XI "C" '922 I was on my 47th ops trip, to Denmark. My targets, shown in the log book, were Aarsmund, Badschotel, Juelsminde, Frederica, and Kiel. As I recall, the first meetings of a peace treaty were being held between the heads of our forces and the German leaders. Anyway, my job was to take pictures which I did – and over Kiel I saw the makings of a large fleet of ships being put together in lines of 10. They were all headed north and in the direction of Norway. Again I recall being very excited about my find, and having on my knee a pad strapped to a small board (I still have it), I started counting – noting in lines of 10 the number of ships. I reached 110 when I looked up (ahead) and saw two Me 262s coming directly at me!

"My height is shown as 20,500 feet in my log. I cannot recall now what action I took – I know I stopped counting ships! I know they didn't hit me! I did, however, get on the radio channel (my call sign was "Quaker 29") and called "Mayday". I reached them and told them of the ships and the two jets. I was told help would be immediate as one of the squadrons was airborne in my area.

"I got home safely, but before landing I heard on the RT that the bombers were already hitting the ships. I would really like to know what happened to the fleet! It was my last ops flight and no one was more relieved and happy just to have come through the whole mess. I might add I was the only married man on the Squadron and possibly on the Wing. I had a three-year-old son, whom I had not seen since he was born, and I was determined I was going back alive. I almost did not, on what I always called the last real day of the war!"

"... Tommy Thompson reported that, off the East Coast of Denmark , there was a convoy of 200 ships which was immediately attacked by aircraft of Coastal Command and 2nd TAF and the latter claimed to have destroyed 23 and damaged 115." *(From: "Thirty Four Wing. An Unofficial Account")*

Venlo Dicer

"I have two other incidents which I have not forgotten.

"The first one has to do with a "dicer", named after our OTU school at Dyce *(more likely derived from the phrase "dicing with death")*. It was a low level flight at Venlo. My log book shows Nov. 6th '44 Spit "T" '845 – target Bridge at Roermond – 1 hour and ten minutes – photos. The Mitchells on Melsbroek field had been bombing this target for over a week, over which the Germans were retreating night and day. The Mitchells had hit everything but the bridge! There had been a lot of cloud and they were bombing from a fairly low level – 3,000 feet or thereabouts.

"I was not sure how to do this dicer and Clyde Heath, one of our Squadron members, suggested I approach at about 10,000 feet up to five miles back from the target, then hit the river and bridge 1,000 yards before target at ground level. The bombers would be overhead at around 3 pm and the Germans should still be in their trenches when I came over at 3.27 pm.

"Everything went as planned except for two things. I couldn't see the ground and when I came out of clouds heading for ground level, I saw the river and bridge directly ahead. Going over 400 mph I had only seconds to turn on my left-side camera. It was not until moments later that I realised *it was not the Maas river but one in front of it!* I just kept climbing and turning – back to a height where I could take another run at Venlo bridge. It did not take long and I was at a record speed when I came alongside the bridge. I pushed the tit (camera button), but in my nervousness felt I had pushed it on and then off. I wasn't sure – but I had time to see the bridge was not down and that the Germans were standing up – a lot of them watching me fly by.

"I then did something I was told never to do, and that was to go over the target a second time at that level. I turned around and approached the target from the opposite direction and this time all hell broke loose. Everything but the kitchen sink came up at me. I did not come to until I was at over 10,000 feet – and at that point I was just coming out of a state of shock. First time I ever experienced this in my life. My mouth-piece was full of water (sweat), my arms and legs were shaking so badly that I had no control over them. It was a nasty experience.

"The next day Clyde Heath had the same target and he followed exactly what he told me to do. But this time the Jerries were waiting for him and passing the bridge they shot him down. We visited his grave in Venlo after hostilities ended. He saved my life and I will never forget him."

Close Encounter

"The final incident has to do with the V-2s. The headlines on the Daily Express newspaper said in large bold type that an American had seen this large, long missile going up in the air, thirty feet long, flames coming out of the rear, etc, etc. A group of RAF boys on the Squadron were sitting around in the flight room saying, 'Wouldn't you know it. The Americans seeing the V-2 first – and all but the name of the manufacturer'. We all had a good laugh.

"Three or four days later I am on a target path that takes me over Enschede and lo-and-behold, there is this stinking great V-2 off my left wing, headed for the moon and looking just as the American had described it. If Intelligence records are still available, then you can read what I said on my debriefing. It was along the lines of '...If anyone tells *anything* to *anybody* in the Mess about this debriefing, *I'm* not going to tell you what I saw'."

Low level ("dicer") damage assessment photograph of the Venlo bridge over the river Maas, taken by P/O Clyde Heath, November 8th 1944. The bombing was carried out by 2 Group medium bombers. *(Photo: "Thirty Four Wing. An Unofficial Account")*

FLIGHT LIEUTENANT J.M. THOMPSON – PL 965 Pilot

F/Lt "Tommy" Thompson outside the operations room at Melsbroek, January 1945. *(Photo: L.L. Cadan)*

F/Lt "Tommy" Thompson joined the RCAF in 1940, and next year trained at 16 EFTS, Edmonton, 34 SFTS, Medicine Hat, and CFS (Central Flying School), Trenton. Later that year he became an instructor at St Hubert, amassing 1,300 hours on Harvards by the middle of 1943. Next year Thompson crossed the Atlantic, posted to the Dallachy Course and subsequently to 14 AFU, Banff, in Scotland.

His PR training as usual took place at 8 OTU (Dyce) during July and August of 1944, followed by a posting to Benson before joining 16 Squadron at Northolt in September. He moved subsequently with his squadron to Amiens (France), Melsbroek (Belgium) Eindhoven (Netherlands) and on detachment to Bückeburg, (Germany). On repatriation in August 1945 he was discharged from the RCAF and has never flown alone since.

Total flying time on Anson, Auster, Bolingbroke, Cessna, Fleet, Harvard, Hurricane, Mosquito, Mustang, Oxford, Spitfire, Tiger Moth, Wellington: 1,881 hours (Spitfire 175).

Sorties in PL 965 (operational):

05.04.45: Ops 1 hr 45 min (no photos)
Total: 1 hr 45 min

PL965 Pilots II

FLYING OFFICER I.E.D. WILLIAMS

Believed to be F/O Idris Williams, alongside a Spitfire PR Mark XI of 16 Squadron. The aircraft's engine air intake has a canvas cover to keep moisture, dust, insects and nesting birds out while it is parked. *(Photo: L.L. Cadan)*

In September 1942 Idris Einion David Williams transferred from the Royal Artillery, where he had been a Second Lieutenant since January 1941. He was immediately granted a temporary commission as a P/O in the General Duties branch of the RAF and subsequently promoted the following March to the war-substantive rank of F/O. In September 1944 he was elevated to F/Lt and he remained in service until Februaruy 1946.

Sorties in PL 965 (operational):

07.04.45: Ops 2 hr 15 min (photos)
Total: 2 hr 15 min

Extract from the 16 Squadron Line Book concerning F/O I.E.D. Williams' sortie on April 7th 1945 flying PL 965. *(From: 16 Squadron archive)*

Continued overleaf >

3043   16/2010:7 APR 45:F20" H 75/23·18000'.

F/O Idris Williams took these photographs of Lüneburg marshalling yards and Lüneburg airfield from 18-23,000 feet using a 20-inch focal-length vertical camera of PL 965 on April 7th 1945. The four large hangars on the airfield are still there today. *(Photos: Air Photo Library, Keele)*

> Continued
from overleaf

16/2010 : 7 APR 45 : F20 K 76/23 - 18000'

4027

FLIGHT LIEUTENANT E. MARTIN DFC

Eric Martin came from a home-counties background and an equestrian family. Granted an emergency commission in March 1942 he was promoted to F/O in October of the same year. March 1944 saw him adding a second ring to his sleeve and he went on to become OC "B" Flight of 16 Squadron. He left the RAF as a F/O in January 1946 but, 6 months later, returned as a F/Lt and was awarded a permanent commission in June 1948. He died in August 1952, while displaying an aircraft (it has been reported) in an RAF Battle of Britain air display.

Sorties in PL 965 (operational):

09.04.45: Ops 2 hr 40 min (photos)
14.04.45: Ops 2 hr 50 min (photos)
16.04.45: Ops 2 hr 30 min
Total: 8 hr

F/Lt Eric Martin DFC, Eindhoven 1945. He is wearing the purple and pale blue ribbon of the DFC, and the dark blue, red and pale blue of the 1939-1945 Star. Eric Martin was killed in a flying accident in 1952. *(Photo: L.L. Cadan)*

Facing page: the heavily bombed German airfield at Zwischenahner lake (near Oldenburg) photographed by F/Lt Eric Martin from 24,500 feet with the 20-inch focal-length vertical cameras of PL 965, on April 14th 1945. *(Photo: Air Photo Library, Keele)*

A/B. 1700 hrs. S/c ~~target~~. Trak photos, too much green light - port camera. Returned to base & landed 1940 without incident

S.20". 25,000'. Airfields - Fassburg, Bremen, Zwischenahuer. Climbed to 25,000'. Photographs Frassburg area to Bremen area and Zwishenahuer Lake airfield. Runs O.K. No incidents. Landed 19.40.

S.36" 30,000' Cover of the Frisians

Extracts from the 16 Squadron Line Book and Operations Record Book concerning F/Lt Eric Martin's sorties on April 9th, 14th and 16th 1945 flying PL 965. *(From: 16 Squadron archive & the Public Records Office)*

A/B 1650 climbed to 28000 Photo of area as reqd. Saw P.R Spit & contrails fly across my bow E to W. No incidents. Returned & landed base 1920

3103   33:...: 14 APR 45 620/K69/25.000

FLIGHT LIEUTENANT J.F.G. RENIER DFC

F/O Joe Renier enjoying a half pint of beer at "Chez Gaston" in wartime London. *(Photo: Georges Lecomte)*

F/Lt Joe Renier DFC was a 2nd Lieutenant in the Belgian Air Force and already over 30 years old when he escaped in January or February 1941 from Occupied France, over the Pyrénées to Spain. He was imprisoned in Barcelona, in the Castel Modelo, sharing a cell with a younger Belgian fighter pilot, Jean Parisse. They were suspected of being the accomplices of the third inmate, an "English spy". In order to expedite his release, Renier later changed his nationality to Canadian. On arrival in UK he was accepted into the RAF, to complete a first tour of duty with 609 Squadron and a second with 140 and 16 Squadrons. His RAF service was recognised with the award of a DFC.

Universally described as a most charming man, he returned to the Belgian Air Force after the war, having been promoted Captain with effect from 1940. Renier commanded 1st Fighter Wing at Beauvechain (Bevekom) in 1952/53 and continued at Air Centre, Fontainebleau, retiring in the early '60s as a Lieutenant-Colonel.

Sorties in PL 965 (operational):

18.04.45: Ops 2 hr 40 min (photos)
23.04.45: Ops 2 hr 40 min (photos)
Total:　　5 hr 20 min

A/B 16"35   s/e A climbed to 28.000. 10/10 clouds but the target was clear. was chased big Me 109 which try to come in my tail I turned on him. The made a half roll & pulled away in a very fast & steep dive. I made 5 runs over target. On my 2d run I saw two unidentified single seat fighters. Two avoid beeing seen, I flew for 4 minutes full out north of Kiel. During the meeting of the Me 109, as a result of avoiding action, I broke the oxygen tube, I flew for 1"30 with the free end of the oxygen tube fixed in my mouth as a cigar & after removing the mask. Landed at base at 19"15.

Extract from the 16 Squadron Line Book concerning F/Lt Joe Renier's encounter with enemy aircraft on April 18th 1945 while flying PL 965. *(From: 16 Squadron archive)*

A/B 8.30. climbed on course to 28000. through clouds. Got 4 airfields out of 7 and through gaps in clouds. Landed at base 11"10. no incidents

Extract from the 16 Squadron Line Book concerning F/Lt Joe Renier's sortie in PL 965 on April 2rd 1945 covering Cuxhaven, Sylt, and Wilhelmshaven. *(From: 16 Squadron archive)*

WARRANT OFFICER E. CHALK

Ernest Chalk enlisted in 1939 as an airman. During the next six years he was Mentioned In Dispatches, accepted for pilot training and flew operationally as an NCO pilot before being commissioned in April 1945. He held the war-substantive rank of P/O until being de-mobbed in February 1946.

W/O Ernest "Chalky" Chalk, Eindhoven 1945. His decorations are the dark blue, red and pale blue ribbon of the 1939-1945 Star and the Oak Leaf for Mention In Dispatches. *(Photo: W.C. Anderson)*

Sorties in PL 965 (operational):

07.04.45: Ops 2 hr 20 min (photos)
Total: 2 hr 20 min

Extract from the 16 Squadron Line Book concerning W/O E. Chalk's sortie on April 24th 1945 flying PL 965. *(From: 16 Squadron archive)*

FLIGHT LIEUTENANT M.A. WETZ DFC

F/Lt Mike Wetz DFC was an RAF special entrant to Oxford in the autumn of 1940, where he began initial training until joining the RAF proper next spring, starting at Regents Park ("where I cleaned all the toilets while I waited for a posting"). Elementary flying training at Booker, Buckinghamshire, began that winter, but in March '41 he "crossed the pond" for primary training at the US Navy Base, Detroit. His US Navy Wings were awarded in December at Pensacola, where he flew several types but finished up on Catalinas. Early 1943 found him on Prince Edward Island, Canada, for a navigation course, which was followed by conversion to single-engined aircraft and return to UK. From 8 OTU Dyce, he was posted to 16 Squadron at Hartford Bridge in November 1943. He remained with the Squadron until it was disbanded in September 1945 (apart from a spell with HQ 34 Wing at the

F/Lts Mike Wetz DFC (left) and Ken Snell outside the 34 Wing Operations Room at Melsbroek. *(Photo: L.L. Cadan)*

YEAR 1945		AIRCRAFT		PILOT, OR 1ST PILOT	2ND PILOT, PUPIL OR PASSENGER	DUTY (INCLUDING RESULTS AND REMA
MONTH	DATE	Type	No.			
—	—	—	—			TOTALS BROUGHT FORW
JUNE	28	SPITFIRE XI	K125	SELF	—	B 151 - 78
"	29	"	R965	"	—	B78 - BLACKBUSH
"	30	"	R965	"	—	BLACKBUSHE - B78
"	30	"	R965	"	—	B78 - 151
SUMMARY		FOR	JUNE			(SPITFIRE
UNIT			16 SQUADRON			
DATE			30/6/45			
		Michael. A. Wetz				

end of his first tour) and was "de-mobbed" (de-mobilised from the RAF) next year. About 320 of his 600 flying hours were on Spitfires, the rest distributed among 13 other types.

Mike Wetz received a special award of the DFC in 1944 for low level communications work with the beleaguered ground forces after the airborne assault on Arnhem.

Sorties in PL 965 (all non-operational):

29.06.45: B78 – Blackbushe 1 hr 10 min
(Parents' Silver Wedding)
30.06.45: Blackbushe – B78 1 hr 15 min
30.06.45: B78 – B151 55 min
11.08.45: Local (B78) 1 hr 10 min
24.08.45: Blackbushe 1 hr 40 min
28.08.45: Blackbushe – Farsfield 30 min
28.08.45: Farsfield – Eindhoven 1 hr
Total: 7 hr 40 min

Entry in the Flying Log Book of F/Lt Mike Wetz DFC recording his sorties in PL 965 during June 1945. *(From: M.A. Wetz)*

SINGLE-ENGINE AIRCRAFT				MULTI-ENGINE AIRCRAFT						PASS-ENGER	INSTR/CLOUD FLYING [incl. in cols. (1) to (10)]	
DAY		NIGHT		DAY			NIGHT				DAY	PILOT
	PILOT	DUAL	PILOT	DUAL	1ST PILOT	2ND PILOT	DUAL	1ST PILOT	2ND PILOT		DUAL	PILOT
(1)	(2)	(3)	(4)	(5)	(6)	(7)	(8)	(9)	(10)	(11)	(12)	(13)
1	405·25	6·15	5·05	12·35	—	16·30	·10			16·35	29·30	28·35
	1·00											
	1·10			(Parents Silver Wedding)								
	1·15											
	·55											
	4·20											
	18·40											

O.C. 'A' FLIGHT

O.C. 16 SQDN.

LIEUTENANT ANDRE ESTARIA

Lt André Estaria (Free French) was a commercial pilot before the war, and a great extrovert, noted for his impressive one-legged squat-to-stand-up performance at Mess parties. When France was liberated (and as soon as he could get through to Rheims) he disappeared in an Anson for several days, apparently on a personal "operation". On return to Northolt, the Anson (very much over-weight) stalled onto the runway and made a very heavy landing. The undercarriage collapsed, and the aircraft ended up on its belly. Estaria, mercifully uninjured, had to be freed from the cockpit, which had been invaded by part of his cargo — which consisted entirely of cases of champagne! Despite the prang, the champagne survived long enough to be enjoyed by his grateful allies. Other "humanitarian" operations involved coffee to the thirsty Belgians and a Spitfire-load of bicycle tubes, which also escaped in the cockpit — but unfortunately turned out to be "Imperial" rather than metric sizes!

He was "a terrible navigator", but nevertheless an accomplished and dedicated pilot. Very popular on the Squadron, he was also a great man with the ladies, with whom he claimed he wasn't unfaithful to his wife (a French nurse), because he never loved them!

Sorties in PL 965 (operational):

25.04.45:	Ops 2 hr 5 min (photos)
Total:	2 hr 5 min

The photograph was taken at Eindhoven in 1945. Note the French pilot's badge on his right-hand breast pocket, and the Lieutenant's bars on his epaulettes. *(Photo: L.L. Cadan)*

Extract from the 16 Squadron Line Book concerning Lt André Estaria's sortie in PL 965 on April 25th 1945, covering Cuxhaven airfield and "gap filling" of mapping survey areas. *(From: 16 Squadron archive)*

"Q-for" Engineering

Flying Officer Edgar "Q-for" Quested was Engineering Officer for 16 Squadron from 1942. Until the formation of 34 Wing and the introduction of the centralised Servicing Echelon system (which was introduced in anticipation of a much heavier battle-damage, repair and maintenance work-load than eventually transpired after D-Day), he was responsible for all servicing and maintenance of aircraft, vehicles, and ground equipment (even trivia such as marquee lighting)

on the Squadron. By the time 16 Squadron was dug-in at Melsbroek, however, his team was concerned with fairly immediate problems of day-to-day "line" serviceability, whereas tasks like propeller-changing, 120-hour checks and engine-changes, which were well within the capacity of his skilled technicians, were being passed on to 6016 Servicing Echelon, which was "crying out for work". It made his job much easier, but not as challenging as it had been in the days of Army Co-op, when his

Melsbroek, first thing in the morning probably of January 5th 1945. An airman with his greatcoat inscribed "ANN THE BEAUTIFUL" has already shovelled snow away from the undercarriage of Spitfire PR Mark XI "T" PL 980. The fitter is in the cockpit warming up the Merlin 70 motor and the warmth of the engine and exhaust ports has melted the snow and ice from the nose cowling. PR Mosquitos of 140 Squadron are dispersed in the background. It is very early in 1945 and red, white, blue and yellow roundels have been applied to the aircraft to make it more identifiable to trigger-happy USAAF pilots. The lighter-painted belly panels show where the black and white (half) "invasion stripes" of 1944 have been obliterated. *(Photo: E. Quested)*

The ground-staff have arrived in force and are preparing Spitfire "T" PL 890 for its first sortie of the day, wiping off the airframe while directing the warm air hose of the de-icer truck to soften snow and ice. Sergeant Bone (left) directs operations. Note the red, white, blue and yellow "C" type roundel on the wing. On January 3rd 1945, HQ 2nd TAF decreed that all 2nd TAF aircraft (including PR types) must carry this version of the national marking. Nonetheless, the 140 Squadron PR Mosquito in the background still bears the old two-colour version on its fuselage. The dark mark painted on the Spitfire's aileron is the sighting mark for oblique photography, used in conjunction with a cross-hair etched on the canopy. *(Photo: E. Quested)*

resourcefulness and ingenuity were constantly being tested.

Teamwork and organisation

"Every PR aircraft was able to fly not just by the lift of its wings and power of its Merlin but also by the endeavours of its capable pilot and a host of terra firma humans – ground-crews, radio and radar operators, camera technicians, meteorologists, intelligence officers, cooks, clerks, etc. A flaw in the links of this chain could put the pilot's life in jeopardy.

"For my part, the serviceability depended to a large part on the welfare of the ground-crews and the organisation of their work and equipment. I look back and am certain that we maintained a high standard of serviceability – others higher up have remarked upon this, and this was helped to a large extent by the team of NCOs and tradesmen that I was fortunate enough to have inherited (and kept) – Sergeants Bone, Read, Parmenter, Shobruck and Talbot are a few of those who gave excellent service.

"I rank as some of my priorities: much attention to the serviceability and availability of the ground equipment, and availability of special and frequently-used tools such as wheel spanners needed for quick wheel-changing, plug spanners, etc. In this respect I found it helpful to have vital tools attached to a wooden backboard prominently displayed at dispersal point and insisted that these were returned as and when used – rather than have them locked or hidden away in a fitter's tool kit when he could not be found.

"Our busiest time was during and after D-Day when very many routine sorties were carried out – serviceability was vital then just to keep things moving – essential to have starter trolleys with fully-charged batteries, diesel engines in good order for lighting various places, field telephones always working efficiently.

"The evening before D-Day the Windmill Girls arrived to give us a show in a large marquee, and just before the show began we had to "tannoy" the lads to report for work. The black-and-white

Warm air from the de-icer truck is now being used on the frozen rudder hinges of "T" PL 980, while an airman works on the port undercarriage. The pilot, S/Ldr Tony Davis DFC (OC 16 Squadron), stamps his feet to keep warm, his maps stuffed into his flying boots. He is wearing a polo-neck sweater ("Frock White") under his battledress blouse, silk glove liners and pressure waistcoat, which will be connected to the oxygen supply in the cockpit *(See: Appendix IV; page 137)*. His flying helmet is lying on the port tailplane. Inside the cockpit below the windscreen is the Type 35 camera control-box, which set the time interval on the cameras. In the distance beyond the truck is a PR Mosquito of 140 Squadron. *(Photo: E. Quested)*

"The Merlin engine behaved well under all conditions, but a headache did occur on one occasion. A particular engine performed perfectly on "run-up" on the ground, but several pilots claimed that it cut out when doing aerobatics. This was eventually traced to a faulty fuel feed-pipe to the carburettor. The pipe had been disconnected from the carb' for a couple of weeks during servicing and fuel had remained in the "U" bend in the pipe, which had apparently weakened the inner wall of the pipe so that, when the engine was given a quick burst of power, the inner wall collapsed, so temporarily shutting off the fuel. The problem was only detected when the pipe was removed and straightened on a level surface, and looked through with a torch light. The news was passed on to HQ and a signal was dispatched to ground all Spits to check the part number of this item and renew it with another of different make.

"O" PL 823 gets similar treatment. The warm air is now being used to free the brakes, while an airman polishes the one-piece windscreen. On the port tailplane is a parachute pack, and the retractable tail-wheel doors are obvious. Beyond the Spitfires of 16 Squadron's dispersal ("K" PM 125 nearest) is a row of B-25 Mitchells. *(Photo: E. Quested)*

stripes had to be painted on the aircraft after collecting drums of white and black oil-bound distemper and dozens of whitewash brushes from the railway station.

"When recalling some of the peculiarities, snags and cures regarding the Mustangs and Spitfires that I worked on, let me not forget the paperwork that had to be attended to at all times. Also the manpower and difficulties involved in attending to visiting aircraft of all types (refuelling and minor servicing) including American Liberators. My praise for the ground "erks" cannot easily be expressed: they often had to work long hours under difficult conditions and to be adept at improvisation, but somehow remained fit and cheerful."

Spitfire snags and solutions

"My respect and praise for the Spitfire XI cannot be exaggerated. It was easy to maintain and spares were easily available. But there were inevitably some problems which needed persistence and ingenuity to overcome.

F/O Edgar "Q-for" Quested, 16 Squadron Engineering Officer, pilot S/Ldr Tony Davis DFC, and an unidentified airman wearing an American greatcoat, snapped shortly before the sortie. Both the camera access hatch on the starboard side of the Spitfire and the access hatch on the port side, with its optically "flat" glazing for the oblique camera position, are open. Davis is wearing a pressure waistcoat, which will be connected to the oxygen supply in the cockpit. This outfit was tailored to fit at Farnborough, but was suspected of being responsible for the loss of a pilot who dived into the ground after climbing to altitude – possibly because in his case the jacket was incorrectly connected to the system. *(Photo: E. Quested)*

With a puff of smoke from the exhaust ports S/Ldr Tony Davis DFC starts up "T" PL 980, while an airman at the wing-tip stands with his finger on the switch of the "trolley-acc." external electrical power supply (kept fully charged by its small petrol motor), which has just been used to activate the Spitfire's starter motor. The chocks are still firmly in place, and an airman is leaning over the tail-end of the fuselage to keep it on the deck when the engine is power-checked. The protective canvas canopy cover lies in the snow beyond. *(Photo: E. Quested)*

"One type of aileron gave us some trouble. It had a raised upper surface, and this caused level flight difficulties to such an extent that they could not be corrected unless both units were exchanged for the same flush type. Normally, slight level adjustment was possible by the upending (by about 2 mm) of the trailing edge using a soft hammer and wooden edge support.

"The Spitfire could easily be tipped on to its nose and this meant a propeller-change and a "clock" reading of the prop' shaft to check for "out of alignment". I had the good fortune to rescue a Spit that had force-landed in a small field in Holland just after the Arnhem episode. It had tipped up and badly damaged one blade. I managed to persuade someone to fly me to the scene in our little Auster aircraft and my decision was to cut 12 inches off each of the blades, shape them and run the engine to test for vibration. It was flown back with valuable pictures aboard and the pilot (who declared that it ran better than before) and the rest of the unit were delighted."

Photographic installations sometimes needed attention, too. For instance, alterations to the camera mounting had to be made for fitting a camera to take special pictures of the coast-line before D-Day. An early problem was that of the optical flats in the belly of the aircraft, which had a habit of becoming oiled over. The accumulated oil from ground-running, which collected in the bottom of the engine compartment, would stream back down the fuselage once the aircraft's tail came up on take-off, and some sorties were useless as the pictures were spoiled. "Q" cured this by cutting a square opening 5 inches by 5 inches under the engine cowling and fitting a hinged flap with a screwdriver screw catch (Dzus clip). A fitter would be dispatched by jeep or motorcycle to the end of the runway when the Spitfire was lined up for take-off. The little panel was simply opened and the accumulated oil (if any) could be wiped away with a rag.

Living and working conditions

For the whole of the war period personnel fared pretty well, according to "Q". They were accommodated in billets (staying in local houses) while at Weston Zoyland, in wooden accommodation huts at Andover and Hartford Bridge, and in tents and marquees at Northolt. On moving to the Continent, tents remained the order of the day until becoming established at Melsbroek

Two airmen tow the disconnected trolley-acc. clear as S/Ldr Tony Davis DFC completes his cockpit pre-flight checks. *(Photo: E. Quested)*

On a snowy early morning sortie at the beginning of 1945, Spitfire "T" PL 980 accelerates down the runway at Melsbroek, flown by S/Ldr Tony Davis DFC .
(Photo: E. Quested)

in the winter of 1944. Here the resourceful "erks" took over lofts and basements of old buildings and built themselves makeshift but weather-proof corrugated iron sheds. The worst memory is of "filthy" wooden huts left by their Allied predecessors at Eindhoven.

At Melsbroek the engineering department was able to renovate buildings left by the Germans and utilise them for workshops.

"We had a few spells of really cold weather on the Continent (especially at the time of the Battle of the Bulge) and occasionally had to clear part of the runway for take-offs – all hands were needed whatever one's trade or rank. On the aircraft we used de-icing equipment sparingly and had to watch for corrosion taking a grip on the phosphor-bronze bushes of ailerons, etc, when "Kilfrost" fluid from 5-gallon drums was used." There was also a special de-icing truck with wide, concertina tubes for blowing warm air, which could be man-handled and directed as required.

January 1945, Melsbroek airfield under snow, and Sharpe, Littler, Quested and Nicholls take a short break. "Q" is wearing the medal ribbons of the MBE (three light grey stripes on pink) and the 1940 campaign medal for France (dark blue, red and light blue) where he served in 2 Squadron before the Dunkirk evacuation.
(Photo: E. Quested)

Daily Inspection Section

At Melsbroek the day began for the ground-crews about 7.00 am with breakfast (unless a "Dawn Patrol" sortie required an earlier start), and the airmen would be on the dispersal site an hour later. All serviceable Spitfires were subject to DIs (Daily Inspections) by different sections such as FM(E)s (Flight Mechanics Engines) and FM(A)s (Flight Mechanics Airframes), Electricians and Photographic and Radio Technicians.

The FM(E) and FM(A) were usually a well-established team and assigned to a particular aircraft. First job was to take the covers off the engine, cockpit and pitot head, and unscrew the pickets which attached the aircraft to the ground as a precaution against strong winds. The FM(A) would then begin his detailed external checks, starting at the cockpit door and working around the Spitfire in a clockwise direction. Meanwhile, the FM(E) would check the Merlin's fuel, oil and glycol coolant levels (and for any signs of leaks), the exhaust manifolds, and intercooler. Normally the aircraft were refuelled immediately after every sortie by the petrol bowser lorry, both to be ready for use and also to prevent water condensation forming in partly-empty tanks.

With external airframe, undercarriage, radiators and cockpit inspected, and flying controls tested by the FM(A), the FM(E) then started and warmed-

"TAFF'S TEA SHOP" "M.I.D. AND BAR" (the proprietor "Taffy" Parnell's MID – Mention In Dispatches – was gazetted June 8th 1944) at 16 Squadron's Dispersal, Melsbroek. FM(A) Ron Parnell brews up for FM(E) Ron Abrahams, FM Albert Littler, and FM(A) Geoff Oldham. Their makeshift flight hut of corrugated iron is homemade, and the tea urn was once a Spitfire oil can. The walls also bear the messages VACANCY APPLY WITHOUT – ONE STOOGE FOR WATER CARRIER; "TYPHOO SPECIAL" NO SECONDS LATE CHITS MUST BE HERE HALF HOUR BEFORE HAND. Parnell was responsible for the artwork on the back of Littler's leather jerkin, which shows a corpse climbing out of a coffin, saying EH! NOT YET!! (Albert's father was an undertaker), and Taffy's own battledress blouse is painted with an oak leaf in honour of his MID. (Photo: R. Abrahams)

"No Smoking" at Eindhoven, scorching summer 1945. Cpl Gilbert FM(A), FMs Hurst, Hinchcliffe and Abrahams taking advantage of the shade. (Photo: H.R. Parnell)

Cameras and battery being fitted to Spitfire PR Mark XI "O" PL 823, Melsbroek early 1945. *(Photo: H.R. Parnell)*

up the engine – checking the magnetos, engine temperatures and pressures at various power settings. Three lucky "erks" would have the cold and windy job of draping themselves over the fuselage and tail-plane to keep it from lifting during the "run-up procedure". If all was well when the FM(E) shut down the engine, they could then make their way to the flight office to sign the "Form 700", which would also have to be signed by all the other tradesmen when they had completed their individual daily routines. If an aircraft was found to be u/s (unserviceable) by any tradesman, the snag was recorded on the '700 and it was not flown until the problem had been rectified.

FM(A) Ron Parnell points out two simple tasks were of particular importance with the PR Spitfire. "Most important for the pilot's view: inspect and clean the windscreen and canopy in and out with perspex polish, making sure that there were no spots visible to distract the pilot. Also, in order to reduce drag as much as possible, it was essential to have a clean aircraft, free of oil and glycol drips (especially around the camera lenses). Any oil was

removed with "Gunk" fluid, and finally the whole aircraft was cleaned with the same stuff, which gave a very smooth finish".

"Not for us the thrill of action,
tension, danger, strain:
But on us relies the safety
of the Spitfire 'plane"

...as the 16 Squadron ground-crew motto ran.

After each sortie the aircraft would be returned to its ground-crew for a further between-flight service, ready for the next flight. "I often put the following question to the pilot, 'How is she flying?' Reply: 'Straight and level with hands off, Taff – perfect'."

It took three to four months of "square bashing", practical work in basic engineering skills, and specialised theory, to turn a conscript into an aircraftsman. In addition to the requirements of a particular job (such as airframe mechanic), the basic theory of flight, aircraft structure, flight instruments and cockpit procedures were covered.

"After inwardly digesting the former and making notes during the instruction classes each day, we were eventually tested at the end of the course," remembers Parnell. "Some failed the examination, others were made up to AC2 (fair), AC1 (very good) and LAC (Leading Aircraftsman – excellent or 100%)." Once posted to a squadron, the airman learned airfield defence with the .303-inch Lee Enfield rifle and Bren light machine-gun, and to carry out day and night guard-duty and aircraft Crash Party duties.

The Bedford fuel bowser driver at Melsbroek. Note the "gas detector tray" in front of the driver's position. *(Photo: H.R. Parnell)*

Changing the plugs on a Spitfire PR Mark XI. The bowser driver looks on while FM(E) Ron Abrahams, FM(A) Ron "Taffy" Parnell, and FM(A) Doug Jacques (on the ground) handle the tools. *(Photo: H.R. Parnell)*

Hartford Bridge 1943. F/Lt Eric Martin DFC in the cockpit of one of 16 Squadron's first batch of Spitfire PR Mark XIs. FM(E) Percy Last manhandles the trolley-acc. external electrical supply past Cpl Douglas, while FM(A) Taffy Parnell brings back the starter plug. FM(E) Ron Abrahams stands in the background. *(Photo: H.R. Parnell)*

"Morning and afternoon breaks were brought around by NAAFI and the Salvation Army to "dispersal", and lunch was in shifts between 12 and 1 pm. Tea was brewed at 4.30 and the day ended at dusk after the last aircraft landed. Guard-duty came around every three to four weeks. On the airfield – two hours on, two off. Playing cards and listening to the radio were the main pastimes, but evening entertainment at Melsbroek was very good. Two trucks were put on to run into Brussels, leaving at 7 pm and returning at 11 pm. You had to make sure you caught the transport back or you were in great trouble. And there were always leftovers in the canteen if a snack was required", recalls Taffy Parnell's "oppo", FM(E) Ron Abrahams. "Not often!" contradicts Parnell.

An aspect of Melsbroek which sticks in Abrahams' mind concerns USAAF Flying Fortresses, which occasionally came in after long-distance daylight bombing raids. "No person was allowed off the 'plane. Injured and dead were flown back to England. You could see the airmen dead over the guns. Not a pretty sight to see".

"All the Yanks would say was, 'Fill her up, boys, we've got a bloody mess on board. We must get back to England tonight'. I often doubted whether they would reach England with their rudders and tail-plane riddled with holes and their forward turrets shot away", muses Parnell.

"Only once did we see major action, which left us a bit shattered", says Ron Abrahams. "New Year's Eve – most of the personnel went down into Brussels for a celebration, a large Service (Malcolm) Club which was open for food, drink and a dance band to listen to. A good time had by all. January 1st – all feeling a little drowsy sitting in the Nissen hut on the airfield. All of a sudden – machine-gun fire. Out of the hut we came to see what was going on. Our field latrine was a nearby trench with containers in the bottom. We just dived into the trench when we saw German aircraft coming down and simply firing at will into our parked Spitfires, Mosquitos, and Wellingtons! One was even flying up and down the runway to stop aircraft from taking-off! By the time they had

finished, many aircraft were on fire, but luckily our trench did not get a burst".

Fitter LAC Ken Holloway tells how "...about 50 Me 109s and Fw 190s strafed us just after 9 o'clock. The airfield looked like Pearl Harbour, everything seemed to be burning, including Mustangs, the little Austers and a Stirling just repaired by an MU gang waiting for a ferry crew. We lost two Spits and two were damaged (sic), but luckily we had no casualties on the Squadron. I was doing my DI engine-run in a Spitfire when they came in. I didn't bother about any slow-running cut-off, I can tell you. I just hit the mag. switch and dived behind a trolley-acc! When the first wave went by, I ran to the slit-trench, which was so full of blokes that when I jumped in I landed on Bill Frencham's back! He never smoked, but 'Give me a cigarette, we'll not see Blighty again!' he cried."

After a "bit of a do" in the Mess the night before, Squadron Engineering Officer F/O Quested was cycling as usual along the perimeter track on his way to the Servicing Echelon when "...I saw

Spitfire PR Mk XI "H" PL 892 of 16 Squadron at Eindhoven, summer 1945, on an ex-Luftwaffe dispersal site. In the background is a pile of aircraft wreckage. The airmen are FM(A) "Taffy" Parnell, FM Bill Frencham, FM(E) Ron Abrahams. The picture distinctly shows how the original faded two-colour wing roundel has been extended with new paint to make it a "C" type (red, white, blue and yellow) and the same thing applies to the fuselage. *(Photo: H.R. Parnell)*

Spitfires PR Mk XI "H" PL 892 and "C" PA 939 of 16 Squadron at Eindhoven, summer 1945, on an ex-Luftwaffe dispersal site. The airmen are FM Bill Frencham and FM(A) Ron Abrahams. The picture also shows how the original faded two colour wing roundel has been extended with new paint to make it a "C" type (red, white, blue and yellow) and the same thing applies to the fuselage. *(Photo: H.R. Parnell)*

Ablutions by the air raid shelter at Northolt while living under canvas in April/May 1944 – FM(E) Ron Abrahams, FM Smith, FM(A) Cpl Gilbert, AC Cockburn, FM(A) Ron Parnell, FM(E) Reg Hinchcliffe, FM(E) Arthur Robinson, FM Bill Frencham, FM(A) Geoff Oldham, FM Rosenburg, FM Percy Last. On the makeshift bench are washing and shaving kits, propped-up mirrors and wash bowls made from half a petrol can. *(Photo: R. Abrahams)*

three low-flying aircraft. Spitfires? Who's up this early in the morning? Then one peeled off and made, as far as I could tell, straight for me. Bullets spattered on the peri-track in front of me as I went into the ditch. When he passed over, I looked over to see the other aircraft drop down to attack the aircraft on the other side of the field. The Wellington boys really suffered because they were caught inside their aircraft doing their daily inspection, and some were burned.

"We had little or no airfield defence: the AA (anti-aircraft) guns were in place for anti-tank use", which had been the case since the scare of the Ardennes Offensive (or "Battle of the Bulge") in December.

When the enemy aircraft had fired off all their ammunition, records the 34 Wing history, "Six Spitfires, six Mosquitos and eleven Wellingtons of the Wing were destroyed (or damaged) and there were 25 casualties, of whom six died. The enemy were so elated that they then gave a rather feeble aerobatic display over Brussels, for which they

Left: Melsbroek, the morning of January 1st 1945. 16 Squadron Spitfires "F", "O" and "N" appear undamaged, but another blazes beyond them. Figures are running about urgently by the tents. The purpose of the vehicle carrying a hut in the foreground is still a mystery. Right: A Wellington of 69 Squadron. *(Photos: E. Quested)*

suffered a severe penalty when they attempted to get back to Germany".

16 Squadron lost three Spitfires: Category E (written off) "M" PL 765, "K" PL 976, "S" PL 905; one Category B (sent for repair at a Maintenance Unit) "J" PL 978; one Category AC (repairable on site) "P" PL 912. All were replaced within the week by 34 WSU.

FMs Hinchcliffe, Hurst and Robinson with "instruments bod" Holmes who is carrying a couple of Spitfire oxygen bottles, Melsbroek 1944. *(Photo: H.R. Parnell)*

A/C Rosenburg with 16 Squadron Spitfire "R" for Robert, at Melsbroek. Whether this photograph was taken in 1944 (in which case the aircraft is likely to be PL 849) or in 1945 (in which case it would be PL 965) cannot be confirmed. *(Photo: H.R. Parnell)*

Farewell 16 Squadron

unfortunate enough to be sitting opposite) with a steely blue-eyed (if slightly glazed) stare, his unwelcome attention eventually unsettled its object to the point where blows were exchanged. Next morning there was no sign of "Scotty" when it was time to check the duty roster. S/Ldr Tony Davis was not impressed and when it was discovered that the missing pilot was being detained by the Belgian police, it was rumoured that his "number was up" on the Squadron.

A grim-faced party was dispatched to bail-out the miscreant and bring him back to face the music. However, on arrival at the Gendarmerie, there was another kind of party in progress! "Scotty" had been proclaimed a local hero for spotting what turned out to be a left-over German soldier who, for reasons best known to himself, had not pulled-out with the rest of his comrades when the area was liberated. "That Bloody Aussie Scotty" (as he describes himself) had got away with it again!

Ubiquitous Dyce

"I had volunteered for fighters, and was posted to 8 OTU, Dyce, Scotland, on 13 June '44 on PRU Spits. Training was fairly intensive – 10 hours Link Training (flight simulation) involving precision blind instrument-flying; numerous lectures covering aerial photographic techniques: the operation of the photographic instruments in the cockpit; the use of various focal-length lenses, eg 5-inch, 14-inch, 36-inch, to obtain different scales; the use of selective time intervals to obtain the correct overlaps, which gave the third dimensional aspect (when viewed by a Photographic Interpreter armed with a stereoscope)."

"On the flying side, there was training in the use of navigational instruments, preparing the flight-path, numerous practice sorties over UK, photographing nominated targets using "line overlap", "mosaic" and low level oblique methods; practice in learning how to turn on to the photographic run; how to flip the aircraft vertically between exposures to ensure you were directly over the target; allowing for wind drift; low level oblique single shots from the side of the aircraft, sighting from marks on the canopy, etc. A high standard of photography and general flying was required before posting onto ops."

"Scotty" Cadan wearing RAAF dark blue battledress. The note on the back of the photo says "hangover". *(Photo: L.L. Cadan)*

PL 965's last 16 Squadron pilot was red-haired Australian "Scotty" Cadan, an unconventional character, but well-loved on the Squadron. A fitness fanatic in comparison with his fellow-pilots, he could often be seen jogging the perimeter track. However, this healthy exercise was offset by occasional sprees among the neighbouring watering-holes, which sometimes brought him under the jaundiced gaze of Authority. On one occasion, recalls his friend Andy Anderson, "Scotty" was returning to Melsbroek airfield by tram from Brussels, just a little the worse for his evening's entertainment. Fixing a "local" (who was

Airborne Assault

"I stayed with 16 Squadron from the day of joining until disbandment on 22nd September '45. During this period, 16 Squadron operated from Northolt, A.12 France (an apple orchard in Normandy), Amiens, Melsbroek (outside Brussels), and Eindhoven in Holland. I did 53 operational sorties with a total of 203 hours on Spit XI, with a few hours on Spit XIX.

"Whilst at Amiens, six of us volunteered to return to England to do a special operation (wanted to see girl friends, etc). The operation turned out to be covering the parachute drop at Arnhem. We were operating from Northolt and these were the most memorable sorties I can recall. It was almost impossible to get photos – aircraft everywhere going down in flames, gliders in their thousands on the deck, getting jumped by aircraft (both sides). Of the six of us, only two survived, me and the OC in charge of that op. ("Thirty Four Wing – An Unofficial Account" records two Spitfires and two Mosquitos under the direction of Sandy Webb. Two pilots went missing, one returned later having been hidden by Dutch people and after many adventures). I was recommended for the Dutch Bronze Cross, but heard nothing further.

"There was a marvellous camaraderie in 34 Wing, of which 16 Squadron was a part. Pilots and ground-crew got on extremely well, with great rivalry between Wellington, Mosquito and Spitfire teams."

Bringing PL 965 Home

Scotty Cadan flew "R" '965 on several occasions (four PR and nine non-operational sorties). On February 22nd 1945 he was forced to abandon an operational sortie in '965 when the engine went u/s, possibly from a magneto packing up. He got home with a very rough motor "but down to a nasty low level".

"I was the last 16 Squadron pilot to fly "R" '965. The evening before 16 Squadron was due to do a fly-past and return to England and disbandment, '965 became temperamental and ground-staff advised me that it was u/s and I would not be able to leave with the rest of the Squadron. I hung around for a couple of days whilst ground-staff laboured mightily, eventually declaring '965 airworthy. Even then, it seemed the old war-horse was reluctant to leave the scene of its gallant exploits.

"Airborne, the radio packed up – frightful weather – so returned to Eindhoven.

"Another attempt the next day. Same story and had to creep into Knocke.

"Next day I kicked '965 smartly on one of the oleos. 'This is it, old boy' – and off we went, up to 38,000 feet over all the weather and presto, made it! I was quite upset to leave my Spitfire all alone at Dunsfold, looking very forlorn."

Strange War

"It was a strange war for me. Whilst at Northolt, we would do our sorties during the day, then repair to the "Old Bill" at Ruislip (our favourite pub), meet our girl friends and generally enjoy ourselves – practically office hours. Whilst on the Continent, this pattern continued. At Brussels we had a most luxurious Mess at one of the Rothschild's residences, our hostesses being the pick of society. Afternoon tea-dances were very popular, and a few of the lads succumbed to the local beauties. At Eindhoven, we also played tennis with the local belles and had some interesting swimming parties. I hope I haven't made it sound like 'a piece of cake', for there were interspersed moments of sheer fright."

16 Squadron Spitfire PR Mark XIs at Eindhoven, 1945. Both have "blister" cockpit canopies (see page 104), so the photograph was taken post war. *(Photo: E. Quested)*

FLYING OFFICER L.L. CADAN (RAAF) – PL 965 Pilot

F/O L.L. "Scotty" Cadan (RAAF) began training in Rhodesia with RAF instructors under the Empire Air Training Scheme in 1941-42. On arrival in England in September '42 he continued at AFUs Acaster Malbis and Leconfield, Yorkshire; AGS (Air Gunnery School) Mona and Castle Kennedy – and inevitably 8 OTU Dyce, Scotland (where he "wiped the port leg off a Spit in approach – very deflating"). Some of this stint in Training Command was spent recovering from a night flying "prang" at Acaster Malbis, near York, which "wrote-off" the aircraft concerned. He joined 16 Squadron at Northolt in August 1944 and remained with the Squadron until it disbanded in September 1945. After repatriation he stayed on in the RAAF, going to Japan with the British Commonwealth Occupation Forces, and returned there when the Korean war erupted, to fly Mustangs and Meteors. His service wound up with postings to Malaya and Trincomalee (Ceylon). In recognition of his efforts he collected a Mention In Dispatches and the American Air Medal (Korea). His Flying Log Book lists 14 types and a total time of more than 2,000 hours, about 250 on Spitfires.

Sorties in PL 965 (operational and non-operational):

22.02.45: Ops 45 min (engine packed up)
14.03.45: Ops 1 hr 50 min (photos)
19.03.45: Ops 1 hr 30 min (photos)
05.05.45: Air test 50 min
31.05.45: Low-level obliques 2 hr
26.06.45: Base (B78) – Hartford Bridge 2 hr 10 min
27.06.45: Hartford Bridge – Base 1 hr 55 min
27.07.45: Local (B78) 50 min
08.08.45: Local 40 min
06.09.45: Hartford Bridge – Base 1 hr 30 min
20.09.45: Base – Bury St Edmunds 2 hr (Bad weather. Returned to Base)
21.09.45: Base – Bury St Edmunds 1 hr 45 min (Weather still duff. Returned to Knocke)
22.09.45: Knocke – Bury St Edmunds 1 hr 10 min
22.09.45: Bury St Edmunds – Dunsfold 30 min
Total: 19 hr 25 min

Entry in the Flying Log Book of F/O "Scotty" Cadan recording his sorties in PL 965 during September 1945. *(From: L.L. Cadan)*

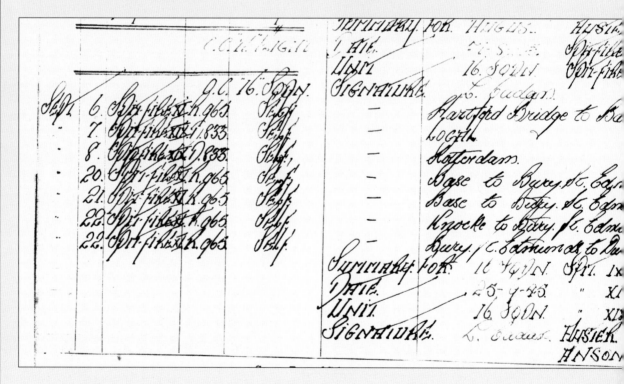

incident at 13.15 hrs.

S.20". 24.000'. Bremen.
Aircraft had 250 mag. drop on ground testing. Airborne
14.30 in hope of engine clearing. Climbed to 24.000',
but motor very rough. Tested switches again over Ruhr, on
port wing engine died. Decided to return to base. Base
O.K.

Extract from the 16 Squadron Operations Record Book concerning F/O "Scotty" Cadan's magneto-drop problems on February 22nd 1945 while flying PL 965. *(From: Public Records Office)*

A/B 1000. s/c + climbed to 27,000'. Photos of all targets, then did nice recce + radioed gen back. Base 1120. NB incidents.
L. Cadan, F/O.

Extract from the 16 Squadron Line Book concerning F/O "Scotty" Cadan's Met Recce on March 14th 1945 while flying PL 965. *(From: 16 Squadron archive)*

Airfields Ruhr.
Over target area 10/10ths. Waited for it to clear, but had
to come down to 15.000' to get below it. Broke cloud over
Gladbach and they threw everything at me, including the
kitchen sink. A terrible amount of markers came up and then
a 262 whizzed below going like the clappers, I did like-wise.
Went back and did a run along the Rhine, photographing a
large smoke screen. Base O.K. 10.10 hours.

Extract from the 16 Squadron Operations Record Book concerning F/O "Scotty" Cadan's encounter with an enemy aircraft on March 19th 1945 while flying PL 965. *(From: Public Records Office)*

.05.
6.25.
2.20.

1.30.
.40.
1.30.
2.00.
1.25.
1.10.
.30.
1.35.
193.10.
8.20.
4.20.

Bad weather. Returned to Base
Weather still duff. Returned to Brooke.

16. Squadron disbands. Good-luck to all my old comrades

4.30.

Spitfire Air Dispatch Letter Service

2nd TAF Communications Wing and BAFO Communications Wing

2nd TAF Communications Wing B.151 Bückeburg summer 1945. The army laid the PSP (pieced steel planking) runways in a matter of days on farmland. The ADLS Spitfire (possibly "D" PL 839) has a "blister" cockpit canopy. Slung beneath the centre-section is the cylindrical fuel tank converted for mail carrying. The airman in the foreground appears to be "laying the dust"! *(Photo: R. Abrahams)*

Several entries in the Flying Log Book of F/Lt Wendelken suggested at first glance that PL 965 was detached to Bückeburg, near Minden, with other Spitfires of 16 Squadron on ADLS duties (Air Dispatch Letter Service, with 2nd TAF Communications Wing, later British Air Forces of Occupation Communications Wing, Bückeburg, Germany). Sorties with "L" '965 were recorded several times, too. Subsequently it became clear that it was a case of mistaken identity as *"L" PL 985* definitely had been converted for this work, but entries in the Log Book of F/Lts Wetz, Stutchbury, and Anderson not only provided no further evidence concerning '965 in this rôle, but

confirmed that it retained its letter "R" throughout its service with 16 Squadron. There the matter rested until a letter from Douglas Petrie revealed:

"I flew Mark XI Spitfires with ADLS from August 14th 1945 to April 22nd 1946. From my Log Book entry I see that I flew PM 965 from Bückeburg to Schleswig-Cuxhaven and return. Flight time 1 hour 55 minutes. Since the few PM series aircraft had low numbers such as 137, 124, 133, 156, I think the PM 965 entry was an error and would more likely have been PL 965. However, there is no means of checking this (date of entry 13.1.46)."

Douglas Petrie had flown PL 965 on only two previous occasions, in January and February 1945

– a year before this date. Its serial number was not familiar to him. In January '46 there were two ex-16 Squadron Mark XIs with BAFO Communications Wing, which had been "C" PL 939 and "E" PL 970, but their digits are not easily confused with 965. There was also a PL 895, but no likely contenders in the PA or PM series of Spitfires Mark XI or XIX, so the possibility remains. It is worth remembering that PL 965 was accepted on charge by 151 RU, Lüneburg, in October '45 and could have been available for use in early 1946.

The ADLS Spitfires are a little-known variety, but interesting enough to justify further investigation. They are clearly described in the 16 Squadron Operations Record Book:

"5.6.45. Notification received by signal from Headquarters 2nd T.A.F. (REAR) that six Spitfire XI aircraft to be flown to 151 R.U. for modification to A.D.L.S. requirements. Fuselage cameras to be removed and plywood bulkheads and covers for flying controls to be fitted to form compartment for mail bags. Under fuselage, cylindrical fuel tanks

The ADLS Spitfire is having its wing leading edge fuel tanks topped-up from the bowser lorry. *(Photo: R. Abrahams)*

to be fitted and nose made removable to enable tank to be used for carrying mail bags. Modifications made will not prevent these aircraft

The ADLS Spitfire is possibly "T" PL 890. In the background is a Lockheed Hudson of RAF Coastal Command. *(Photo: W.J. Wendelken)*

Running up ADLS Spitfire "L" PL 985. In the background are Avro Ansons. *(Photo: W.J. Wendelken)*

ADLS Spitfire "K" PM 125 taxies from dispersal. Note the "blister" canopy. *(Photo: W.J. Wendelken)*

being re-converted to P.R. rôle at a later date. These aircraft will be completed by A.M. Monday, 10th June. They will remain on our strength... A detached flight of six Spitfire XI aircraft, together with pilots and maintenance personnel to B.151 (Bückeburg) ...will come under the Operational Control of O.C. 2nd T.A.F. Communications Wing. The maintenance personnel will be provided by 6016 S.E."

Eventually seven Spitfires appear to have been used, possibly because while at Bückeburg a new Merlin engine was flown in and a Spitfire re-engined and subsequently tested and flown back to UK for major overhaul. FM(E) Ron Abrahams, one of the party of flight mechanics supplied from 16 Squadron, is justifiably proud that he and his colleagues (who were not trained for such radical work) completed the task on site – particularly under the scorching heat of the summer of 1945. The seven ADLS aircraft were: "D" PL 839, "H" PL 892, "K" PM 125, "L" PL 985, "S" PL 964, "T" PL 890 and "V" PM 147. According to its movement records, PL 964 was unserviceable Category AC from a flying accident in August 1945, which falls within the period which ran from June 10th to September 12th. All the ADLS Spitfires (which still belonged to 16 Squadron) were returned, and flown to Dunsfold for disbandment. The ADLS unit continued in existence and subsequently became known as BAFO Comm. Wing.

ADLS Spitfire "L" PL 985 with trolley-acc. attached, ready for another urgent delivery. *(Photo: J.M. Thompson)*

Dutch Air Force Spitfire

On May 10th 1940 German forces invaded the Netherlands and for five days the Dutch LVA (Luchtvaart Afdeling – Aviation Division of the army) resisted bravely. However, its 29 fixed-undercarriage Fokker D.XXI front-line fighters were of a different generation from its Luftwaffe opponents, and the survivors ran out of ammunition after three of the five days of fighting. Nevertheless the LVA, with its obsolescent aircraft of all types, still managed to score almost two for one against Europe's most powerful and aggressive air force, an undeniable tribute to the skill and bravery of its officers and men. By May 15th they had to decide whether to obey orders and destroy all equipment before surrendering, or try to escape and continue fighting elsewhere. Eventually about 300 did escape to England, of whom about 20 were pilots, 75 student pilots and more than 50 ground engineers. Some travelled directly by sea, some drove and others simply walked into France, before crossing the Channel via Dunkirk. A very few managed to commandeer aircraft and fly out, including a complete flying school – that unfortunately then had to leave its aircraft in France.

RAF Coastal Command was quick to form two Dutch units, 320 and 321 Squadrons, at Pembroke Dock on June 1st 1940. The former squadron

A serious group of Luchtmacht Techniche School (LTS) student engineers at Deelen. The patched-up markings on the Spitfire in the background suggest that this is perhaps 1947 or '48. The Mark XI in the foreground may well be PL 965 (the only Mark XI to remain intact for long). *(Photo: H. van der Meer)*

utilised some Fokker T.VIII-W floatplanes, which had escaped with their MLD (Marine Luchtvaart Dienst - Naval Aviation Service) crews, but which were eventually replaced by Lockheed Hudsons. The latter squadron flew Avro Ansons. These two UK-based squadrons amalgamated in 1941, but a new 321 Squadron was formed in August 1942 in the Far East to patrol the Indian Ocean in Consolidated Catalinas. In 1943 320 Squadron was transferred to Bomber Command and re-equipped with Dutch-owned North American Mitchells.

On June 12th 1943 the Dutch personnel of 167 Squadron, which already fielded an all-Dutch "B" Flight, were formed into 322 (Dutch) Squadron at Hornchurch. HRH Prince Bernhard of the Netherlands, who was in exile in UK with the Dutch Royal Family, lobbied vigorously on behalf of the Squadron. A pilot himself, HRH had a Spitfire IIa at his disposal. 322 Squadron was immediately operational and fought in England, the Netherlands and Germany, using Spitfires Marks Vb, LF IXb, XIV, and LF XVIe in a wide variety of operations including "Ramrods", "Rhubarbs", "Jim Crow" and "Anti-Diver" patrols, "Armed Recces" and dive-bombing (See: Glossary; page 147). In October 1945 the Squadron was disbanded at Wunsdorf, but its number was revived when it became a founder unit of the post-war LSK (Luchtstrijdkrachten – the air combat force of the Dutch army). On March 27th 1953 the LSK became an independent service, entitled KLu (Koninklijke Luchtmacht – Royal Air Force).

Three other Dutch flying units operated within the British forces during the Second World War: 860 Squadron, Fleet Air Arm, commissioned in June 1943 and operating Fairey Swordfishes from Merchant Aircraft Carriers; 6 Air Observation Post (AOP) Squadron, formed in December 1944 and equipped with Austers for liaison work with the liberating armies in Europe; and 1316 (Allied) Flight RAF, autonomous at Hendon from July 1944 in the communications rôle.

In Holland everyone knew the Spitfire. Expatriate Dutch airmen who flew Spitfires may have had admiration and affection for the aircraft, but Dutch people on the ground did not necessarily share the romantic reaction to the name "Spitfire" so universally held in Britain. If they had watched with approval as Spitfires remorselessly harried the occupying German forces, they had also all-too-often been caught in the line of fire, as Spitfires pounced indiscriminately on anything which moved by road, rail or canal. A symbol of liberation it might be, but to the Dutch it was, first and foremost, a weapon which in certain circumstances had claimed the lives of friends and relations. However, with large numbers of Spitfires surplus to post-war RAF requirements, it was the obvious choice in 1946 with which to equip the new LSK 322 Squadron and the JVS (Jachtvlieg School – fighter flight school).

55 Spitfire Mark IXs were acquired from the RAF by the Netherlands, of which 35 were used at home by 322 Squadron and the JVS (plus three two-seat T.9s for dual instruction), and 20 went with 322 Squadron to the Dutch East Indies in 1947. In the Indies, nationalist forces were rebelling against the resumption of Dutch administration after liberation from Japanese occupation.

In July 1946 an interim Technical Training Establishment (TOI – Technische Opleidings Inrichting) was established at RAF Langham in England. The unit received eleven Spitfires of various Marks (along with several aircraft of other types), which were handed back to the RAF when the unit moved to the Netherlands in 1947 to become the Luchtmacht Technische School (LTS). Eventually there were eight ground-instructional Spitfires on charge, of which there were two Mark XIVs, two Mark XVIs and four Mark XIs. In 1959 the LTS combined with the Luchtmacht Elektronische School (LES) to form the Luchtmacht Elektronische en Technische School (LETS) – the Air Force Electronics and Technical School.

PL 965 with the LTS/LETS, Deelen 1947 to 1960

In May 1947 the first group of technical instructors arrived at Deelen air base from RAF Langham. They had come home after surviving the privations of a most severe winter, at times cut off by deep snow and reduced to burning carpets and tyres to keep warm. At Deelen, the Luftwaffe had left a very large airfield about 5 kilometers north of Arnhem, with plenty of buildings and a network of runways, taxi-ways and roads, which could be used for the new technical school.

During the summer, personnel, ground equipment and instructional material were transferred from Langham, the last shipment arriving on September 24th. However, this did not include aircraft, which were not considered worth the expense of shipment. Instead a fresh batch, including at least eight Spitfires, was purchased from the British Air Ministry. Legend has it that each aircraft cost only £25.0s.0d, on the promise that it would never fly again!

On July 10th the Spitfires were flown in from Germany to Twenthe Air Base (which is half-way down the Dutch border with Germany) near the town of Enschede. The ferry pilots were supplied by the RAF. In the case of Spitfire Mark XI PL 965, it was probably delivered from 151 RU, Lüneburg, where its Air Ministry "Form 78" (which records an aeroplane's transfer from unit to unit) places it on October 11th 1945. 151 RU was a very large establishment with a pool of spare aircraft and comprehensive maintenance facilities for the benefit of BAFO. It was formed in 1943 as a totally self-sufficient, mobile salvage and repair organisation, dedicated to 2nd TAF for the period of the invasion and liberation of Europe. During the campaign it comprised more than 3,000 officers and men. PL 965's "Form 78" records:

"Netherlands School of Technical Training 8.7.47.

SOLD TO DUTCH Authority BAFO Serial 2 10.7.47".

The July 1947 entry in the ORB of 151 RU confirms: "Aircraft dispatched to Netherlands: 6". Another aircraft was sent from Lüneburg to "Dutch Royal Air Force" in October.

Twenthe air base was the home of the JVS, where 322 Squadron was just completing its working-up to operational standard before embarkation for the Indies. Even at this date there was a shortage of some spares for their Spitfires, so the Spitfires from Germany were detained at Twenthe for a short time while various useful parts were swapped for time-expired or worn counterparts. When the technical school at Deelen

KAPTEIN J.W THIJSSEN – PL 965 Pilot

Kaptein J.W Thijssen of 322 Squadron LSK adjusting his parachute straps alongside Spitfire LF Mark IXc MJ 893 (latterly H 69), probably at Semarang, Java, 1948 or '49 (MJ 893 was ex-312 and 302 Squadrons RAF and subsequently sold to Belgium in 1952 to become SM-42). *(Photo: H. van der Meer)*

	22	SPITFIRE	H1.	"	–	Opschieten A'doorn - Terwolde.
	22	SPITFIRE XI	965	"	–	Base - Deelen
	22	Oxford	C.6	Lt. t Hart	–	Deelen - base
	23	Harvard IIA	12?	Zeis	Lt Wieltz	Tw - Valkenburg - Tw

Entry in the Flying Log Book of Kaptein J.W. Thijssen recording PL 965's ferry flight from Twenthe to Deelen on July 22nd 1947. *(From: H. van der Meer)*

Mark XI PL 912: ex-"P" 16 Squadron; sold to LSK 08.07.47; reduced to instructional parts; scrapped 1952.

Mark XI PL 965: ex-"R" 16 Squadron; sold to LSK 08.07.47; engine ground-running; to Overloon museum 1960; extant.

Mark XI PL 998: ex-400 Squadron and BAFO Communications Wing; sold to LSK 08.07.47; stripped to framework for undercarriage study; scrapped 1952.

Mark XI PM 133: ex-400 Squadron and BAFO Communications Wing; sold to LSK 08.07.47; reduced to instructional parts; presumed scrapped.

Mark XIV MT 853: ex-36 and 26 Squadrons; sold to LSK 10.07.47; brief engine ground-running, exhibition use, and later gunnery target; scrapped 1959.

Mark XIV RB 155: ex-350 Squadron (MN-C); sold to LSK 31.07.47; brief engine ground-running, later fire drill practice; burned 1950.

Mark XVI TD 264: ex-421 and 416 Squadrons, Communications Flight Berlin, 164 and 63 Squadrons; sold to LSK 08.07.47; engine ground-running; scrapped 1956.

Mark XVI TD 402: no operational service; sold to LSK 08.07.47; engine ground-running; scrapped 1952.

was ready to receive them, the Spitfires made their last flight. Pilots with type experience were detailed to fly the Griffon-powered Mark XIVs, but the XIs and XVIs were flown on a "first come first served" basis. It is said that the Spitfires were ferried to Deelen in formation and before landing, the traditional airfield "beat-up" was executed. The pilot of PL 965 was Kaptein J.W Thijssen from 322 Squadron. His Log Book records a 30-minute flight on July 22nd 1947.

At Deelen the Spitfires were intended for training ground engineers, so some of the Rolls-Royce Merlin-powered Spitfires were soon

NCOs (one from the MLD) and men possibly with PL 965, LTS Deelen, November 11th 1949. *(Photo: H. van der Meer)*

dismantled for training purposes. The Mark XIVs were of no practical use, because the LSK did not operate Griffon-powered variants. One ended its days on the fire-drill practice dump, and the other survived for some time as a display item, before an ignominious end on an army shooting range. As luck would have it, Mark XI PL 965 and the two Mark XVIs were selected for engine ground-running practice and thus remained intact.

The Spitfire Mark XIs were supplied with "blister" cockpit hoods, which were normally specified for the PR Mark IV and VII. The reason for this is not known, but photographs show Spitfire Mark XIs of 16 Squadron at Eindhoven and on ADLS detachment at Bückeburg during the summer of 1945 similarly modified. Perhaps these canopies were fitted post-war as a safety measure to improve forward visibility when taxying, or to aid visual navigation, or even for their original purpose which was to check that a photographic target was directly below. In peacetime, any extra drag in flight, or delicacy of structure would be of less consequence. Wartime photographs of operational Mark XIs on 16 Squadron invariably show standard canopies.

Interestingly, the blister was the invention of Australian adventurer Sidney Cotton, father of the RAF's Photo Reconnaissance Unit (who also designed the "Sidcot" flying-suit). Before the war, as a "free agent" he was flying secret, joint operations for the French Deuxième Bureau and the Air Intelligence Branch of MI6. Two modified Lockheed 12As were used principally to photograph Germany's defences. In 1939 he was placed in command of the Heston Flight (with the rank of Wing Commander), with a brief to develop high-speed photo-reconnaissance methods and equipment. He was already a strong advocate of the Spitfire for this rôle. His special "blister" canopy was designed in May 1939, patented, and licensed to Triplex. He sportingly never accepted his 10/- (50p) royalty on every canopy produced.

Soon after their arrival, Dutch national markings were applied to the Spitfires. The rozetten (red, white and blue rosettes with an orange central disk) were simply sized to the red, white and blue RAF roundels on the fuselage and applied over the top, although the yellow outer ring was carefully painted out. The roundels on the upper wing surfaces seem to have been obliterated and substantially smaller rozetten applied instead. The RAF fin-flash was painted out, as was the serial number, which was replaced by a number in the series 01 to 05. PL 965 is believed to have been re-designated 03. At a later date the national markings were regularised to a standard LSK format, which probably required a substantial amount of repainting, if not a complete respray. The new scheme included smaller, repositioned fuselage rozetten, the driekleur (tricolour) on the fin, and large rozetten above and below the wings.

1948 also marked the introduction of the Gloster Meteor jet fighter into LSK service, and with that the days of the Spitfire were truly numbered. With only one Spitfire fighter squadron (which was presently away in the Indies) and the JVS training machines, ground support for Spitfires was no longer a priority. By 1950 type-rating at LTS was phased out in favour of the Harvard and Meteor and the Deelen Spitfires were of little use.

At the end of 1949 322 Squadron returned from overseas. Thereafter, Spitfire flying with the JVS was reduced to little more than the maintenance of currency for weekend Reservists, albeit under the name of 322 Squadron. Flying continued initially from Twenthe, but from August 1951 Soesterburg became the last operational base of LSK Spitfires. By September 1953 the Spitfire was obsolete and withdrawn from use in the new, fully autonomous service, the KLu.

At Deelen also, the Spitfires were dumped. But all was not lost! Ten years after the end of the war, a new batch of officers and instructors had replaced the generation who were perhaps over-familiar with the Spitfire. Someone, who obviously harboured respect and nostalgia for the legendary Spitfire, convinced his superiors that a Spitfire would be a suitable "guardian" for the Sergeants'

Spitfire Mark XI (with a "blister" canopy) which is chocked and tied down at the tail for engine-running practice at Deelen. This is almost certainly PL 965, which was used for that purpose. The roughly painted-out fin flash and serial number, together with the rozetten obviously applied over the RAF roundel, suggests that the date is 1947 or '48. Note the two-digit Dutch serial number. *(Photo: H. van der Meer)*

Mess. A small grassy area lay alongside the Mess and here, in 1955, a Spitfire was resurrected.

Most of the airframe was provided by PL 965, with some parts (mainly cowling panels) scavenged

Almost certainly PL 965, being pushed back into an LTS hangar at Deelen in 1948 or '49. Note the later, standard LSK markings, including rozetten underneath the wing and the driekleur on the fin. The cockpit canopy is of the "blister" variety. *(Photo: H. van der Meer)*

PL 965 after salvation and restoration, on display outside the Sergeants' Mess at Deelen between 1955 and '60. Mistaken for a Mark IX, it is painted roughly to represent a Spitfire of 322 Squadron RAF. Note the oranje driehoek (orange triangle), which was the pre-war Dutch national insignia, on the cockpit door. *(Photo: H. van der Meer)*

The chocks and rear fuselage tie-down identify this Spitfire as PL 965, which was used for engine-running exercises at Deelen. *(Photo: H. van der Meer)*

from the remains of PM 156, PL 998 and TD 402. In honour of Dutch wartime association with the Spitfire, PL 965 (which was mistaken for a Mark IX) was painted in camouflage style to represent an aircraft of 322 Squadron RAF. In those days people relied upon their memory in such matters, so the result was not particularly accurate. All the elements were there, but the position, size, style, etc, of the markings were completely mixed-up, as can be seen from the accompanying photograph which was taken sometime between 1955 and 1960. The inverted orange triangle with a black outline was the old national insignia displayed, for instance, by the Fokker D.XXIs in 1940. It was occasionally used during the war on aircraft presented by donors of Dutch or Dutch Colonial origin, flown by Dutch pilots, or operated by expatriate Dutch squadrons. In such circumstances however, it would not have been so prominent.

Overloon 1960 to 1987

PL 965 being dismantled at Deelen for transportation to the National War and Resistance Museum, Overloon, in December 1960. *(Photo: Sectie Luchtmachthistorie)*

In 1955 plans were laid for a new Dutch National Aeronautical Collection, and the hunt began for suitable aircraft to exhibit. A North American B-25 Mitchell was flown in to Deelen for preservation and PL 965, which was standing alongside the Mess at Deelen, was also earmarked. The museum opened its doors in 1960, with a display of ten aircraft and several engines, in the old terminal area of Schiphol airport. However, Spitfire Mark IXc MJ 143 was supplied by the KLu (it is now on display at the Luchtmacht Museum, Soesterberg), and PL 965 was once again redundant. Both the B-25 (which was too large) and PL 965 needed a new home, or their inevitable fate would be the scrap-yard. Indeed, in 1960 half a dozen Spitfires in Holland were scrapped!

Luckily, there was an alternative site to consider. As early as 1945 the Nederlands Nationaal Oorlogs- en Verzetsmuseum (National War and Resistance Museum) was founded on the tank battlefield of Overloon, in the south-east near

PL 965 at Overloon, probably during the winter of 1960-61, just as it was received from Deelen. Note the blister fairing for an F24 5-inch camera outboard of each wheel-well, and the lack of any roundels painted under the wings. *(Photo: H. van der Meer)*

The firewall serial number found by Harry van der Meer on April 12th 1972 (photographed at Brüggen three years later). *(Photo: H. van der Meer)*

PL 965 at Overloon about 1971. The erroneous 3-W paint scheme is obvious, as is the "blister" canopy, and signs of fabric deterioration. *(Photo: H. van der Meer)*

the border with Germany. The collection had no aircraft and jumped at the offer of the two Deelen veterans. The Spitfire (which was now anonymous because of several layers of paint overlaying its RAF serial number) was sold on November 22nd 1960, and arrived at Overloon on December 9th. It was soon on display (erroneously described as a Mark IX) on a small knoll among the trees, behind a low fence.

Standing in the open, with inadequate protection from both the weather and the public, the condition of the Spitfire soon began to deteriorate. Adults and children were able to climb

all over it, and the thin, "blister" canopy was an early casualty. Some time in the early '60s a former Air Force officer advised the Museum that their Spitfire was incorrectly painted. It certainly was a time when little was known or published about such historical detail, as the subsequent redecoration confirmed.

The new paint scheme obliterated all previous markings with a representation of camouflage, and the only fuselage markings were a large white "3" and "W", widely spaced on either side of a big orange triangle with a bold black outline. Similar triangles were painted on the wings. For the next few years the anonymous Spitfire stood outside in all weathers, and continued to be subjected to marauding tourists.

Perhaps the greatest single contribution to European aircraft preservation since the Second World War occurred in 1968, when the film "Battle of Britain" was released. A veritable fleet of Spitfires had been assembled for the making of this epic, mostly through the efforts of G/Cpt Hamish Mahaddie. Many of the Spitfires alive and well today owe their continued existence to the film, and not only the participants, but also many neglected airframes lying around all over the world, which suddenly became re-imbued with the glamour which was once their due. Ageing ex-RAF "types" and also a new generation of younger pilots suddenly wanted to own and fly the legendary fighter. Groups of relatively penniless enthusiasts began to gather together, determined to salvage and protect the remains of their local Spitfire.

PL 965 at Overloon about 1972. Note the driehoek painted under the wing, and extra fencing which did not keep the vandals at bay. *(Photo: H. van der Meer)*

PL 965 in a poor state at Overloon before restoration by Harry van der Meer and Fred Vinju, which was accomplished in August 1973. *(Photo: H. van der Meer)*

In Holland, Harry van der Meer (now Technical Curator at the Aviodome Museum, Schiphol) became infected by "Spitfire madness" and began to collect information and artefacts concerned directly with Dutch Spitfires. When he made contact with Peter R. Arnold, who was among the earliest British "Spitfire Survivor" gurus, he was enjoined to seek out all the Spitfires remaining in Holland and identify them by serial number. Guided by Arnold, and rapidly gaining experience through research in Belgium and at home, van der Meer knew what to look for among the tell-tale groups of numbers to be found either stamped on data plates or stencilled on out-of-the-way bits of airframe. On April 12th 1972, armed with authority from the museum to search the aircraft, van der Meer and fellow enthusiast Henk Otsen went to Overloon to try to formally identify the Spitfire. His letter to Peter Arnold says it all:

"This one was found so easy and fast, that it was a little disappointing. In fact there was no camera hatch, but on the same place a little hatch, too small to see anything or push your hand through. So after studying the wing underside, we found that there was a wing fairing held on its place by a few bolts. We removed them, and could easily access the firewall. On the wing mount assembly there was a bolt measurement plate, but no serial. Also on the wing formers was a plate with bolt sizes but no serial. On the fire wall was no plate as usually found on the other aircraft.

"So we started to see what was on the fuselage in the place where the serial could be. But after removing some paint, only the original PR blue was found, but no white or grey of the serial. We

tried also the other side with no success. Next try was the normal place (on Dutch aircraft) of serials, below the fin-flash. But still no sign of a serial."

The two detectives then returned to the fairings under the wings, adjacent to the engine compartment, one of which they had removed earlier.

"We tried the other wing fairing but no bolt would move a little millimetre. Back to the open fairing. Looking inside we saw lots of oil and birds' nests. After removing lots of it we could see more

Overloon, July 30th/31st 1973. Fred Vinju dismantling the damaged "blister" canopy. *(Photo: H. van der Meer)*

Overloon, July 30th/31st 1973. Harry van der Meer using extreme methods to cut through the layers of paint before re-finishing. *(Photo: H. van der Meer)*

August 1973. Fred Vinju begins the process of transformation using a gallon of PR Blue paint supplied by the Shuttleworth Collection. *(Photo: H. van der Meer)*

August 1973. Two-week transformation complete, apart from cockpit glazing and elevator repair. *(Photo: H. van der Meer)*

Resistance Museum with a formal offer to refurbish its Spitfire, which was by now in a very poor state. The cockpit was seriously smashed, paint work peeling and the fabric control surfaces in tatters. Van der Meer was rapidly becoming the Dutch Spitfire expert. The previous year he had identified a Spitfire at Delfzijl (LF Mark IXc MJ 271) and been instrumental in setting up a restoration scheme. Also in 1971 he identified the Spitfire displayed at Eindhoven air base (LF Mark IXc MK 959).

The museum was delighted, therefore, with the prospect of practical assistance from a knowledgeable and vigorous source, particularly as the proposal included technical as well as cosmetic aid. The offer was formally accepted in October by the Administrateur, P. Klaassen, on behalf of the

October 18th 1975. RAF engineers take a strong line with the recalcitrant wing bolts – which prove more than a match for technology. *(Photo: H. Lambeck)*

of the fire-wall and approx half way up there were black letters stencilled. My friend took a lamp and so made clear what was on the wall: PL 965. The letters were approx two inch high and 1.5 inch wide. But black and with lots of oil on them."

Never one to let the grass grow under his feet, in the same letter he mentions awaiting a replacement canopy, possibly windscreen too and plans to remove and refurbish the control surfaces and repaint the Spitfire in more authentic colours.

In August 1972 he approached the Administrateur of the Overloon National War and

October 18th 1975: Heavy lifting gear stands by, but the propeller was the only part to be lifted that day. *(Photo: H. Lambeck)*

installed, and finally painted according to an official Supermarine drawing for PR aircraft. The paint was a gallon of PR blue from the Shuttleworth Collection.

"When finished the aircraft really looked smart – ready to fly away."

Although for a time van der Meer's restoration slowed down the fatal effects of weather and marauding sightseers, it quickly became obvious that a much more radical overhaul was really needed if the Spitfire was not gradually to crumble where it stood. Within months of completing the job, the propeller blades began to split apart and, during the next two-and-a-half years, the canopy was shattered again and a new one had to be ordered and fitted. The next major casualties were the exhaust stubs, which began to corrode away. All this in spite of periodic maintenance on paint-work and minor repairs.

In May 1975 Flight Lieutenant Len Woodgate, who was currently Motor Transport Officer at RAF Brüggen, West Germany, (and who later became Curator of the RAF Cosford Aerospace Museum), visited Overloon and was struck by the condition of PL 965. Having already had experience with museum aircraft, he wrote on May 20th (on behalf of his Commanding Officer) offering the extensive engineering facilities of RAF Brüggen in order to restore it. The offer was gratefully accepted by Directeur G.J.H. Spitz in July, with the work scheduled to be done between October and April

Directors. It was agreed that the work should be postponed until the following summer, but "niet op zondag!" (not on Sunday!).

In 1973 there was no such thing as an aircraft preservation movement in Holland and not many enthusiasts were inspired even to work on Spitfires. But Harry van der Meer and his brother-in-law Fred Vinju spent their summer holiday at Overloon. In two weeks (minus Sundays of course!) the Spitfire was fully cleaned, painted internally, greased, oiled, fabric control surfaces repaired, plexiglass repaired, a new canopy and new windscreen (made of hammer-resistant lexan)

RAF Brüggen, 1976. PL 965's wings and fuselage stripped for restoration. *(Photos: H. van der Meer)*

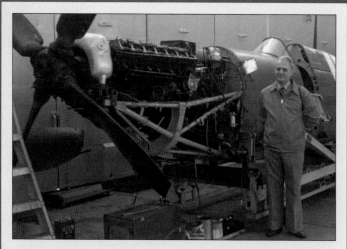

F/Lt Len Woodgate at RAF Brüggen with the engine he almost managed to run. This Merlin 70 (number 182411) was PL 965's second power-plant and was part of contract SB23303/C.28(a) for 482 engines, from number 182409 to 183371. It passed test originally at Rolls-Royce's Crewe works on January 8th 1944 and was delivered on February 2nd, and presumably installed in an aircraft until a major overhaul at Rolls-Royce was required. As far as PL 965 is concerned, however, the significant entry on its record is for December 7th 1945, when it was noted at 7 MU, Quedgeley, which was the same place to which PL 965's first Merlin was returned on December 12th. Presumably the replacement engine was fitted at 151 RU, Lüneburg, where PL 965 had been in residence since October. *(Photo: H. van der Meer)*

1st 1976 (before the Easter holidays). Spitz also introduced Harry van der Meer to Woodgate, and soon a good working relationship developed between them, which matured into friendship.

On Saturday October 18th, the first attempt was made to dismantle the aircraft. The propeller unit came away easily but, despite a week of soaking in oil, the wing bolts refused to budge. It took three

RAF Brüggen, 1976. PL 965 complete in its high-gloss paintwork. *(Photo: H. van der Meer)*

weeks to shift them, working carefully to avoid damaging or distorting them.

At last the aircraft could be loaded onto a "Queen Mary" and moved to Brüggen where, under the supervision of Len Woodgate, an extensive restoration took place. Most of the vital parts like wings, flaps, main landing-gear and engine-mount were removed. The fuselage was paint-stripped and repainted, and protected by a heavy coat of clear varnish to help weather-proof it. As is often the case, the group of volunteers dropped away as the months went by, which limited what could have been achieved. Nevertheless, had he been able to free the last of the 12 cylinder barrels, Woodgate would have tried to run the engine!

Individual credit for the work done by volunteers, including members of 431 MU, is detailed in "Spitfire Survivors" by Gordon Riley and Graham Trant:

"The fuselage was restored by C/T (Chief Technician) John Atkey and Cpl Pete Nash, with assistance from other members of the Armament Servicing Flight, RAF Brüggen; the rebuilding of the cockpit area was performed by Sgt Pat Coyne and C/T Jim Anderson; the Merlin 70 was cleaned up and restored to near-running order – apart from one rusty cylinder – by C/T 'Chalky' White and members of the Engine Repair Bay; Sgt Pete Sharp of the Armoury manufactured fibreglass exhaust stubs, to replace the corroded originals, and a replica signal pistol for the cockpit; the wings were restored by Sgt C. F. 'Oscar' Smedley, Cpl Tony Edwards and other members of the Aircraft Servicing Flight, whilst Sgt Bob Botwood of 431 MU made up dummy elevators and a rudder to replace the missing original items. 'Chalky' White repaired the propeller, Oscar Smedley and Tony Edwards restored the spinner, and the wheels were a joint effort by the RAF Brüggen Tyre Bay and No.25 Squadron. The final high-gloss paint finish in PRU blue plus invasion stripes was the work of Cpl Les Brimmer and SAC (Senior Aircraftsman) Tony McGlynn of Station Workshops."

When the aircraft returned to Overloon there was a celebration, but no one suspected that after a few years the gleaming varnish would crack and peel away from the paint work, the fibre-glass replacement parts fall away and, eventually, even the propeller blades would be lost.

An interim low budget face-lift was done in 1982, but by '85 corrosion was advancing apace.

PL 965 being re-assembled at Overloon after restoration at Brüggen. April 10th 1976. *(Photo: H. van der Meer)*

There was no more money to save the Spitfire; so, in order to rescue what remained, Harry van der Meer resurrected an old scheme to try to swap the Mark XI for an exhibit more relevant to operational Dutch Spitfire history. He suggested to the Museum that he be allowed to organise an exchange, perhaps for the empty shell of a Mark XIV, a type in which 322 Squadron had chased the V-1 "Doodle-bugs" on the south coast of England in 1944. As it happened, the museum already had a real V-1, and the two would make a complementary display.

The idea was accepted and English restorer Steve Atkins affirmed that he could supply a Mark XIV. In the event, the contract was to be completed (after a couple of deadline extensions) by another Spitfire restorer, Nick Grace, and the new exhibit arrived on March 13th 1987.

PL 965 returned home, after 43 years away, next day.

March 13th 1987. PL 965 about to leave Overloon after being swapped for Mark XIV NH 649. Nick Grace is wearing the bright blue overalls, on the right of this photograph. *(Photo: H. van der Meer)*

Rochester Restoration

by Lewis Deal, Managing Director, Medway Aircraft Preservation Society

February 1992, PL 965's Packard Merlin 266 installed and ready for test-running at Rochester. *(Photo: L.E. Deal)*

In 1976 the Medway Branch of the RAeS (Royal Aeronautical Society) formed an Aircraft Preservation Group. At that time the group comprised some 30 members, many of whom had worked at the Short Brothers' factories on the River Medway or at Rochester Airport. Others had seen service with the Royal Air Force, both during and after the war, and a few with companies in the Medway Towns linked to the engineering and metal-working industries.

The group has built up a reputation over the years for the quality of its restoration work, much of which has been undertaken (at no cost I would add) on behalf of the RAF Historic Aircraft Committee. Restorations have included Spitfire Mark XVI TB 752 and Hurricane Mark IIc LF 751, both now permanently housed at RAF Manston. Other projects have included a Meteor Mark 8 and a Republic F84-F Thunderstreak, as well as a "brace" of Merlins – a "20" and a "35". A Junkers Jumo 400 jet engine was restored for the Science Museum, and a section of a Short Stirling fuselage and the radio dome from the Short "Golden Hind"

flying boat. Many other artefacts too numerous to mention have been restored for various museums throughout Southern England.

The size of the group and its activities led to the formation of a Limited Company in 1988 entitled the Medway Aircraft Preservation Society Ltd. The Company was still voluntary and non-profit-making but, mainly because of insurance and indemnities, the formation of MAPSL became essential.

Mr E.N. (Nick) Grace had been a member of the Medway Branch of the RAeS for some years and we had grown accustomed to Nick "popping in" to our (by now) two workshops to see what we were working on. Sometimes he would drive to Rochester, but more often than not he would fly-in his Spitfire T 9 "Vicki" and we undertook one or two little repair jobs on split cowlings, fairings, etc. Nick had hinted that he was hoping to obtain a Spitfire from Holland and as the time approached (by now it was towards the end of 1976), he asked whether we would be interested in restoring the Spitfire fuselage only.

We readily agreed as, on the face of it, the project could quite easily be contained within the group's existing restoration commitments. Nick emphasised that there was not a time factor, and

PL 965's Packard Merlin 266 on the test-run bench at Vintage V-12s' facility in the Mohave Desert, California. *(Photo: R Eatwell)*

that he would provide materials, drawings and finance and personally offer any necessary advice and expertise. For its part, the group was to rebuild the Spitfire from the firewall up to the fin. The Spitfire's engine-bearers, wings, fin, tail-plane and rudder, etc, would be restored by others. All in all, a very pleasant working arrangement.

In February 1987 Nick advised us that the deal for bringing the Spitfire over from Holland was virtually complete. He then revealed that the aircraft was a rare example of the breed – a photographic-reconnaissance Mark XI, of which only three examples were known to survive at the time. The aircraft's serial was PL 965 – and that was all he knew. We had no information on the Spitfire's condition other than that it had been standing outside on display for over 30 years.

As the time approached to receive PL 965, the group busied itself in making up special supporting jacks and trestles and, in general, ensuring that there would be no "hiccups" when the whole aircraft was unloaded at Rochester. By then Nick had asked us – in his own inimitable fashion – if we could disassemble the whole aircraft at Rochester so that the various components could be "farmed-out" to various sub-contractors for rebuild. Again, this did not appear to be too onerous a task.

On the (late) evening of the March 17th 1987 Spitfire PR XI PL 965 arrived on a lorry, having been shipped from Holland by ferry. Even on the ferry the cockpit area had been vandalised – not that there was a lot left to be vandalised!

The group was quite used to restoring corroded wrecks – but this was a wreck with a capital "W"! As we unloaded '965, even in the dark she looked bad – and the following morning's daylight strengthened our apprehensions of the previous evening. Nick was always the optimist, and under his direction and over the following months the Merlin 70 engine (seized) was removed together with the engine-bearers, which you could see daylight through. The rudder and the elevators were composed of tin sheet and corrugated cardboard; the undercarriage and main wheels were a total write-off, as were the radiators. The retracting tail-wheel was corroded beyond belief.

The fuselage interior was an inch thick in grime with bits of electric wiring and hydraulic and pneumatic tubing poking out of the grime – and out of virtually everywhere else for that matter!

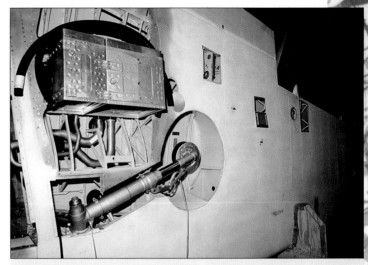

Starboard radiator and undercarriage leg, fully restored, December 1991. *(Photo: G. Lancaster)*

Gradually PL 965 was stripped, with every component job carded, photographed and recorded. A pitifully small number of components were saved but, by some miracle, the throttle quadrant and undercarriage selector appeared to be salvageable.

There was no cockpit seat or control column but, conversely, the rudder bars proved to be in good order. Here and there, as components were removed, there was a gleam of bright metal – and this gleam kept the group's spirits high and they worked with considerable enthusiasm and speed – perhaps goaded by Nick's insistence that it was "a piece of cake". A prophetic expression indeed, as in the autumn of the same year we were approached by the makers of the TV drama of that name for use of PL 965's fuselage and other bits to make up "props" for the film.

'965 was removed to Elstree Studios on December 23rd 1987 so that fibre-glass moulds could be taken, and we were invited to go to Elstree on three occasions to ensure that the aircraft was being treated properly – as indeed it was. The Spitfire was not returned until late March and the final dismantling started again.

Some cleaning of the fuselage interior and general tidying up revealed a far from pristine "cylinder" but, overall, the fuselage's condition was far better than the first indications. The fuselage was moved into the main workshop and a careful programme of panel removal, cleaning, assessment, replacement and rivetting

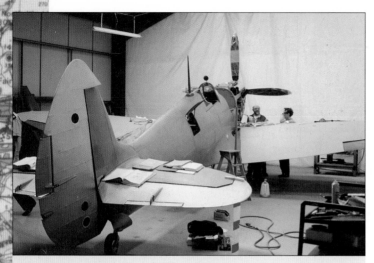

The Rochester hangar May 13th 1992, just before engine runs began. Note the polythene curtain which kept dust and draughts at bay. *(Photo: H. van der Meer)*

commenced. Gradually PL 965's fuselage took shape and she began to take on the beautiful lines that only a Spitfire has. As work progressed, the number of visitors increased and with them the inevitable question, "When's it going to fly?" Our usual patient (?) reply was "When it's ready!".

Nick Grace's inimitable optimism was always a great boost to the group and it was with total disbelief that, on October 14th 1988, MAPSL members heard of his death in a car crash. Only 48 hours before, Nick had been with us to take the

The Rochester hangar May 13th 1992. Note the modern external electrical power source for engine-starting purposes. *(Photo: H. van der Meer)*

engine-bearers away. Nobody could accept that such a vibrant person was no longer with us and this continued even after several of us attended Nick's funeral at Chichester.

We had no idea what was to happen next, but we assumed that '965 would leave Rochester perhaps for rebuild in the hands of another owner. We had no clues as to future ownership or, indeed, the Spitfire's fate. A very, very sad time for everyone.

After a gap of several weeks we were approached by Mr Christopher Horsley – the new owner of PL 965, who had been Nick's associate in "Tangmere Wing" – to ask whether MAPSL would be prepared to undertake the responsibility for the whole project up to final assembly, which obviously we were not licensed to undertake. MAPSL needed time to assess the implications of the proposal, bearing in mind that ours was a voluntary part-time body and what was being asked of us normally demanded the attention of four or five full-time professionals for approximately four years.

After two weeks Mr Horsley was informed that MAPSL would undertake responsibility to rebuild. Nothing was put in writing and no contracts etc, were even exchanged: the whole rebuild and all its implications were being undertaken on the basis of trust on both sides. Surprisingly, this worked! Being a non-professional group we were ultra-careful in our approach to the expanded project. Job cards were meticulously completed and work signed-off by Mr John Froud, who had responded to an approach by MAPSL to become the licensed engineer for the project. I must add that John was always very helpful and objective during the course of the rebuild and his previous experience on Seafires stood him (and us) in good stead.

A job programme was established and gradually various components left Rochester for expert rebuild elsewhere. The wings went to Air Repair Ltd on the Isle of Wight for re-sparring and the installation of wing tanks: on the PR Spitfires the wing leading edge contained fuel, but the Civil Aviation Authority (CAA) did not view continuation of this design feature with any enthusiasm, bearing in mind the Spitfire's habit of ground-looping! The engine-bearers and tail-plane were dispatched and orders placed for a new broad-chord rudder and new elevators.

In the meantime Mr Horsley had placed an order for a Packard Merlin 266 engine from Vintage-V12s, based in California. The Merlin arrived in the UK towards the end of 1990 – and what a gleaming picture it looked with its chromed rocker-box covers and light grey enamelled finish. It really looked "the business"!

An unexpected bonus proved to be the propeller hub. X-rays showed the unit to be airworthy and this initial check was later confirmed by Dowty-Rotol Ltd. Material Measurements Ltd at Redhill proved to be very helpful in the x-raying of literally dozens of components from '965.

Microscan Ltd of Long Eaton, Nottingham, supplied new fuselage spars as well as the new mountings for the engine-bearers and the (rear) wing attachment fittings.

As far as possible we maintained external authenticity and original appearance for a Mark XI Spitfire but, after seeking advice and bearing in mind the possibility of "bird-strike", we opted to fit a fighter-type armoured windscreen in place of the original Mark I-type wrap-round screen. This may not have pleased the so-called purists and experts amongst our visitors, but we always took the view that safety and not originality was paramount. At some future date a pilot would be placing his life on the line and anything we could do to improve pilot safety we did. For example, the fire-wall was rebuilt using stainless steel in lieu of the original aluminium and asbestos sandwich; the lower fire-wall skirt was also fabricated in stainless steel. All the forward hoses were manufactured by A.F. Saywell Ltd of Littlehampton, using modern air-liner techniques in relation to the use of flexible lines for fuel, hydraulics and pneumatics.

New 10¼-inch main wheels were obtained from Goodman-Broady Ltd and, fortunately, a new pair of main-wheel brake assemblies from another source. Tyres came from Watts Aviation Services, but one of our major problems related to the almost non-existence of tubes. Nobody seemed prepared to produce them anymore, when literally dozens of sets were needed. Propeller blades arrived from Hoffmann Propellers along with new hub-bearings, and the whole package was dispatched to Dowty-Rotol Ltd for assembly and balancing.

As I mentioned earlier, the undercarriage was a total write-off but, with the kind assistance of Dick Melton, good legs were obtained together with enough bits and pieces to make up a new tail-wheel assembly. The cockpit area was now receiving attention, and gradually instrumentation of the correct era and fit was obtained: a boxed

May 15th 1992. Bob Eatwell runs up the engine for the first time while the traditional three-man team holds down the tail. *(Photo: H. van der Meer)*

compass was found and re-calibrated by SIRS Navigation at nearby Dartford. An order was placed with Cambridge Radiators for new "rads" and, on arrival, they looked an absolute picture.

All the time this was going on, the fuselage and fire-wall were proceeding well and it is nice to record that one of the more experienced Spitfire engineers pronounced that "this aircraft has some of the neatest rivetting I have ever seen". Praise indeed for MAPSL and the standard of work! By now also the paint-sprayers were increasingly in action as dozens of components were etch-primed and painted in readiness for installation.

If this all sounds like a full-time activity, it virtually was! I do not think that anyone could have realised the enormous pressures placed on a group of part-time volunteers inexperienced in the terms of restoring an aircraft to flying order. Paper-work and telephone and fax messages were the order of the day to maintain the impetus, but somehow it was maintained, so that towards the end of 1990 it became increasingly necessary to appoint a full-time engineer to undertake final assembly of the Spitfire.

Kent is not one of the "hot-beds" of Spitfire or "war-bird" restoration and suitable engineers are very few and far between, but again we were fortunate in obtaining the services of an engineer who literally lived on the door-step at Rochester

Rochester Airport, December 23rd 1992. Test-pilot Mark Hanna, of The Old Flying Machine Company, opens up the Merlin for PL 965's first take-off since July 22nd 1947. *(Photo: L.E. Deal)*

Airport. Robert (Bob) Eatwell was appointed and took up duties on January 1st 1991. He was presented with a "Meccano Set", comprising a virtually complete Spitfire but at this stage without wings, which were still with Airframe Assemblies Ltd.

Also at this time there was another piece of good fortune in the bespectacled form of Peter Jennings, who literally walked into the workshop one day and declared himself as being interested in taking on the Spit's electrics, avionics, radios, etc. As a very experienced man in this field, Peter's offer was welcomed with open arms. I must also add that Peter undertook all this in his spare time.

Work-space was becoming more and more critical and, as it was obvious that we did not have enough room even to fit the wings, an approach was made to GEC Avionics Ltd (who administer Rochester Airport) for space to be made available in the company's new No.4 Hangar. This was readily agreed and, in April 1991, PL 965 took up residence at the rear of the hangar, occupying a space measuring 45 feet square, together with a caravan containing tools, paper-work – and Bob Eatwell.

Forward progress was maintained but, as usual, there were the usual "war-bird" problems of components not arriving on time or not being available, etc. Bearing in mind that we were supposedly in the middle of an economic recession, I could never understand the attitude of some companies who either did not seem to want work or, if they did accept it, could not be bothered to complete it on time. Very, very frustrating – and then, to top it all, they charged ridiculously high prices. We soon learned who to approach – and who not to approach! I feel I must mention a small local engineering company, R.T. Lane, who gave invaluable and prompt service. A total contrast to some of the larger firms.

The year passed, but with each month '965 looked more and more complete – but like a butterfly without wings. However, on January 18th 1992 fitting of the wings began, accompanied by all the relevant problems of reaming the spars (both fuselage and wings) and driving home the 14 wing-spar bolts. This was accomplished after three days of very careful work – and much head-scratching – but achieved it was, and now '965 took on all the curvaceous beauty that only a Spitfire possesses.

The undercarriage quickly went on and retraction and lowering tests continued during

February. These were completed to everyone's satisfaction later that month and attention turned to the engine and propeller department.

I'm cutting a long story short, but by mid-April 1992 PL 965 was on her undercarriage and being prepared for first engine-runs for over 40 years. As usual, there were a couple of minor snags which occupied time, but eventually the first run did take place. Modest engine revs were obtained after the Packard Merlin fired-up at the second attempt, and the evocative sound of the legendary engine echoed around Rochester Airport. Incidentally, we had fitted the original pattern of "fish-tail" exhaust stubs as opposed to the more normal open exhaust. The fish-tails certainly gave the Merlin more of a crackle than the other type.

After a number of runs, disaster struck when a supercharger bearing seized. This resulted in the engine having to be removed and sent back to the 'States. Vintage V-12 responded marvellously and the engine was totally rebuilt and tested and was back in the UK in just over 8 weeks. For some reason the "new" engine sounded even crisper

than before. The engine was quickly re-installed but, of course, everything had to be checked and re-checked with fresh undercarriage, electrical, hydraulic and pneumatic tests. All this was time-consuming but very necessary – and at the same time very frustrating.

Considerable thought had been given to the final paint scheme for "Stella", as PL 965 was known. The decision was made (in agreement with Mr Horsley) that the aircraft be finished in the colours of the US Eighth Air Force's 14th Photo Squadron (7th Reconnaissance Group), which operated from Mount Farm near Oxford. 1992 was of course the 50th anniversary of the operational entry into the European war of the "Mighty Eighth". PL 965 would be finished in RAF "PR Blue" with yellow serial numbers on the fuselage, which would be repeated in larger format on the fin and rudder. The "Stars and Bars" would be painted on each side of the fuselage plus the port upper- and starboard under-wing surface. Together with all the essential instructional stencils such as "DO NOT WALK", "FIRST AID", etc, this took quite some

Rochester Airport, December 23rd 1992. PL 965 lifts clear of the very wet runway at Rochester Airport into a gloomy winter sky. *(Photo: N. Blake)*

December 1992. Members of the Medway Aircraft Preservation Society Ltd and Tangmere Flight, with Michael Wetz once more in the cockpit of PL 965. *(Photo: Classic Photographic Services)*

Together with OFMC's resident engineer Roger Shepherd, Mark commenced his own engine runs and other tests in November and hopes were high that '965 would take to the air either later that month or in early December. The roar of the Merlin could be heard all over the airfield and its surrounds but, surprisingly, no objections were raised by the guests in the adjacent Crest-Forte hotel, which on several occasions felt the full force of '965's backwash and the Merlin's strident note as Mark increased boost on the Merlin to +10 and 3,000 rpm. How the cups and saucers must have rattled! It was a good job that we had six steel spikes (each four feet long) embedded in the ground to keep the tail down. Even then, Stella "bucked" all over the place in an effort to break free.

December 21st 1992 saw Charlie Channon rivet the last of the fasteners on to the engine cowlings and there seemed to be every hope that Stella would take to the air the following day, but a persistent oil-leak, which was both difficult to locate and to rectify caused abandonment that day. This was particularly frustrating for former 16 Squadron pilot Michael Wetz and engineering officer Edgar Quested, who had travelled specially to Rochester to see the first flight of their old Squadron's Spitfire.

In contrast to the weather the previous day, December 23rd dawned frosty with fitful sunshine and worst of all, a cloud base of only some 400-500 feet. However, after a last-minute panic over engine documentation, Mark commenced his final checks of the aircraft towards noon. By now the ice had cleared off the apron but cloud conditions were, if anything, slightly worse. Just after noon he climbed into the cockpit, was strapped in and, after a final polish of the windscreen, the Merlin was fired-up. Probably because of the cold and damp the engine was reluctant to start first time, as we had become accustomed to expect. The second start was successful and PL 965 vibrated to the power of the Merlin.

Chocks away, and Mark weaved slowly along the apron fronting the main hangar, checking instruments and gauges as he went. Out to the main runway and to the concrete "hold", where 50 years ago four-engined Stirling bombers from the nearby Short Brothers' factory also undertook their final "run-ups" and final checks. Everyone could feel the tension as Mark exercised the engine and propeller. Slowly he edged the aircraft forward,

time. The actual spraying was undertaken in the poorest conditions imaginable: a dusty hangar floor (although we had sealed our portion), uncertain temperatures, and with pilots starting up their engines and blowing in even more dust through the ever-open hangar doors. The job was achieved only by erecting a tent of plastic-sheeting over the aircraft, and it says much for the skill and patience of the paint-sprayer and his helpers that such a fine finish was obtained.

Engine runs and other tests continued, with the major problem being inconsistent oil pressure. Barely adequate pressure was being maintained and it was only after exhaustive checks that the problem was located. A pre-oiler motor had been fitted in the root of the starboard wing and with this by-passed the pressure rose by 100% – the problem then was to reduce oil pressure.

Mark Hanna from the Old Flying Machine Company (OFMC) based at Duxford Airfield, Cambridgeshire, was given responsibility for test-flying PL 965 from Rochester. The grass runways being some 900 metres in length were considered of sufficient length by the CAA for the test flights and, as it proved later, were more than adequate.

opened the throttle and to everyone's surprise (and delight), lifted off from the wet and sodden runway into the murk. It was later established that take-off was achieved within 85 yards. Visibility was such that the Spitfire almost disappeared from sight before the undercarriage was tucked away into the wings! But Stella was in the air and the urgent note of the Merlin did not pass unnoticed in the GEC Avionics facility as faces appeared by the dozen at its windows.

Mark banked slowly to port and the engine note changed as he selected coarse pitch. At no time in the first circuit did the Spitfire reach more than 500 feet and every movement of the aircraft was watched with a certain amount of apprehension by the onlookers, who increased in numbers by the minute. But the Merlin sounded beautiful and gradually our fears and anxieties began to dissipate. Mark selected "undercarriage down" on the second circuit and it was obvious that, because of the weather conditions, he was curtailing the first test-flight. At the conclusion of the third circuit he brought Stella in fairly fast and flared out over the threshold to get the landing line exactly right.

Stella touched down in a flurry of mud and water from the sodden runway: she seemed reluctant to land for, after all, 45 years without flight is a long time for any Spitfire. However, she did settle and Mark taxied her back to the apron with the aircraft spattered and, in some places, caked with mud. He swung her round at the end of the apron and shut the engine down.

At first it was uncannily quiet, but after a minute or two the realisation of what had been seen and achieved began to sink in – and 50 different views of that first flight were expressed. For some members of MAPSL the emotion and fears had been all too much and many faces were turned away to hide strong fellings – mine included. Some could not bring themselves to watch the flight, and I can well understand their sentiments. Together MAPSL and Tangmere Flight had put machine and man into the air successfully. What a Christmas present!

For the record, Mark Hanna took-off at 12.16 pm and landed at 12.19 pm, adding up to just 30 seconds for each year we worked on the Spitfire!

Some people achieve very little or indeed nothing in their lives. We could all be proud – but

Duxford, July 25th 1993. PL 965 is a static guest at the 50th birthday of another veteran Spitfire, The Old Flying Machine Company's Mark IX, MH 434. *(Photo: P.R. Arnold)*

Three generations of Horsley fliers. Air Marshal Sir Peter Horsley flew Mosquitos with 21 Squadron in 1944 on 140 Wing, his grandson James, who began flying training in New Zealand in 1994, and his son Christopher, who owns PL 965 which stands behind them. The aircraft is in black and white "invasion stripes", for the 50th anniversary of D-Day. (Photo: C. Horsley)

Because of Mark's other commitments, flight testing was not resumed until February 1st 1993, when he arrived unexpectedly. Few MAPSL members were therefore present for the second flight. The Merlin started first time and the all-blue Spitfire took off into a beautiful blue sky – a total contrast to the conditions on the previous flight. At 12.23 pm Mark lifted her off and now had the perfect opportunity to put the Spitfire through her paces. As his confidence in the aeroplane grew so did the noise of the Merlin, as residents in the Medway valley were treated to the rare sight of a Spitfire performing loops, rolls and finally a stall over their heads.

Our pilot had already promised a couple of fly-bys if he was happy with the aircraft and its handling – and we were not to be disappointed. His short display had the effect of blocking roads adjacent to Rochester Airport and stopping work at GEC while this loveliest of "war-birds" performed against the perfect blue back-drop.

Stella was alive and in her own element again in the hands of a superb display pilot. But it was also a bitter-sweet occasion for us, as we knew that, after post-flight checks and re-fuelling, PL 965 would be leaving for a new home at Duxford. Mark landed at 12.35 pm and was back in the air at 13.12 to complete a couple of circuits and a low pass before rounding off with a victory roll and disappearing from sight towards the blue horizon.

The excited chatter soon subsided and was replaced by a deep feeling of sadness that the aircraft which had been the centre of our lives for over six years had finally gone. Some 45,000 man-hours were expended by MAPSL and Tangmere Flight in the rebuild. We knew it had been worth it.

at the same time we remembered sadly Nick Grace and Arthur Colver, who were not there to share the credit and the satisfaction. Always the perfectionist, Arthur rebuilt the flattened spinner and made a superb job of it, and his skills will always be evident whenever we see PL 965 in future. Doubtless Nick was having a quiet chuckle somewhere.

There were some first flight problems: for example, the ASI (Air Speed Indicator) fluctuated, the undercarriage selector was stiff and the ailerons over-responsive. Someone later told me that the chord of the aileron on the Mark XI's wing was some 1½ inches deeper than on the standard Spitfire wing. We were even learning on test-flight day.

Members of Medway Aircraft Preservation Society Ltd and Tangmere Flight:

Medway Aircraft Preservation Society:			
David Bowles	George Elsegood	Ray Sealey	Frank Wood
Brian Bowling	John Homer	Oslo Schine	John Young
Alan Briggs	Albert Lock	John Semark	Trevor Young
Michael Butler	Edward Mankey	Albert Short	
William Channon	Iain Miller	Christopher Sturgeon	**Tangmere Flight:**
Philip Cole	Ken Oakes	Colin Walder	
Arthur Colver	Sidney Page	William Waldock	Robert Eatwell assisted by:
Alan Covel	George Prager	David Ward	Nigel Eatwell
Lewis Deal	Alfred Richards	Peter Watson	Mark Farmer
	Paul Roberts	John Webb	David Harwood
	Stuart Robinson	Robert Wheeler	Peter Jennings
	Alan Rowe		

From 1994 PL 965 was operated from Duxford by the Old Flying Machine Company. First camouflaged to represent a Spitfire Mark IX, "Invasion Stripes" were added for the D-Day celebrations which were replaced in 1995 with the PR blue scheme it would have worn (minus "R") on delivery, October 2nd 1944. *(Photos: J. Dibbs)*

MARK HANNA – PL 965 Pilot

Mark Hanna with Hans Dittes' Messerschmitt 109G-10 and PL 965 accompanied by LF Mark IX MH 434 both painted-up for the BBC TV-Movie "Over Here" in 1995. Note the different nose and tail profiles of the 1943 Mark IX and the 1945 Mark XI. *(Photos: John Dibbs)*

Mark Hanna's first flight was in a Tiger Moth, a start which befits the son of an ex-leader of the Red Arrows, the "crack" display team of the RAF. At the age of 17, as a student pilot he flew his first military type, a Beechcraft Mentor. Clearly the Service was in his blood and he was accepted for officer training at OCTU (Officer Cadet Training Unit), Henlow, the following year. Mark began his military flying training at 1 BFTS (Basic Flying Training School), Linton, in the summer of 1978 on Jet Provosts, going on to 4 AF(T)S (Adavanced Flying Training School), Valley, in '79 where he flew Hawks. Posted north to 2 TWU (Tactical Weapons Unit), Lossiemouth, for tactical training on the classic Hunter, he was introduced to the type he was destined to fly operationally at 228 OCU (Operational Conversion Unit), Coningsby – the Phantom. As a Squadron Pilot from July 1981, he continued to fly Phantoms with 111(F) Squadron, Leuchars, and 23(F) Squadron, Port Stanley. With 56(F) Squadron, Wattisham, and 29(F) Squadron, Coningsby, he was also Air Combat Leader. His RAF career closed with a spell on the Phantom Simulator at Wattisham in autumn 1988, and some 1,600 hours RAF flying under his belt.

In 1981 a display-flying organisation, which was later (in 1984) to be called "The Old Flying Machine Company", was formed by his father Ray Hanna. Mark's first vintage military type the same year was the Pilatus P-2, an ex-Swiss Air Force trainer of the late 1940s, and his first airshow appearance in the P-2 was a year later at Yeovilton. In another year he was at home in the Spitfire Mark IX. Throughout the '80s he flew the display circuit as and when his RAF duties allowed, becoming very involved by 1985. On leaving the RAF he was able to enter the business on a full-time basis, the work-load of airshow and film display flying steadily increasing. The 1993 season, for example, involved 36 shows, 360 sorties and 180 hours flying.

His list of types is exotic, particularly for someone born well into the jet age. Apart from those mentioned above, he has time on; Avenger, Bird Dog, Chipmunk, Boomerang, Broussard, Corsair, Flying Fortress, Fokker Dr.1 and Fokker D.VII (replicas), Harvard, Invader, Jaguar, Jungmann, Jungmeister, Kittyhawk, Lockheed T-33, Morane 733, Mustang, Nieuport 24 (replica), Piper Cub, SE5a (replica), Sea Fury, Spanish-built Messerschmitt 109, Stearman, Tornado, Trojan, Vampire, Yak-11, Yak-50, and Yak-52.

Mark declares his equal favourite piston types are the Merlin-powered Spitfire and the Kittyhawk, and his best-loved jet is the Phantom.

Rare Wartime Colour Photographs

taken by F/Lt J.M.C. Horsfall

Melsbroek, September 1944. S/Ldr Tony Davis DFC and Spitfire PR Mark XI "R" PL 848. Note the fresh paint blotting out the upper part of the "invasion stripes" and the retractable tail-wheel's doors. *(Photo: RAF Museum)*
See chapter: Officers Commanding, Sq L/dr Davis; page 68.

Spitfire FR IXs of 16 Squadron at Melsbroek, autumn 1944. They are painted pale pink for low altitude work below cloud, and are fully armed. The hangar has been disguised as a row of cottages and inside its door there is a row of long-range fuel tanks or bombs on stands. *(Photo: RAF Museum)*
See chapter: PR Problems and Solutions; page 37.

Melbroek, autumn 1944. Pilot F/Lt "Tommy" Thompson and F/Lt Derek Wales discuss aerial matters with ground-crew Rae, Pate and Hellier on board Spitfire PR Mark XI W-for-William. Note the battered and faded paintwork. *(Photo: RAF Museum)*
See chapter: Tommy and the '262s; page 69.

"Scotty" Cadan at Melsbroek in September 1944, with Spitfire PR Mark XI "H" MB 953. Note the essential submariner's polo-neck sweater and sheepskin-lined flying boots (against the cold at high altitude) and the khaki Heavy Duty Dress (a precaution against baling out over Germany, where RAF survivors in uniform were believed to have been killed out of hand, or alternatively being shot by partisans or trigger-happy Allies mistaking air force blue for German *"Feldgrau"*). The black and white "invasion" half-stripes on the aircraft (originally completely encircling the fuselage during June only) were applied for recognition purposes to all Allied aircraft for D-Day); the two-colour roundel and the sunshine confirm this was taken in the late summer 1944 (this aircraft had been with 16 Squadron since November '43 and left after a minor accident in September '44).
See chapter: Farewell to 16 Squadron; page 94.

No.16 Squadron RFC and RAF

The motto means "Hidden things are revealed" and the black and white keys represent the capability to reveal hidden enemy positions by day and by night.

1915-1919 Corps Squadron

In 1914 the RFC (Royal Flying Corps) went to war with a scratch force consisting of a Headquarters Unit, four squadrons and an Aircraft Spares unit. The RFC was slow to expand, but in February 1915 16 Squadron was formed in France at St Omer from Flights provided by 2, 5 and 6 Squadrons. Its birthplace gave rise to the Squadron's nickname – "The Saints" – and to the matchstick man symbol adopted in later years from Leslie Charteris' crime-fighting hero.

The new unit was provided with a motley collection of aircraft – Blériot XIs, Martinsyde Scouts, RE5s and a Vickers FB5 Gun Bus. Later on, these were supplemented by, or exchanged for, Maurice Farman "Shorthorns", Henri Farman Voisins, BE2cs and a BE2. As specific defence against

the marauding Fokker *Eindecker*, a Bristol Scout arrived late in the autumn. Interestingly, the second CO of 16 Squadron was a certain Major H.C.T. Dowding, who was later to become a household name as Commander-in-Chief of Fighter Command during the Battle of Britain.

The Squadron's primary rôle from its nine French bases during the First World War was reconnaissance and artillery ranging, with ground-attack as its secondary contribution – including day and night bombing. Its expertise in aerial photography and target spotting for the guns was particularly appreciated by the Canadian Corps in the assault on Vimy Ridge during the spring offensive of 1917. From that point onwards the Canadians insisted that 16 Squadron (Royal Air Force after April 1918) move with them wherever they went – and that was the case until the Armistice. Other types flown during the war were Armstrong Whitworth FK8, BE2e, f and g, BE9, Bristol Scout C and D, Bristol F2B and RE8 (see Glossery page 147).

By the beginning of 1919 the Squadron was based for the first time in England, at Fowlmere, Cambridgeshire, but was disbanded there at the end of the year.

1924-1943 Army Co-Operation Squadron

16 Squadron RAF was re-formed five years later at Old Sarum, Wiltshire, as an Army Co-Operation squadron, working with British Army Southern Command on tactical reconnaissance and aerial photography, spotting troops, vehicles, shot and shell. The type provided was the Bristol F2B "Biff". The Squadron practised a growing use of radio (which it had pioneered in 1915) and ground-attack gunnery and bombing at seasonal camps and on exercises with the army. During the next ten years, experimental artillery observation methods were tested for the School of Artillery, and a variety of proposed army co-operation aircraft types evaluated.

In 1931 the shades of the First World War finally faded when the Bristols were replaced by the Armstrong Whitworth Atlas, which was itself superseded at the end of '33 by the Hawker Audax, the Army Co-Operation version of Sydney Camm's classic Hawker Hart light bomber. Technological innovations also led to the Squadron's pilots learning to fly half-a-dozen autogyros.

16 Squadron broke away from the School of Army Co-Operation to become an independent Army Co-Operation squadron in 1934; but little changed at Old Sarum, the pre-war build-up of the RAF being concentrated on Bomber and Fighter Squadrons, which were also being first served with the new generation of monoplane aircraft. Despite requests from the Army Co-Operation squadrons for a semi-fighter type, in 1938 16 Squadron was presented with Westland Lysanders – which it had previously tested and judged unsuitable for warlike purposes! A year later the Squadron took them to war.

During 1939 a number of experienced crews were posted to squadrons earmarked for defensive duties in northern France and pilot strength had to be maintained by the secondment of army officers. Meanwhile, one of the less glamorous jobs the Lysanders were asked to practise was the spraying of anti-personnel gas – just in case it was needed.

At last, in preparation for a move to France, 16 Squadron relocated to Hawkinge, Kent, in 1940. In April it was established in tents at Bertangles as part of the Air Component of the RAF, with the task of providing tactical reconnaissance and photography. But the "Phoney War" came to an abrupt end in May, with the Germans' fierce and successful drive through the Ardennes to the Channel coast. After twelve days of bitter fighting, 16 Squadron pulled-out and retired to Lympne, Kent, from where its Lysanders flew tactical reconnaissance covering the Dunkirk evacuation.

Throughout the rest of 1940 and into 1941 the Squadron was engaged in coastal dawn and dusk anti-invasion patrols from a string of locations including: Redhill, Surrey; Teversham, Cambridgeshire; Okehampton, Devon; and finally Weston Zoyland, Somerset, where it was to remain for a year and a half. In 1942 North American Mustangs arrived, which, although lacking in performance at altitude, were far ahead of the Lysanders (a couple of which were retained for vertical photography – later replaced by Curtiss P-40 Tomahawks). And also two Fairey Battles were used for bombing with the local Army Battle School.

The Squadron now began to train with Fighter Command at Middle Wallop, Hampshire, in preparation for convoy patrols, shipping reconnaissance patrols, photo-recces and strikes against coastal targets west of the Cherbourg peninsula, which commenced in November. The Mustang's long-range capabilities made it particularly suitable for such operations, although they put it beyond the protection of fighter escort. Operations were extended deeper into Britanny in 1943 from Andover, Hampshire, and Ford, Sussex, which meant the Mustangs of 16 Squadron were required to fly "Rhubarb" offensive sorties against military installations, port facilities, and communications targets. The trains on the Rennes to Brest line received regular attention. Conversely, June '43 also provided a hectic round of "Anti-Rhubarbs" to counter hit-and-run raids made by the Luftwaffe's Messerschmitt Bf 109 and Focke-Wulf Fw 190 fighter-bombers.

On June 1st 1943 the Squadron also moved to Middle Wallop, which coincided with the disbandment of the old Army Co-Operation Command. A new organisation, dubbed 2nd TAF, was formed the same day to constitute the main air weapon for the projected invasion of Europe. The reconnaissance requirements of what was eventually to become General Montgomery's 21st Army Group and Air Vice-Marshal Coningham's 2nd TAF demanded the formation of a specific unit dedicated to fulfilling those needs. On July 1st 16 Squadron moved to Hartford Bridge, Hampshire, to join 140 Squadron, which was to be the focal point of the new 34 Photographic Reconnaissance Wing.

1943-1945 Photo-Reconnaissance Squadron

For its part, 16 Squadron was going to change its rôle from low level tactical to high level reconnaissance operations. Both the Mustangs and some of the pilots were temperamentally unsuited to the change of operational ceiling, so changes in both establishments were necessary. The intention was to re-equip with Spitfire PR Mark XI aircraft, but at present those were in short supply, as the main production lines were still concentrating on fighter variants. In the meantime, the Squadron was lent some well-used Spitfire PR Mark IVs by 140 Squadron, who were also in the process of converting to PR Mosquitos for day and night work. During this period of changes, "Rhubarbs" continued until high level photographic sorties began to take over in September, the last Mustangs leaving next month.

During the winter, the Squadron brought back photographs pin-pointing the V-1 sites under construction in the Pas de Calais and began preliminary coverage of the Normandy beaches and sea bed. The tempo of operations increased with the New Year and the work-load expanded to include damage-assessment pictures after bombing raids. It was vital to know that the isolation of Normandy was being maintained by cutting road, rail and air links with the rest of Occupied Europe. Neither were underground headquarters, fuel and ammunition dumps neglected by the Spitfires' cameras.

At the beginning of April the Wing moved to Northolt, Middlesex, to be closer to the main user of visual intelligence – SHAEF. In May, 69 Squadron arrived from Malta to convert to Wellingtons for night visual reconnaissance and low level photography. 34 Wing now consisted of 140 Squadron with Mosquitos, 69 Squadron with Wellingtons and 16 Squadron with Spitfires.

As the weeks counted down towards D-Day, every rail-head in Europe was covered, 16 Squadron routinely flying 16 damage-assessment sorties a day. Soon the Normandy beaches were being photographed every three days. On June 6th the Squadron flew 17 sorties but, owing to cloud cover, only the low level operations were productive. The next five days provided only low level work over the Allies' "Mulberry" floating harbours and various rail marshalling yards to monitor attempts by the Germans to reinforce their troops in Normandy. The Wing was also required to observe railway lines and enemy airfield reconstruction and continue bombing-assessment operations. Casualties were sustained.

At the end of August the Allied armies broke out of the Cherbourg peninsula and advanced rapidly to the river Seine. 34 Wing moved shop to an airstrip south of Bayeux, known as "A12" Balleroy. It was at this stage that 16 Squadron acquired pale pink Spitfire IX fighters equipped with a single port-facing oblique camera, for low level tactical operations. Most of the sorties were to spot ammunition dumps, or over the Channel ports, where pockets of resistance often lingered on the flanks, or even in the rear, of the Allied front line. In September the Wing moved on to Amiens-Glissy, from where two Spitfires and two Mosquitos were detached to Northolt to cover Operation "Market Garden" – the ill-fated airborne assault on Arnhem and Nijmegen. After only two weeks the PR Wing leap-frogged on to Melsbroek, near Brussels, where it dug in for the winter.

At the end of 1944 16 Squadron was flying all the daylight reconnaissance sorties (except for a small amount of survey work), as the Mosquitos were thought to be too vulnerable to the Messerschmitt Me 262 jet and Me 163 rocket fighters. The tell-tale condensation trails of V-2 missiles were also beginning to be seen and trying to keep tabs on their launching sites soon became another job for 16 Squadron. There were also dangerous low level sorties flown to the few remaining bridges over the river Maas still open to the enemy. Several pilots were lost during the winter of 1944-45.

The last year of the war began with a bang, when much of the remaining strength of the Luftwaffe was flung at the Allied front-line airfields, including Melsbroek. On New Year's Day Operation *Bodenplatte* (or "Hermann" as it was more popularly known) cost 16 Squadron three Spitfires completely destroyed and three badly damaged of the 22 aircraft wrecked at Melsbroek. None of the casualties suffered by the Wing were from either 16 Squadron or 6016 Servicing Echelon.

The early months of 1945 were filled with mainly high level operations, often deep into

Germany. Particular attention was paid to V-2 launch sites, airfields suspected of harbouring jet aircraft, midget submarine bases and lines of communication. After the British and Canadian 21st Army Group crossed the Rhine towards the end of March, 16 Squadron's last major task was to reconnoitre and report on German North Sea and Baltic ports, where the enemy were attempting to evacuate troops by land and sea. In April a move was made to Eindhoven, in the Netherlands.

On May 7th Germany surrendered unconditionally, and the Squadron's final sorties of the Second World War revealed "Signs of liberation everywhere..."

16 Squadron remained at Eindhoven during the summer, taking delivery of a few Spitfire PR Mark XIXs. However, it received notification to proceed first to Bury St Edmunds, Suffolk on September 19th, then to Dunsfold, Surrey on 20th, where disbandment subsequently took place.

By some twist in the "red tape" at more or less the same time, both 268 Squadron (at Celle, Germany) and 487 Squadron (at Epinoy, France) were renumbered 16 Squadron, but then disbanded before the end of October. Eventually, and more permanently, in April 1946 56 Squadron at Lüneburg Heath became the new 16 Squadron in the fighter/ground-attack rôle with Hawker Tempests. The Squadron number has remained in existence ever since, with only short periods of lapse and based in Germany until 1991. Its last operational base was Laarbruch, flying Tornados. Here it celebrated its 75th Anniversary in May 1990, and from here it participated with honour in the Gulf War, the Officer Commanding, W/Cdr Ian Travers-Smith, receiving the DSO.

16 Squadron disbanded at Laarbruch on September 11th 1991, but reformed on November 1st 1991 at RAF Lossiemouth, Grampian, taking over from 226 Squadron in its rôle of the Jaguar Operational Conversion Unit. As this was a Reserve Squadron, 16's title is now No.16 (Reserve) Squadron. All the Squadron's documents and memorabilia are housed in a special room within the No.16 (R) Squadron Operations Building.

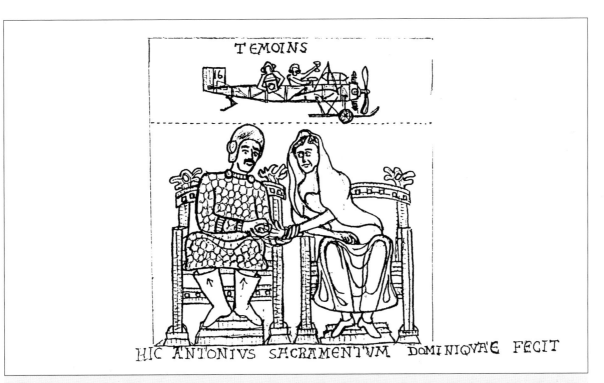

Sketched design by Jimmy Taylor of a ceramic tile he gave to Tony Davis as a Wedding gift. Taylor and Mike Horsfall were invited to be witnesses (Témoins). The evocation of the Bayeux Tapestry goes back to September 1944 and the A-12 (Balleroy) airstrip days of 16 Squadron, when Taylor and Mike Horsfall visited Bayeux Cathedral. The design shows their gallant commander, in flying helmet and boots, putting the ring on Dominique's finger. Above a 16 Squadron Blériot is piloted by a mustachioed Mike while Jimmy takes a photo from the rear seat.

Supermarine Southern Region Dispersal Scheme

Premises occupied for Spitfire production, July 1940-December 1945
Commander James Bird, General Manager
W. Elliot, Works Superintendent
L. Gooch, Works Manager

Hursley Park House

Chiswell's Garage, Winchester	Press shop and sheet metal details
Ekin's Garage, Kenilworth	Transport centre
Experimental Shops	Prototype build
Garratt's Garage	Transport, transport workshop and repairs
Hendy's Garage	Pre-production build
Hursley Park	Design department, drawing office and experimental
Hursley Park House	Administration
Hursley Road Stores	Central stores, raw materials and finished parts
Leigh Road Cable Works	Stores
Moore's Garage, Bagshot	Transport centre
RNAS Worthy Down	Final assembly, flight test and experimental flight test
Short's Garage, Winchester	Machine shop
Sleepy Hollow Barn	Accounts, records, stores
Southend House	Accounts
Wonston Stores	Embodiment loans (parts supplied by the Air Ministry)

Southampton, Manager, A. Nelson

Austin House Garage	Tank covering and training
Bishops Waltham Brick Works	Finished parts stores
Botley Store	Finished parts stores
Hants & Dorset Bus Garage	Wing assembly
Hendy's Garage, Southampton	Fuselage assembly and tank manufacture
Holly Brook Stores	Stores
Holt House	Inspection and AID (Aeronautical Inspection Directorate)
Lowther's Garage	Machine shop, toolroom
Marwell Hall	Finished components store
Newtown Works	Woodwork and metal assemblies
Park Place House	WVS (Women's Voluntary Service) rivet sorting
Seward's Garage	Fuselages equipped
Sholing Store	Finished parts stores
Sunlight Laundry	Details and sub-assembly
Weston Rolling Mills	Tanks and pipes

Salisbury, Manager, W. Heaver

Anna Valley Garage	Tail units, sub-assemblies
Assembly Rooms	Canteen
Castle Garage	Transport
Castle Road No 2 Factory	Wing leading edges, wings
Castle Road No I Factory	Canteen
Castle Road No I Factory	Fuselages, engine installation
Castle Road Office	Accommodation, administration
Chattis Hill Airfield	Engine overhauls

Chattis Hill Racing Gallops	Final assembly and flight test
High Post Aerodrome	Communications flight and experimental flight test
High Post Aerodrome Hangar	Final assembly
High Post Hotel	Canteen and accommodation
W H Smith High Street	Canteen
Wessex Garage	Fuselages, tail units, wing leading edges
Wilts & Dorset Bus Garage	Wings

Trowbridge, Manager, V. Hall

Bolton Glove Factory	Westbury area assembly
Bradley Road Factory	Wings, sub-assemblies, tool room, mould loft
Currie's Garage	Completed fuselage store
Eyken's Garage	Transport department
Forestreet Garage	Details and fittings
Haverton Cloth Mills	Raw material, finished parts stores
Hilperton Road Factory	Sub-assemblies and details
Moore's Garage	Transport department
RAF Keevil Aerodrome	Final assembly and flight test
Red Triangle Club	Canteen
Rutland Garage	Pipes and coppersmiths
Southwick Steam-roller Works	Wing leading edges

Newbury, Manager, T. Barby

Baughurst Garage	Stores
Hungerford Garage	Machine shop
Mill Lane Works	Sub-assemblies
NIAS No.1 Garage	Toolmakers
NIAS No.2 Garage	Stores
Pass Garage	Process department
Shaw Works	Press and machine shop
Stradling's Garage	Detail fittings
Venture Bus Garage	Stores

Reading, Manager, K. Scales

Caversham Works	Fuselages, engine installation
Central Garage	Canteen
Great Western Garage	Wings
Henley Aerodrome	Final assembly and flight test (Not suitable for PR XI and later Marks)
RAF Aldermaston	Final assembly and flight test
Vincent's Garage	Fuselages, details, sub-assemblies

The Merlin 70 — Developed for superior performance at altitude

Rolls-Royce Merlin 66 engine, externally similar to the Merlin 70. *(From: Rolls-Royce Heritage Trust)*

It is possible to say that the development of the aircraft engine played a more vital part in the struggle to achieve air supremacy than any other single factor. However, the problem of performance is more complex than might first appear. Obviously an aircraft engine must be capable of producing considerable power when required, but this cannot be achieved simply by having a bigger engine, with larger or more numerous cylinders. Aerodynamic considerations aside, this would bring with it an increase in mass, which would result in a less effective acceleration, plus an increase in fuel consumption – thereby either restricting the range or further increasing the weight of the aircraft.

Supercharging

During the war, it was vital that combat aircraft (and especially photo-reconnaissance variants) should be capable of operating effectively at considerable altitude, often in excess of 30,000 feet, and this is where the big problem lay. At low altitude it is possible to increase power by using bigger engines. But higher up this strategy does not work, simply because the air is too thin. In very simple terms, the power developed by an engine is directly related to the mass of fuel that it burns per second. "Burning" is a process in which the hydrocarbon molecules of the fuel combine with oxygen molecules from the air. This results in the release of a large amount of energy in the form of heat, which pressurises the gases in the cylinder, which then forces down the piston. Now, roughly speaking, for every kilogram of fuel which is burnt, three kilograms of oxygen are needed, which means that about 15 kilograms of air must be acquired by the engine. In a "normally aspirated" engine this air is obtained by the "suction" created when the piston moves down on the "induction stroke". As this happens, the air is pulled through a narrowing tube in the carburettor (the venturi) where its pressure falls, so that fuel is drawn into the air-stream.

At low altitude the air is sufficiently dense for sufficient oxygen to be obtained in this way, but at 30,000 feet the air is very thin, its density being only $1/3$ of that at sea level. This means that, on each stroke of the piston, only $1/3$ of the amount of air is drawn into the engine, so only $1/3$ of the fuel can be burnt, resulting in a considerable loss of power. The answer to this problem is "supercharging". This can be looked at in two ways (which come to the same thing). A supercharger can be thought of either as artificially increasing the density of the air by compressing it – or as forcing more air than normal into the cylinder every time the piston moves down.

By the beginning of the 1930s, supercharging was being developed for the Schneider Trophy racing aircraft, and the Rolls-Royce "R" engine had a single-stage supercharging compressor. The purpose of this was not to increase performance at altitude, as the race took place at sea-level, but to get even more power out of the engine without increasing its size. The Rolls-Royce Merlin was developed out of this engine, and up to 1940 the single-stage compressor was adequate.

Of course, supercharging is not without its problems, the worst one being detonation, loosely referred to as "knocking". When an engine is run with a "low octane" fuel, or on a lean mixture, or at high temperatures, or even worse a combination of all three, there is a tendency for the fuel/air mixture to ignite unevenly and/or too quickly in the cylinder. Instead of a flame spreading rapidly through the mixture from the spark plug, as is normal, a high-pressure shock-wave, similar to an explosive detonation, shoots through the mixture at high speed, causing considerable forces on the piston and the rest of the engine. The potential

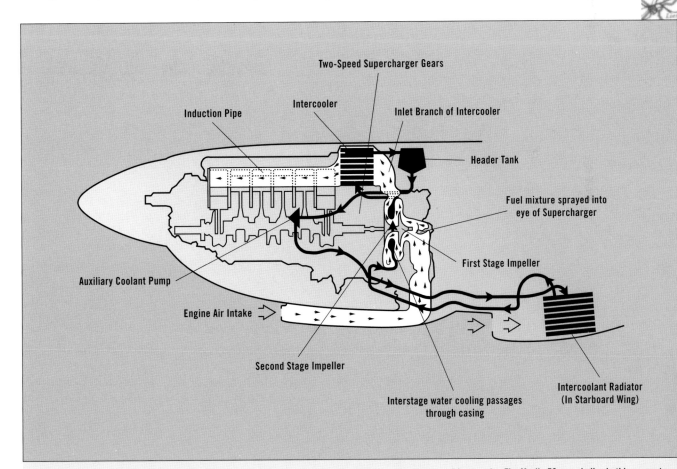

Cut-away diagram of the Rolls-Royce Merlin 66 engine, showing air/fuel flow through the supercharger and intercooler. The Merlin 70 was similar in this respect.

damage from "knocking" is so great that it should never be allowed to happen in an aircraft engine.

In order to further "boost" performance, particularly at high altitude, in about 1940 Rolls-Royce started to develop a two-stage supercharger. As we have seen, the more the air can be compressed, the more fuel can be burnt. The compression can be increased by making the supercharger impeller rotate faster – and in order to do this a *two-speed* gear-box had already been developed. The engine rotated at about 3,000 rpm, and the impeller needed to rotate at something like 30,000 rpm, which was achieved by use of a gear-box. To give the engine a better performance at even higher altitudes, the gearing was enabled to be changed to a higher ratio when a barometric capsule detected that the aircraft had reached a certain altitude. Unfortunately there was a limit to the speed that the impeller could rotate. Quite apart from stress considerations, as the tips of the impeller approached the velocity of sound, there started to be a loss in efficiency – mainly because the behaviour of the gases changed dramatically as their velocities approached, and exceeded, the sound barrier.

Rolls-Royce overcame this limitation by using a *two-stage* compressor in the Merlin 60-series engines, and the later Merlin 70-series used the same system. This was in effect two compressors, the second one compressing the air that had already been compressed by the first one. This meant that greater compression could be obtained at lower impeller speeds.

However, higher supercharger, or boost, pressures brought with them another problem. As anyone who has ever used a bicycle pump knows, when gases are compressed suddenly they heat-up. When the gases emerged from the supercharger, their temperature could have been increased by as much as 200°C (360°F). There was a danger of these gases being ignited before they reached the cylinder. But apart from this, when gases of such temperatures took part in the normal combustion process, there was a considerable danger of "knocking" taking place in the cylinder. These problems were overcome by the "intercooler". This was a heat exchanger placed between the supercharger and the inlet manifold, which worked in a similar way to the radiator in a car. In addition to solving the problems already mentioned, there was another benefit from having the incoming gases cooled. As they cooled they

became denser, so an even greater mass of fuel/air mixture could be crammed into the cylinder. An external manifestation of the extra cooling requirements of the Merlin 60 and 70-series engines was the identical-looking radiator housings under each wing, which replaced the asymmetrical arrangement of earlier Spitfires. Inside the port housing was the oil cooler and main radiator, and the starboard housing was shared by the other main radiator and an intercooler radiator.

The problem of "knocking" could also be alleviated by running the aircraft on a "fuel-rich" mixture. This cooled the cylinder to some extent and "knocking" was less likely to occur with a cooler and richer mixture. However, the biggest contribution to the "anti-knocking" campaign was the introduction of various additives into the fuel, mainly tetra-ethyl lead and methyl analine.

The "octane" rating for fuels is a direct measure of their "anti-knocking" properties, rather than the amount of energy they can release when they are burnt.

Aviation fuels were given two ratings, one based on a lean mixture, the other on a rich mixture. In the early days of the war the fuel was rated at something like 91/98 octane, but later on 100/130 was developed and eventually 105/150. This meant that, as knocking was less likely to occur because of the nature of the fuel, the pressure developed by the supercharger could be increased even more.

What is "boost"?

"Boost" is the increase in air pressure at the inlet manifold of the engine due to the supercharger. Although often not stated in full, the unit for boost measurement is psi (pounds per square inch) but, in practice, it is typically referred to as "lbs (pounds) boost". Normal air pressure is about 14.5 psi at sea-level, so a boost of "+15" provides a little more than double the pressure of air at the inlet manifold.

The supercharger is permanently connected to the crankshaft via centrifugal clutches and a gear-box. The purpose of the clutches is to temporarily disengage the supercharger (which is geared up to about 10-times engine speed) when the engine is throttled-back, so that no damage is done to the supercharger by the sudden reduction in crankshaft speed. Though sudden reduction in engine speed can be tolerated by the engine's components, deceleration of the supercharger components would be 10 times greater and would lead to catastrophic failures without the protection of the centrifugal clutch.

At slow engine speeds the supercharger is turning, but can actually hinder the flow of air into the cylinders. This is displayed on the boost gauge in the cockpit as "negative boost". At cruising speeds, the boost reading is typically in the region of 7 psi. The throttle governs the boost setting, and the CSU (Constant Speed Unit) control determines the engine speed, by altering the pitch of the propeller blades. Once set, the CSU alters the pitch of the propeller blades to maintain a constant propeller speed irrespective of the boost setting. In later versions of the Spitfire the engine revolutions and boost were interconnected. At 19,500 feet in the climb (for the Merlin 70), the speed of the supercharger impeller must be increased to cope with much thinner air. As explained above, this is done automatically by a barometric capsule which switches the gears to a higher ratio (from Medium Speed or "MS" to Fast Speed or "FS"). Conversely, at 18,000 feet in the descent, the supercharger automatically reverts to the lower ratio.

The throttle-lever moves in a quadrant which has an adjustable stop ("the gate") at about 75-80% travel. This is set to give climbing boost (+12 psi). For training and normal loads, take-off boost is between +7 and +9 psi. For maximum take-off power and combat-rating, the lever is moved slightly sideways, allowing it to pass the stop, so maximum travel (+18 psi boost) can be obtained. Hence the expression "going through the gate".

Superior carburettor performance

During the Battle of Britain, the Spitfire engine developed the embarrassing habit of "fluffing" when the pilots pushed the nose down to go into a dive. These engines had a (relatively) standard carburettor with a float-chamber controlling the flow of fuel into the venturis. When the aircraft first went into negative g, it immediately resulted in fuel starvation. It was as if the float-chamber had been inverted, so that for a brief period there was air (rather than fuel) at the *outlet* nozzle. Shortly after that the chamber would fill up with fuel, and because the float was still not closing off the *inlet* into the chamber, fuel was forced through to the venturis at pump pressure resulting in a fuel *rich* mixture. This situation was actually aggravated by the aircraft going into slightly less negative g.

Several modifications were developed to overcome the problem. One, developed by Miss Shilling at RAE (Royal Aircraft Establishment, Farnborough) was to introduce a restrictor into the fuel line – very like a washer – the aperture of which had been carefully calculated so that the maximum flow of fuel through the orifice was the same as the maximum rate ever needed by the engine. At times of great crisis, when the engine was at maximum power already, this worked very well. But at less than maximum power, a fuel rich mixture could still be produced.

Another modification consisted of taking the outlet from the SU carburettor, not from the bottom as was the convention, but from the side, exactly half way up. This meant that the fuel could flow equally well under negative, or positive g. However, if the aircraft happened to be going through exactly zero g (as it must do inevitably, if it goes from positive to negative or *vice versa*), then once again there were fuel flow problems.

These irritations were overcome on a number of marks of Merlin (including the 66 and 70) by using the Rolls-Royce version of the American Bendix carburettor. In this device, there is a twin-choke "carburettor" in the air supply just before the supercharger. Each choke has two venturis but, unlike a conventional carburettor, the fuel is not fed into the air-stream at these venturis. They are used to detect the air flow rate into the engine and the pressure in them (which is related to the airflow) is fed back to the D chamber. A complicated series of diaphragms (made out of a sort of rubberised canvas) and levers controlled the amount of fuel, which was pumped along a fuel line to some spray nozzles just in front of the inlet to the first stage of the supercharger (the "eye"). Part of the carburation process also involved sucking air up to these nozzles as well, so that when the fuel came out it was efficiently atomised before it went into the supercharger.

The spray nozzles at the eye of the supercharger have been likened to the arms of a star fish. At low engine speeds the fuel emerges out of a central nozzle, but as the fuel pressure builds up at higher engine speeds, a spring-loaded valve comes into play, which allows the fuel to flow down the arms of the star and come out of nozzles on the underside of the arms (called a duplex system).

This design overcame the "fluffing" problems because at no stage in the process was the flow of fuel dependent upon gravity. The fuel was actively pumped into the air-stream and the flow rate was determined by pressure differences detected at suitable points, but mainly in the venturis of the carburettor.

Even this system was not without its problems, the worst one being due to air getting into the D chamber. This chamber, which was part of the fuel metering system, should be flooded with fuel (with no air in it at all). Normally this was the case, but some aircraft were fitted with long-range drop tanks and, to get the maximum range from them,

pilots preferred to run them dry before jettisoning them and switching over to the main tanks. Unfortunately, this meant that air would be sucked in and an air lock would develop in the D chamber. This was particularly difficult to clear. Eventually a vent was fitted to the chamber, and the type of fuel pump was changed to a design that was more capable of pushing the air out.

In later marks, the Bendix system was replaced by an SU fuel injection system, and then by an injection system designed by Rolls-Royce.

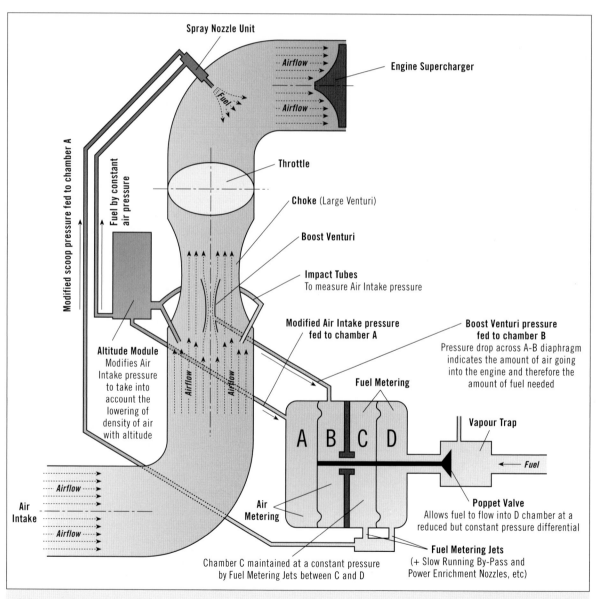

A diagrammatic representation of the Rolls-Royce Bendix-Stromberg carburettor

Breathing Problems at High Altitude

The unarmed photo-reconnaissance Spitfires were often called upon to navigate and work at great height in order to avoid interception by fighters or, even better, to observe the enemy completely undetected. In the reduced ambient atmospheric pressure pilots were exposed to two physiological hazards, namely hypoxia and decompression sickness.

Hypoxia

Hypoxia is having too little oxygen in the lungs and blood, which can fatally impair the judgement of an aviator. The symptoms of hypoxia include reduced performance, euphoria, aggression, delusions, hallucinations, total disregard for personal safety, loss of consciousness, and eventually death. The primary means of avoiding hypoxia is the efficient delivery of sufficient oxygen to the lungs throughout that part of a sortie where either stressful exertion (during combat, for instance), operation above 10,000 feet, or a combination of the two is experienced.

The Oxygen Economiser

During 1940 the RAF Physiological Laboratory ("the Lab") at the RAE, Farnborough, designed the economiser system to optimise the rate of consumption of oxygen and to improve the efficiency of its delivery to the user. By early 1941 the device was being incorporated into all new Spitfires (and other aircraft) and fitted retrospectively, where necessary, to aircraft already in service.

Hitherto, a high flow of oxygen to an ill-fitting and leaky face-mask (the Type D) had made short work of the gas available in the aircraft's oxygen bottles. These metal cylinders were very heavy and it was therefore undesirable simply to fit more of them aboard the aircraft to increase the quantity of gas available and increase the time that aircrew could fly at high altitude in safety. The continuous flow of oxygen into the mask passed directly to waste when the wearer was breathing-out, while ambient air was still drawn into the lungs when he was breathing deeply-in. So despite the unregulated flow of oxygen hypoxia remained a problem, curtailing the duration of high level operations.

The RAF's economiser was a fairly simple device. It was fed from the regulator (which passed a relatively low flow of oxygen from the storage bottles) and it consisted of a rubberised fabric bag maintained under pressure by a spring-loaded plate (or bag-crusher). The bag outlet was controlled by a valve, which remained closed either until the pressure of unused oxygen in the bag forced it open, or until there was suction from the mask at the beginning of inspiration. Once the bag outlet valve was open, it stayed open until either the bag was empty or the mask pressure rose again with the start of expiration. Expired air was vented through an expiratory valve in the mask. If the system was turned-on but no one was breathing from it, it puffed oxygen at you, which earned it the nick-name of "Puffing Billy". An advantage was, that if breathing became too shallow for any reason, bag pressure would build up and automatically force open the valve at the outlet of the bag and oxygen would flow to the mask.

Oxygen Mask Improvements

At the same time as the economiser was being developed, a close-fitting moulded rubber mask (the Type E) was designed at the Lab which (unlike the Type D) could be relied upon to create sufficient pressure-drop in the mask on inspiration to open the economiser's valve. Further modifications followed (in the experimental Type F) which were incorporated later in the Type E*. These included: the provision of an inspiratory valve through which air entered the mask after the bag of the economiser was emptied, thus topping-up the oxygen with air; improvement of the mask's suspension from the helmet; and the provision of saliva and condensation drainage (the "gob duct") to counter the tendency of the valve at the inlet of the economiser to ice-up, in the extreme cold of high altitude.

In 1942 production of the Type G began, and this mask differed radically in construction by ducting the oxygen from the inlet to the top of the mask, away from where condensation and saliva collected at the bottom of the mask. The Type G was also smaller, which increased the wearer's field of vision and made it less of a hindrance when moving the head constantly in order to maintain vigilance in the cockpit. This was the mask most commonly used by 16 Squadron in 1944 and 1945. The Type H mask was developed from the Type G in 1943 and went into production in 1944. It was even smaller, had a better face seal, a pair of low resistance expiratory valves and a new smaller, light-weight microphone.

Decompression sickness

Decompression sickness is caused by nitrogen, dissolved in the tissues of the body, coming out of solution as bubbles of gas. Bubbles forming in the tissues around the joints can cause pain which is called "the bends", more usually associated with deep-sea divers. Bubbles of gas in the blood-stream can also block the small blood vessels in the lungs, causing difficulty in breathing, coughing and a choking sensation known as "the chokes". In addition to familiar symptoms of nausea, vomiting and fainting, the Farnborough doctors also identified other alarming problems during experiments in their altitude-simulating pressure chamber. Caused by gas bubbles obstructing blood vessels supplying the brain, they included partial paralysis of a limb and partial (sometime total) blindness. Fortunately decompression sickness is rare at altitudes below 25,000 feet and most symptoms, apart from the visual ones, tend to disappear during descent to that level, but clearly it is most hazardous to aircrew in an unpressurised aircraft operating at high altitude.

The Lab was able to prove that lightly-built, fit young men were less likely to be affected than older, fatter ones and a programme of aircrew testing was initiated in order to select the best candidates for high-flying operations. These were known as "bends runs" and explain why, when 16 Squadron ceased low level Army Co-Operation work in 1943, a number of its pilots were not considered suitable "for medical reasons" for its new photo-reconnaissance rôle.

A valuable method of reducing the occurrence of decompression sickness, which was researched extensively at Farnborough and in the United States, was pre-breathing oxygen sometime before flying at altitudes above 25,000 feet. This lead the RAF Physiological Laboratory to recommend the breathing of 100% oxygen at *low altitude* to reduce the risk of decompression sickness at *high altitude*.

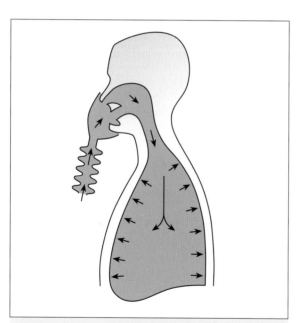

NORMAL BREATHING: where air is drawn into the lungs by the contraction of the inspiratory muscles, which expands the lungs and lowers the pressure within them. Air is driven out of the lungs during expiration by relaxation of the insiratory muscles and the elastic recoil of the lungs.

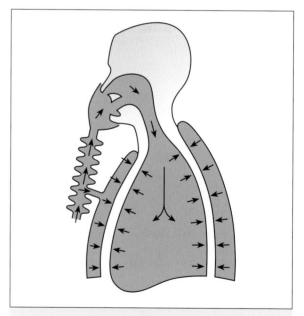

PRESSURE BREATHING: is required to raise the pressure of oxygen in the lung gas at high altitude. Oxygen under pressure is fed to the lungs and to the waistcoat, which applies counterpressure to the chest, thereby preventing overinflation of the lungs and making inspiration easier.

Pressure Breathing

Unfortunately, severe hypoxia will occur above 40,000 feet even when the oxygen is supplied at 100% concentration. The reduced ambient atmospheric pressure (in unpressurised cockpit cabins) simply does not provide sufficient pressure to force enough oxygen into solution in the blood to preserve consciousness. And the obvious answer of increasing the pressure of the oxygen supply risks physical damage to the lungs.

A further complication is that the muscles involved in respiration find themselves working "the wrong way", having to work hard to drive the gas out of the lungs in expiration (rather than working to inflate them for inspiration in the normal way). Respiratory fatigue is the result. A possible solution to this problem, discussed at Farnborough at the end of 1941, was the application of an external counter-pressure of some kind to the chest and abdomen as a substitute for the physical benefits of "normal" atmospheric pressure. It was feared however, that the maximum pressure at which oxygen could be inhaled with external counter-pressure applied, would be determined by the restricting effect which such counter-pressure had upon the return of blood to the heart.

Professor Henry C. Bazett

H.C. Bazett was involved in early aviation medicine during the First World War when he served in the Royal Army Medical Corps and under the Air Board Research Committee (Medical), where he conducted research on altitude hypoxia. Between the wars he became eminent in physiology at Oxford and the University of Pennsylvania, from where he joined what became the Royal Canadian Air Force Institute of Aviation Medicine, Toronto, at the beginning of the Second World War. During 1940 he carried out preliminary work on his own concept of continuous pressure breathing, employing a pressure-sealing oxygen mask and a "pressure waistcoat" to apply counter-pressure to the chest. He worked closely with the team at the Lab, which adopted the Canadian pressure waistcoat which he had developed. Bazett spent several months at Farnborough working with Squadron Leader Harry Roxburgh to adapt the Canadian system to RAF oxygen systems and to develop aircrew training procedures. The Lab was already experimenting with ways to increase the altitude at which aircrews could operate.

Bazett's pressure waistcoat equipment was tested in prototype form by PRU pilots in 1942-43 and went into production in 1944 after successful completion of the trials. 16 Squadron pilots were personally fitted with these garments at Farnborough in August, while they were based at Northolt.

Pressure Breathing Equipment

In 1944 a document on pressure breathing equipment was issued to relevant personnel by the RAF Physiological Laboratory's Flying Personnel

"Bunny" Holden of 16 Squadron at Northolt in 1944 wearing the Bazett pressure waistcoat. In his left hand he is holding his knee-pad, gauntlet-style gloves, Type C flying helmet, and a modified Type H oxygen mask. The small diameter tubing which links the Spitfire's oxygen supply to the waistcoat "T-piece" connector is also visible. His maps are tucked into the tops of his 1943 pattern "escape" boots.

Research Committee. The extracts below summarise clearly the practical outcome at squadron level of the research at Farnborough.

Pressure Breathing Equipment – Instructions for Aircrew*

Summary

a) The purpose of pressure breathing equipment is to provide you with sufficient oxygen to fly safely at altitudes between 35,000 and 45,000 feet without using a pressure cabin or a complete pressure suit. It may also be used as an emergency safety device in case of pressure cabin failure while at high altitudes.

b) Pressure breathing equipment raises your ceiling by keeping the pressure in your mask above the pressure of the surrounding air and thus forcing more oxygen into your lungs.

c) The equipment described here has, in addition to a pressurised mask, an inflatable jacket which is kept at the same pressure as the mask. Besides assisting breathing, this jacket acts as a large reservoir for oxygen and also as a Mae West.

d) The advantages of using this pressure breathing equipment are:

(i) It increases your ceiling by 4,000 feet.

(ii) It prevents the possibility of air entering your mask.

(iii) The sensation of pressure about your body keeps you constantly informed that pure oxygen is flowing to you.

(iv) The large reservoir of oxygen permits you to breathe very deeply without any danger of emptying it.

(v) The jacket is a floatation device which is neat and light.

e) Since you may suffer from "bends" when flying at altitudes requiring pressure breathing, some information is given on the use of oxygen to prevent these pains.

Purpose

Even the use of pure oxygen with an ordinary oxygen mask will not enable you to fly at very high altitudes because the low pressure does not force oxygen into your blood fast enough to keep your body working properly. Therefore, even if you have a perfectly sealed mask, you must have some form of increased pressure about your body in order to fly at extreme altitudes. By using pressure breathing equipment you can increase your ceiling by 4,000 feet without the use of a pressure cabin or a complete pressure suit.

A very air-tight mask will supply you with sufficient oxygen to fly safely as high as 40,000 feet for short periods, if you take no exercise, but slight ascents above this altitude result in serious ill-effects from lack of oxygen, so that at 45,000 feet you will become unconscious in a few minutes. Pressure breathing equipment increases the safety of flying between 35,000 feet and 40,000 feet, and makes possible extended flights at 42,000 feet and shorter flights as high as 45,000 feet. It may also be used as an emergency safety device in case of pressure cabin failure while at high altitude.

Principle

The simplest type of pressure breathing equipment consists of a special mask in which the pressure is kept higher than the pressure of the surrounding atmosphere. Such a mask forces oxygen into the lungs at a higher pressure than the ordinary mask and enables you to go safely to higher altitudes.

Normally you use the muscles of the chest to breathe in, and you simply relax to breathe out. If however extra pressure is applied to the inside of the lungs by using a pressure mask, this normal breathing process is reversed. That is, you just relax to breathe in, but you use the chest muscles to push the breath out. This forcible breathing out, being unnatural, becomes tiring if you employ a very useful amount of pressure in the mask. In order to maintain normal comfortable breathing the equipment used by the RAF has, in addition to a pressurised mask, an inflatable jacket which is kept at the same pressure as the mask. This jacket covers the chest and abdomen making the pressure inside and outside the lungs equal and thus allowing natural breathing to continue. The inflatable compartment of this jacket acts as a large reservoir for oxygen and replaces the economiser. Another inflatable compartment in the jacket is fitted to act as, and to replace, the Mae West.

The Use of Oxygen to Prevent "Bends"

Since pressure breathing equipment gives no protection against "bends", those of you who use it and who therefore fly occasionally at extreme altitudes may suffer at times from "bends" even though you have been selected for high altitude flying by low-pressure chamber test.

The term "bends" refers to the limb pains you may get at high altitude, but does not include the pains in the abdomen which result from the expansion of gas in the intestines. "Bends" are caused by the formation of bubbles from the nitrogen gas which is dissolved in the body.

These pains may be prevented by "washing out" the nitrogen by the breathing of pure oxygen for some time before going to high altitude. This breathing of oxygen can be done on the ground or at altitude. Breathing it at any altitude of up to 20,000 feet is about as useful in preventing "bends" as breathing it at ground level, but above 20,000 feet its value gradually decreases. So, if you wish to get the greatest possible protection from "bends" by breathing pure oxygen while flying, you should stay below 20,000 feet. However, you get some protection by spending time at any altitude below the level at which you get "bends".

For those of you who have been selected for high altitude work by tests in the low-pressure chamber, one hour of oxygen breathing will be sufficient to protect you from any uncomfortable "bends". Unselected men may require longer periods, which can only be found out by experience either in the low-pressure chamber or in the aircraft.

Pressurised Mask

The H-Type mask was specifically modified for use with the pressure waistcoat to make a better seal on the face (the pressurised mask refered to above). In addition the two simple mushroom expiratory valves were replaced by a single large low resistance valve which could be spring-loaded by rotating a control knob by hand. When in operation, the spring-loading raised the pressure at which the expiratory valve opened, thereby raising the pressure in the mask, the waistcoat and the lungs. A three-position knob adjusted the spring-loading of the valve so that it could be used "normally" up to 35,000 feet, at "Low" up to 40,000 feet and "High" above 40,000 feet. The modified mask eventually became the J-Type.

* "Pressure Breathing Equipment – Instructions for Aircrew" A.M. Fraiser. Flying Personnel Research Committee Report No: 628, RAF Physiological Laboratory 1944.

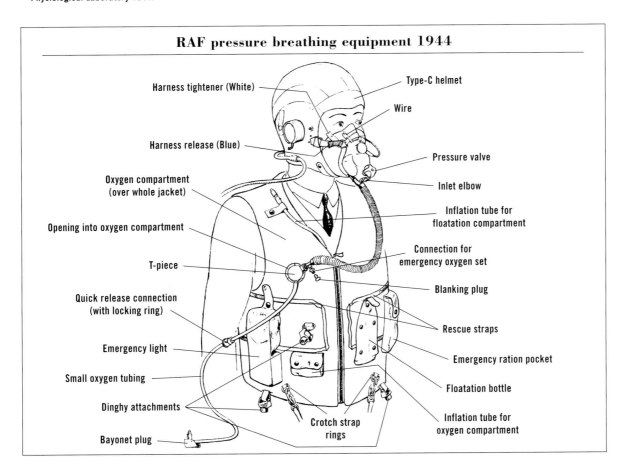

RAF pressure breathing equipment 1944

Harness tightener (White)
Type-C helmet
Wire
Harness release (Blue)
Pressure valve
Oxygen compartment (over whole jacket)
Inlet elbow
Inflation tube for floatation compartment
Opening into oxygen compartment
Connection for emergency oxygen set
T-piece
Blanking plug
Quick release connection (with locking ring)
Rescue straps
Emergency light
Emergency ration pocket
Small oxygen tubing
Floatation bottle
Dinghy attachments
Inflation tube for oxygen compartment
Bayonet plug
Crotch strap rings

Photo-Recce Sorties of PL965

Sources: AIR 26/50 34 Group Operations Record Book (Appendix) and Pilot Log Books

Date	Ops.No.	Pilot	Height	Camera	Duration	Target	Notes	Photos
21.01.45	16/1613	Snell	16,000	20"	–	Mechernich railway yard	–	P
06.02.45	16/1668	Willshaw	–	20"	–	Osnabrück Detmold	Cloud	NP
14.02.45	16/1703	Barker	–	20"	–	Lingen Bremerhaven	Cloud	NP
21.02.45	16/1734	Willshaw	25,000	20"	1540	Vechta-Hoya-Nienburg-Diepholz	–	P
22.02.45	16/1739	Moody	27,000	20"	1115	Lippe Seiten Canal Wesel to Olfen	–	P
22.02.45	16/1752	Cadan	–	20"	1415	Bremen-Papenburg	Engine U/S	NP
02.03.45	16/1798	Wendelken	18,000	20"	–	Dunkirk Calais	–	P
02.03.45	16/1798	Wendelken	2,000	5"	–	–	–	P
13.03.45	16/1828	Burton	–	20"	–	Dortmund Hamm	Cloud	NP
14.03.45	16/1829	Cadan	27,000	20"	1100	Deventer Rheine	–	P
15.03.45	16/1849	Godfrey	26,500	20"	1630	Husum-River Elbe-Bramsche	–	P
18.03.45	16/1859	West	25,000	5"	1245	Utrecht-Zwolle-Apeldoorn	–	P
18.03.45	16/1863	Godfrey	26,000	20"	1630	Zwolle Groningen	–	P
19.03.45	16/1869	Cadan	25,000	20"	0930	Ruhr-Xanten-Wulfen	–	P
21.03.45	16/1891	Bellerby	26,000	20"	0840	Hanover (Hannover)	–	P
21.03.45	16/1891	Bellerby	26,000	5"	–	–	–	P
21.03.45	16/1899	Anderson	27,000	20"	1400	Meppel-Deventer-Amersfoort	–	P
21.03.45	16/1899	Anderson	27,000	5"	–	–	–	P
22.03.45	16/1910	Willshaw	26,000	20"	1100	Hamm-Bielfeld-Paderborn-Detmold	–	P
23.03.45	16/1920	Bowen	24,000	20"	1100	Rheine-Osnabrück-Meppel	–	P
24.03.45	16/1937	West	25,000	20"	1030	Meppel-Oldenburg	–	P
02.04.45	16/1973	Barker	–	20"	–	Lingen-Osnabrück	Cloud	NP
04.04.45	16/1983	Davis	28,000	20"	0830	Zwischenahn-Lemwerden-Bremen	–	P
05.04.45	16/1996	Thompson	–	20"	–	Bremen	Cloud	NP
07.04.45	16/2010	Williams	23,000	20"	1800	Löningen-Rotenburg-Lüneburg	–	P
09.04.45	16/2030	Martin	25,000	20"	1820	Soltau-Ülzen-Wittengen	–	P
10.04.45	16/2040	West	26,000	20"	1554	Ülzen-Wittenburg (Wittenberge?)	–	P
14.04.45	16/2063	Martin	24,500	20"	1815	Fassburg-Bremen-Zwischenaher Lake	–	P
16.04.45	16/2078	Martin	27,500	20"	1815	Hamburg Area	–	P
17.04.45	16/2082	Barker	17/19,000	20"	1145	Hamburg-Lübeck-Parchim-Pritzwalk	–	P
18.04.45	16/2090	Renier	27,500	20"	1810	Kiel	–	P
19.04.45	–	Moody	27,000	20"	–	Hague-Parchim-Perleberg-Woodstok	–	P
23.04.45	16/2106	Renier	26,000	20"	1000	Emden-Denmark A/Fs	–	P
24.04.45	16/2114	Chalk	27,000	20"	1100	Stade-Neumünster-Lübeck	–	P
25.04.45	16/2124	Estaria	26,000	20"	1100	Rendsburg-Kiel	–	P
26.04.45	16/2134	West	20,000	20"	1200	Schwerin-Rechlin	–	P
07.05.45	–	Bellerby	500/5,000	14"	–	Shipping Survey and Copenhagen	–	P
12.05.45	–	Bellerby	–	14"	–	BDA Ijmuiden-The Hague-Amsterdam	–	P
31.05.45	–	Anderson		14"	–	Ruhr-Münster	–	P
31.05.45	–	Cadan	–	14"	–	Low-level obliques	–	P

Spitfires with 16 Squadron in 1945

Code Letter	Serial Number	Dates on 16 Squadron		
A	PL 770	06.05.44 – 11.08.44	&	18.01.44 – 28.06.45
A	PS 835	15.03.45 – 20.09.45	&	01.11.45 – 09.04.46
B	PL 994	13.12.44 – 19.03.45		
B	PS 849	15.03.45 – 20.09.45	&	01.11.45 – 02.05.46
C	PL 922	12.10.44 – 21.12.44	&	02.01.45 – 15.03.45
C	PA 939	05.04.45 – 08.11.45		
C	PS 853	15.03.45 – 20.09.45	&	01.11.45 – 31.03.46
D	PL 839	04.01.45 – 20.09.45		
D	PS 833	21.03.45 – 20.09.45		
E	PL 853	05.10.44 – 14.01.45		
E	PL 970	17.01.45 – 20.08.45		
E	PS 834	22.03.45 – 20.09.45		
F	PL 854	14.09.44 – 24.03.45		
F	PL 826	29.03.45 – 27.07.45		
F	PM 579	17.08.45 – 20.09.45	&	01.11.45 – 09.04.46
G	PL 830	23.07.44 – 26.07.45		
H	PL 892	09.11.44 – 20.09.45		
H	PM 577	29.08.45 – 20.09.45	&	01.11.45 – 18.04.46
J	PL 978	21.12.44 – 21.09.45		
J	PM 580	29.08.45 – 20.09.45	&	01.11.45 – 11.06.46
K	PM 125	11.01.45 – 20.09.45		
L	PL 985	30.11.44 – 20.09.45		
M	PM 123	07.01.45 – 19.03.45		
N	PA 838	03.11.43 – 14.06.45		
N	PA 839	09.08.45 – 20.09.45		
O	PL 823	08.06.44 – 15.07.45		
P	PL 912	28.09.44 – 20.09.45		
R	PL 965	14.01.45 – 22.09.45		
S	PL 964	03.02.45 – 05.08.45		
T	PL 890	18.01.45 – 20.09.45		
V	PM 147	08.03.45 – 20.09.45		
W	PA 949	04.01.45 – 03.08.45		
Y	PM 580	16.10.45 – 20.09.45		
–	MB 903	– . – .44 – 12.10.44	&	02.03.45 – 20.03.45
–	MB 957	12.10.44 – – . – . –		

Movement Details

Movement Card A.M. Form 78 (Facsimile – Original missing) and Data Plate

Type of Aircraft SPITFIRE		Mark P.R. XI.	R.A.F. Number P.L. 965.
Contractor V.A. A.F.	Contract No. 1877 C 23 C	Engine installed :— MERLIN 70 Maker's airframe No. :— 6S 504719	

Unit or Cat'y/Cause	Station or Contractor	Date	Authority	41 or 43 Gp. Allot.
	9.M.U.		2.10.44	
	I.I.P. Benson		5.1.45	
	34 Wing		11.1.45	
	16 SQD		18.1.45	
	151 R.U.		11.10.45	
	HOME CENSUS	MARCH 1946.		
8.7.47	Sold to R.Neth.A.F. B.A.F.O. Serial 2		10.7.47	

A.M. Form 78

The data-plate of PL 965 with its "6S" (Supermarine) prefix, was fixed to the right-hand side of the cockpit interior, just below the top longeron and above the landing-gear selector. Size: about 3 inches (75 mm) long.

Acknowledgements

Published Sources

Aeroplane Monthly (IPC Magazines)

Andrews, C.F. and Morgan, E.B. *Supermarine Aircraft Since 1914* (Putnam 1981)

Babington Smith, C. *Evidence in Camera* (Chatto & Windus 1974)

Bowyer, C. *Supermarine Spitfire* (Bison Books 1981)

Brookes, A.J. *Photo Reconnaissance* (Ian Allan 1975)

Cormack, A. *The Royal Air Force 1939-45* (Men-at-Arms: 225) (Osprey Publishing 1990)

Cotton, F.S. and Barker, R. *Aviator Extraordinary* (Chatto & Windus)

Curtis, L. *The Forgotten Pilots* (Curtis 1982)

Curtis, L. *Forty Years On. A Spitfire Flies Again* (Nelson & Saunders 1985)

FlyPast Magazine (Key Publishing)

Gibson, T.M. and Harrison, M.H. *Into Thin Air. A History of Aviation Medicine in the RAF* (Robert Hale 1984)

Greer, L. and Harold, A. *Flying Clothing* (Air Life 1979)

Henshaw, A. *Sigh For a Merlin* (John Murray 1979)

Jackson, P.A. *Belgian Military Aviation 1945-1977* (Midland Counties 1977)

Jackson, P.A. *Dutch Military Aviation 1945-1978* (Midland Counties 1978)

Lewis, P.L. *The British Fighter Since 1912* (Putnam 1979)

Middlebrook, M. and Everitt, C. *The Bomber Command War Diaries* (Viking 1985)

Morgan, E.B. and Shacklady, E. *Spitfire. The History* (Key 1987)

Nowarra, H. *The Focke Wulf 190. A Famous German Fighter* (Harleyford 1973)

Price, A. *The Spitfire Story* (Janes 1982)

Pyner, A. *Air Cameras RAF & USAAF* (1988)

Quill, J. *Spitfire. A Test Pilot's Story* (John Murray 1983)

RAF Museum *The Spitfire Mk V Manual* (Aston Publications 1976)

Rawlins, J.D.R. *Coastal Support & Special Squadrons* (Janes 1982)

Rawlins, J.D.R. *Fighter Squadrons of the RAF* (Janes 1969)

Riley, G. and Trant, G. *Spitfire Survivors* (Aston Publications 1986)

Robertson, B. *Spitfire. The Story of a Famous Fighter* (Harleyford 1961)

Robertson, B. *Wheels of the RAF* (Patrick Stephens Ltd 1983)

Rouse, W. *Born Again. Spitfire PS 915* (Midland Counties Publications 1989)

Salmaggi, C. and Pallavisini, A. *2194 Days of War* (Windward 1979)

Smallwood, H.R. *2nd TAF Spitfire* (British Aviation Heritage 1985)

Smith, J.R. and Kay, A. *German Aircraft of the Second World War* (Putnam 1972)

Swanborough, G. and Green, W. *The Focke Wulf Fw 190* (Pilot Press 1976)

Taylor, J.W.R. *Combat Aircraft of the World* (Ebury Press & Michael Joseph 1969)

The Jewish Chronicle

van der Meer, H. *Dutch Spitfires* (Airnieuws Nederland 1986)

van der Meer, H. and Hooftman, H. *Spitfires! Nederlandse Vliegtuig Encyclopedie* (Cockpit 1976)

van der Meer, H. and Melchers, T. *Dutch Spitfires. A Technical Study* (Repro Holland bv 1988)

van der Veen, B. *The Observer's Military Vehicles Directory. WW II* (Frederick Warne)

van Ishoven, A. *Messerschmitt – Aircraft Designer* (G.B. 1974)

Unpublished Sources

2 Squadron Operations Record Book (PRO: Air 27/20)

8 OTU Dyce Operations Record Book (PRO: Air 28/235-41)

"16 Squadron History 1915-1990"

16 Squadron Operations Record Book (PRO: Air 27/224 /225)

26 Squadron Operations Record Book (PRO: Air 27/319)

34 Wing Operations Record Book, and Appendices (PRO: Air 26/48, /49, /50)

83 Group Disbandment Unit Operations Record Book (PRO: Air 29/823)

151 Repair Unit Operations Record Book (PRO: Air 29/ 825)

268 Squadron Operations Record Book (PRO: Air 27/1564)

412 Repair Unit Operations Record Book (PRO: Air 29/810)

1697 A.D.L.S. Flight (Communications Flight 2nd TAF) **Operations Record Book** (PRO: Air 29/637)

"A Brief History of No.16 Squadron RAF"

A.D.L.S. Squadron SHAEF Operations Record Book (PRO: Air 27/2347)

Air Publications (RAF Museum archive – various APs, on Spitfire Airframes, Air Cameras, Oxygen Equipment)

Aircraft Movement Cards, (Form 78) (RAF Museum archive)

Gibson, T.M. and Harrison, M.H. *"British Aviation Medicine During the Second World War — Part 1"* (IAM Report N0.594), (RAF Museum)

RAF Benson (PRO:Air 28/61) *"Thirty Four Wing an Unofficial Account"* **Rigby, Major H.** (via ex-RAF Aircrew)

Vickers-Supermarine Drawings (RAF Museum archive)

Institutions

1 Wing, Belgische Luchtmacht, Bevekom, Belgium

16 Squadron Association, England

16 (R) Squadron, RAF Lossiemouth, Scotland

Air Historical Branch of the MoD, London, England

Air Photo Library, University of Keele, England

Aviodome Museum, Schiphol, Netherlands

Bureau Central d'Incorporation et d'Archives de l'Armée de l'Air, Chartres Cedex, France

Cambridge University Library (Vickers Collection), England

Commonwealth War Graves Commission, Maidenhead, England

Department of Defence Discharged Personnel Records, Canberra, Australia

Imperial War Museum, Lambeth, London, England

Ministry of Defence RAF Personnel Management Centre, Innsbrook, England

Public Records Office, Kew, London, England

Quadrant Picture Library, Sutton, England

RAE Farnborough, Hampshire, England

RAF Battle of Britain Memorial Flight, Coningsby, England

RAF Museum Department of Research and Information Services, Hendon, England

RAF Museum Reprographic Services, Hendon, England

Rolls-Royce Heritage Trust, Derby, England

SEPEG International Defence Media, Bruxelles, Belgium

Spitfire Pilots Club, Belgium

The Returned Services League of Australia, Canberra, Australia

The Spitfire Association, Australia

Individuals – Technical/Historical

Arnold, P.R.
Cordery, J.V.
Curtis, E.L.
Deal, L.
Ernsting, J.
Farrel, K.
Gunston, C.P.
Hague, S.P.
Kenton, M.J.
Lamboit, P.
Lecomte, G.
Melchers, T.
Mulelly, I.S.
Nicholls, Dr. M.
Pyner, A.
Soupart, R.
Scrope, H.
Thomas, A.
Trant, G.
Van Der Meer, H.
van den Briel, J
Walton, S.
Welburn, J.P.

16 (R) Squadron

Boyd, F/Lt.
Formoso, F/Lt.

Individuals – Rolls-Royce

Birch, D.
Evans, M.H.

Individuals – Witnesses

Abrahams, R.
Anderson, W.C.
Bellerby, G.
Bertram
Bladt, R.
Bowen, P.
Cadan, L.L.
Curtis, E.L.
Davis, P.
Dutt, E.R.
Efford, F.H.C.
Forrester, R.A.
Godfrey, E.N.
Goodale, E.M.
Grace, E.N.
Greville-Heygate, D.
Hanna, M.
Holden, A.P.G.
Holloway, K.
Horsfall, J.M.C.
Horsley, C.P.
Long, A.
Lousada, C.R.
Pallot, A.G.
Parisse, J.
Parnell, H.R.
Petrie, D.
Prévot, L.
Puttick, G.
Quested, E.
Quill, J.
Rosenburg, H.
Sampson, D.W.
Stutchbury, D.
Taylor, H.J.S.
Thomson, J.M.
Wendelken, W.J.
Wetz, M.A.
Williams, D.J.

Glossary

2nd TAF – Second Tactical Air Force, formed June 1st 1943 to be the British contingent of the Allied Expeditionary Air Force during the invasion of Europe.

AA – Anti-Aircraft guns or gunfire.

A/C or **a/c** – Aircraft.

A/F or **a/f** – Airfield.

AC1 – Aircraftsman grade 1.

AC2 – Aircraftsman grade 2.

ADLS – Air Dispatch Letter Service.

ADGB – Air Defence Great Britain, preceded (1925-1936) Fighter Command in defence of UK and the name to which Fighter Command reverted (1943-1944) on the formation of 2nd TAF.

ADU – Aircraft Delivery Unit.

AE – Air Efficiency award.

AEAF – Allied Expeditionary Air Force, formed November 15th 1943 to have overall control of all Allied offensive air forces associated with the invasion of Europe eg, ADGB, 2nd TAF, IXth USAF and (temporarily) Bomber Command and USSTAF VIIIth and 15th Air Forces.

AFC – Air Force Cross.

AFTS – Advanced Flying Training School.

AFU – Advanced Flying Unit.

AGS – Air Gunnery School.

AID – Aeronautical Inspection Directorate.

Anti-Rhubarbs – defensive action against small scale air attacks.

Anti-Diver – operation (usually a patrol) against V-1 flying bombs.

AOP – Air Observation Post.

Ardennes Offensive – German counter-attack between December 16th 1944 and January 20th 1945 in the region of St Vith and Bastogne, also known as the Battle of the Bulge.

Army Co-Op – Army Co-Operation Command or Squadron.

Arnhem – the Allied airborne assault on bridges in the Arnhem area of Holland, launched on September 17th 1944.

ASI – Air Speed Indicator.

ASR – Air Sea Rescue.

ATA – Air Transport Auxiliary.

AVM – Air Vice Marshal.

AW – standard prefix to the type number of aircraft manufactured by Armstrong Whitworth eg, AW FK8.

BAFO – British Air Forces of Occupation, replaced 2nd TAF on July 15th 1945.

BE – Bomber Experimental, prefix to the type number of an aircraft manufactured by the Royal Aircraft Factory eg, BE2e.

Bf – standard prefix to the type number of aircraft designed by *Bayerische Flugzeugwerke* eg, Bf 109.

BFTS – Basic Flying Training School.

BFTS – British Flying Training School.

BFW – *Bayerische Flugzeugwerke*, the company from which *Messerschmitt AG* was formed in 1938.

bhp – brake horse-power.

Biff – nickname of the Bristol FB2 fighter of the First World War (also "Brisfit").

Blighty – serviceman's name for Great Britain.

Bodenplatte – *Luftwaffe* attack against Allied airfields, January 1st 1945.

Boost – see Appendix III.

Browned-off – bored and disenchanted.

Brown jobs – soldiers.

CAT.A – repairable on site (Cat. = Category).

CAT.A/C – repair beyond the unit's own capacity (but may be repaired on site by another unit or contractor).

CAT.B – repairable at an MU or contractors works).

CAT.E – a write-off

CB – Companion of the Bath.

CFS – Central Flying School.

CO – Commanding Officer.

Cpl – Corporal.

CT – Chief Technician

Croix de Guerre – French and Belgian gallantry decoration.

D-Day – June 6th 1944, when the Allies invaded German-occupied Europe.

De-mobbed – de-mobilised from the forces at the end of the war.

DFC – Distinguished Flying Cross.

DI – Daily Inspection.

Dicer – low level reconnaissance operation ("dicing with death").

Dispersal – an area designated for parking aircraft, usually widely spaced or camouflaged to make air/ground attack more difficult.

Doodle-bug – Fieseler Fi 103 pulse-jet flying bomb, also known as the V-1, with a maximum operational speed of 645 km per hour (400 mph) and an 850 kg (1,870 lb) warhead.

DR – Dead Reckoning, navigational position arrived at by compass course and elapsed time.

Dzus clip – quick-release fastener for removable inspection panels on an airframe.

E/A or **e/a** – enemy aircraft.

EFTS – Elementary Flying Training School.

Eindecker – monoplane eg, Fokker E.III *Eindecker*.

Erks – non-flying airmen.

ETA – Estimated Time of Arrival.

F – Fighter, eg Spitfire F IX.

(F) – Fighter, eg 111 (F) Squadron.

F/Lt – Flight Lieutenant.

F/O – Flying Officer.

F/Sgt – Flight Sergeant.

Feldgrau – German field-grey uniform colour.

Fitter IIA – more practically and technically qualified airframe tradesman.

FK – standard prefix to the type number of aircraft designed by Frederick Koolhoven eg, AW (Armstrong Whitworth) FK8.

Flak – German anti-aircraft guns or gunfire, from *Flieger Abwehr Kanone*.

FM(A) – Flight Mechanic (Airframes), sometimes called a "rigger".

FM(E) – Flight Mechanic (Engines), sometimes called a "fitter".

Form 78 – Air Ministry record of an aircraft's movements from unit to unit.

Form 541 – Air Ministry record sheet of individual sorties by aircraft (as part of the ORB).

Form 540 – Air Ministry monthly record sheet summarising daily operations of an RAF unit (as part of the ORB).

Form 700 – Air Ministry form signed by all relevant tradesmen confirming an aircraft is fully serviceable.

FR – Fighter Reconnaissance (armed aircraft).

ft – feet.

FT & ADU – Ferry Training and Aircraft Delivery Unit.

Fw – standard prefix to the type number of aircraft manufactured by *Focke-Wulf Flugzeugbau GmbH* eg, Fw 190.

g – technically, the acceleration of gravity, but usually used to denote how many times more (or less) than the normal force of gravity a pilot or aircraft is being subjected to during a manoeuvre eg, +4g (or -4g).

G/Cpt – Group Captain.

Glycol – engine coolant.

Gremlins – apocryphal creatures held to be responsible for inexplicable mechanical problems with aircraft.

GSU – Group Support Unit.

Gunk – proprietary de-greasing agent.

Homing – course to steer for home supplied by base controller.

In clear – uncoded RT transmission.

Interdiction – offensive sorties against communication targets such as road, rail and canal.

IP & IP – Initial Preparation and Installation Photographic.

JVS – *Jagchtvlieg School* (Fighter Flight School).

Kenway – an RAF ground control radio station in Belgium.

kg – kilogram.

KLu – *Koninklijke Luchtmacht*, the Dutch Royal Air Force, independent successor to the LSK.

LAC – Leading Aircraftsman.

Lagoons – shipping reconnaissance.

lb – pounds (weight).

LES – *Luchtmacht Elektronische School* (Air Force Electronics School).

LETS – *Luchtmacht Elektronische en Technische School* (Air Force Electronics and Technical School).

LF – Low Fighter, or aircraft optimised for operations at low and medium level eg, Spitfire LF IX.

Link Trainer – flight simulator for instrument-flying practice.

LSK – *Luchtstrijdkrachten*, the air combat force of the Dutch army, which became the independent KLu in 1953.

LTS – *Luchtmacht Technische School* (Air Force Technical School).

Luftwaffe – German air force.

Mae West – generic term for aircrew life-jackets (flotation) in honour of the vital statistics of the Hollywood actress.

Malcolm Club – social club for RAF servicemen.

Market Garden – the Allied airborne assault on canal and river bridges in the Arnhem area of Holland, launched on September 17th 1944.

Mayday – international distress call, from the French *m'aider*, or "help me".

MAPSL – Medway Aircraft Preservation Society Ltd.

MBE – Member of the British Empire.

Me – standard prefix to the type number of aircraft designed by *Messerschmitt AG* eg, Me 262.

MET or **Met** – Meteorology, Meteorologist or weather.

mm – millimetre(s).

mph – miles per hour.

MU – Maintenance Unit.

Mulberry – floating harbours of concrete towed to the invasion beaches of Normandy in June 1944.

NAAFI – Navy, Army and Air Force Institute which provided canteen facilities to the troops.

NCO – Non-Commissioned Officer.

OC – Officer Commanding.

OCTU – Officer Cadet Training Unit.

OCU – Operational Conversion Unit.

Oppo – friend, colleague or work-mate.

ORB – Operations Record Book consisting of daily summary of operations of an RAF unit with appendices.

OTU – Operational Training Unit.

P/O – Pilot Officer.

Penman – 34 Wing ground control radio station.

Peri-track – Perimeter track around the edge of an airfield.

PI – Photographic Interpretation.

Piece of cake – something very easy to accomplish.

Populars – photographic reconnaissance of the French coast.

PoW – Prisoner of War.

PR – Photo(graphic)-Reconnaissance.

PRU – the Photo-Reconnaissance Unit, RAF Benson.

psi – pounds per square inch.

Quaker – sometime 16 Squadron aircraft callsign, eg "Quaker 29".

Queen Mary – low-loader truck for transporting aircraft.

(R) – Reserve, eg 16 (R) Squadron.

RAAF – Royal Australian Air Force.

RAE – Royal Aircraft Establishment.

RaeS – Royal Aeronautical Society.

RAF – Royal Air Force.

RCAF – Royal Canadian Air Force.

RE – Reconnaissance Experimental, prefix to the type number of an aircraft manufactured by the Royal Aircraft Factory eg, RE8.

Red tape – obstructive bureaucracy or paperwork.

RFC – Royal Flying Corps.

Rhubarbs – small-scale offensive sorties against targets of opportunity.

RNZAF – Royal New Zealand Air Force.

RP – Rocket Projectile.

rpm – revolutions per minute.

RT – Radio-Telephone.

RU – Repair Unit.

SAC – Senior Aircraftsman.

Salvation Army – Christian charity run on military lines which looks after the physical and spiritual welfare of the poorest people and in wartime also the troops.

SE – Servicing Echelon.

SFTS – Service Flying Training School.

Sgt – Sergeant.

S/Ldr – Squadron Leader.

SHAEF – Supreme Headquarters Allied Expeditionary Force.

Shaky do – extremely hazardous occurrence.

Snags – faults found with an aircraft or its systems while testing or flying it.

Square-bashing – military drill practice.

SU Carburettor – a make of carburettor.

Tac.R – Tactical Reconnaissance.

Tannoy – a loudspeaker for public address.

TMPFFGH – a pilot's acronym for take-off checks: Throttle; Mixture; Propeller pitch control; Fuel; Flaps; Gyros; Horizon (or Hydraulics) – variable to suit different aircraft types and personal requirements.

TOI – *Technische Opleidings Inrichting* (Technical Training Establishment).

Trolley-acc – electrical ground support unit consisting of accumulators charged-up by a small petrol-engine generator.

Type – as in "RAF type" or "PR type", means a typical sort of chap.

u/s – unserviceable.

Uffz – *Unteroffizier*, equivalent to RAF rank of Corporal.

USAAF – United States Army Air Force, which preceded the independent USAF (United States Air Force formed in 1947).

USSTAF – United States Strategic Air Forces.

V-1 – German Fieseler Fi 103 pulse-jet flying bomb, also known as the Doodle-bug, with a maximum operational speed of 645 km per hour (400 mph) and an 850 kg (1,870 lb) warhead.

V-2 – German rocket-propelled missile, also known as the A4, with impact velocity of 2,900 km/hour (1,800 mph) and a 975 kg (2,145 lb) warhead.

Vickers – Vickers Ltd, a financial holding company, the main subsidiary of which was Vickers-Armstrongs Ltd.

Vickers-Armstrongs – Vickers-Armstrongs Ltd, which acquired two subsidiaries in 1938, Vickers Aviation Ltd and The Supermarine Aviation Works (Vickers) Ltd which became Vickers-Armstrongs Ltd Aircraft Section (Weybridge Division) and (Supermarine Division) respectively.

Viz – visibility.

W/O – Warrant Officer.

Wingco – Wing Commander.

WSU – Wing Support Unit.

WWI – World War One.

WWII – World War Two.

Markings for Spitfire PR Mark XI of 16 Squadron 2nd TAF, Belgium and Holland 1945

Upper and lower surfaces painted uniformly matt PR Blue. Propeller spinner matt Black.

Wing roundel as applied to 2nd TAF Spitfires after January 3rd 1945, until close of hostilities. Source: PRO Document Air 2/8029: 2nd TAF order issued January 3rd 1945: "**All roundels red, white blue, yellow (type 3, DTD 360 C.1. type roundel).**" Confirmed by Air Ministry directive January 7th 1945.

Dimensions: interpolated from photographic evidence from fighter, fighter-reconnaissance and photo-reconnaissance squadrons including *pictures of PR Spitfires of 16 Squadron, Eindhoven May 1945*:

Wing roundels: upper surface only, no roundels on lower surface.
Diameters:
Red (dull brick red) – 22 inches
White – 28 inches
Blue (dark dull blue) – 52 inches
Yellow – 56 inches

Fuselage roundels (Normal day fighter style):
Diameters:
Red (dull brick red) – 12 inches
White – 16 inches
Blue (dark dull blue) – 32 inches
Yellow – 36 inches

Identification letter:
on fuselage side, 12 inches aft of roundel, was white. Dimensions: 17 inches by 10 inches.

Serial numbers:
were 4 inches high, in white.

Tail flashes:
12 inches square.
Dimensions of stripes:
Red (dull brick red) – 12 inches by 5 inches
White – 12 inches by 2 inches
Blue (dark dull blue) – 12 inches by 5 inches

Under the nose: behind the spinner was this 8 inch by 5 inch white identification letter.

NB: No invasion stripes were carried in 1945.

For colour reference see *"British Aviation Colours of World War Two"* (Arms and Armour Press 1976).

Key: Red ▧ White ☐ Blue ■ Yellow ☐ PR Blue ▨

Spitfire PR Mark XI Side Elevations and Details

Early production PR Mark XI a/c and converted Mark IX a/c were fitted with standard Mark IX rudder as shown below. Eg, serial range EN652-EN685. Rudders and elevators are fabric-covered, light alloy frames.

Rudder trimming tab. Actuating rod and fairing starboard side only.

White light.

Broad chord pointed rudder, fabric covered, as fitted to all late production PR Mark XI a/c. Fabric stitching is sealed off by tape.

Front view of canopy with blisters for improved downward view (Ref. dwg. 36530 SHT. 5G.)

Access hatch to radio equipment and rear fuselage. Radio type TR1133 or TR1143.

Access hatch to rear vertical camera.

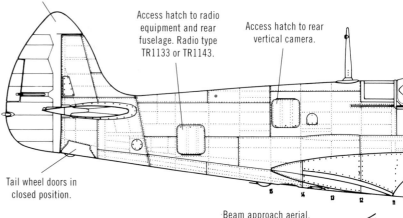

Tail wheel doors in closed position.

F24 cameras could be fitted with 5, 8, 14 and 20-inch lenses. Postwar, a 3¼-inch extra wide angle lens was also introduced.

Universal camera installation: Standard high-altitude camera installation in rear fuselage was a pair of F52 cameras fitted with 36-inch lenses, mounted in tandem between frame 13 and 15. (see section B.)

Beam approach aerial.

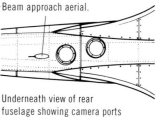

Underneath view of rear fuselage showing camera ports fitted with optical flat glass, for high level photography.

Williamson type F24 aerial camera fitted with 5-inch wide angle lens and type A magazine for 140mm wide air film, allowing 125 exposures. The type C magazine for 250 exp. could also be fitted. Cameras were driven by a 12 or 24 volt electric motor, via a flexible drive to the type E of F gearbox on top of the camera body. Cameras were operated from the cockpit using a type 35 control box on the upper instrument panel and a selector unit situated in the lower port cockpit area. (Camera not drawn to scale with other aircraft parts on this page)

Four-blade Rotol airscrew. Type R12/4F5/4 with Hydulignum blades.

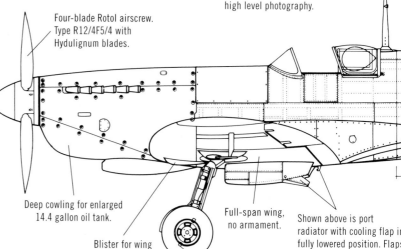

Deep cowling for enlarged 14.4 gallon oil tank.

Blister for wing fuel tank booster pump.

Full-span wing, no armament.

Creep marks.

Shown above is port radiator with cooling flap in fully lowered position. Flaps were operated automatically depending on engine temperature. Fitted aft of radiator, is hook, one per wing, to swing slipper tank clear of a/c after jettisoning.

General specifications Supermarine Type No. 365:

Overall length: 31' 4.5" (9563 mm)
Wingspan: 36' 10" (11227 mm)
Height: 12' 7.75" (3854 mm)
Power unit: Roll-Royce Merlin 61, 63 63A, 70

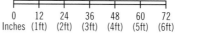

```
0    12   24   36   48   60   72
Inches (1ft) (2ft) (3ft) (4ft) (5ft) (6ft)
```

R.A.F. colour Scheme: Overall PRU Blue, (titanine cellulose lacquer); 40-inch dia. Type B upper wing roundels, 30-inch dia. Type B fuselage roundels, no underwing roundels. Serial no, 4-inch high, red or grey. Squadron markings, if applied, 24-inches high, 16-inches wide. (Ref. dwg. 36564 SHT.14C. 22.2.43) *(NB: For 1945 markings, see page 149)*

Note: Combined heater and filter attachments were fitted to the front of the lenses and electrically heated muffs were fitted to protect the magazine when adequate hot air heating from radiators was not available. A heated electrical sleeve could also be fitted to 14, 20 and 36-inch cones.

Section A below shows alternative "G" type camera installation. Oblique F24 8-inch or F24 14-inch camera. Forward, vertical F24 5-inch and aft, vertical F24 14-inch camera. Type 25 mountings. Section B, shows universal camera installation. Two F52 36-inch cameras in type 38 mounting, each offset 5° 20' to vertical.

PR Mark XI a/c were fitted with the standard Mark IX bubble canopy, or a flat-sided canopy with blisters on both sides.

One piece curved, perspex windscreen.

Fairing on all late production PR Mark XI a/c.

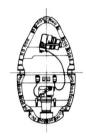 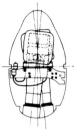

Section A.   Section B.
Views on frame 13, looking aft.

Underwing blister for oblique F24 camera with 5-inch lens, fitted to both wings, on some PR Mark XI a/c in RAF service. Blisters were 'handed', and often varied in shape and size.

Some PR Mark XI a/c had a F24 8-inch camera in a forward facing blister, under each wing.

Electric motor   F24 5-inch camera

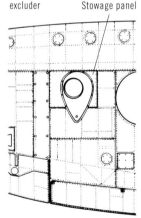

Forward view of blister fairing as fitted to PL 965. Flat glass camera port, diameter 215 mm. Draught excluder and mud flap not fitted.

Draught excluder   Stowage panel

Retractable tail wheel fitted to late production a/c.

Side view of late production PR Mark XI showing, aft of cockpit, camera port in access door fitted with optical flat glass, for oblique camera mounting. Door also offered access to forward vertical camera. Also shown is position of 18-inch (475 mm) invasion stripes.

Front and side view of 30 gallon slipper tank. 45 and 90 gallon slipper tanks could also be attached to PR Mark XI a/c.

 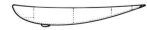

Note: Camera ports in lower fuselage and in underwing blisters were fitted with draught excluders and mud-flap release controls operated manually, from cockpit, after take-off.

Underneath and forward view of the starboard wing showing standard blister-fairing fitted to most PR Mark XI a/c. F24 5-inch camera was mounted in a modified type 45 mounting, offset 10° to wing centre-line. Blister attached to forward hinging stowage panel. (Ref. Supermarine drawing 36564 SHT 25G and dwg. 36564 107-8H.)

Index

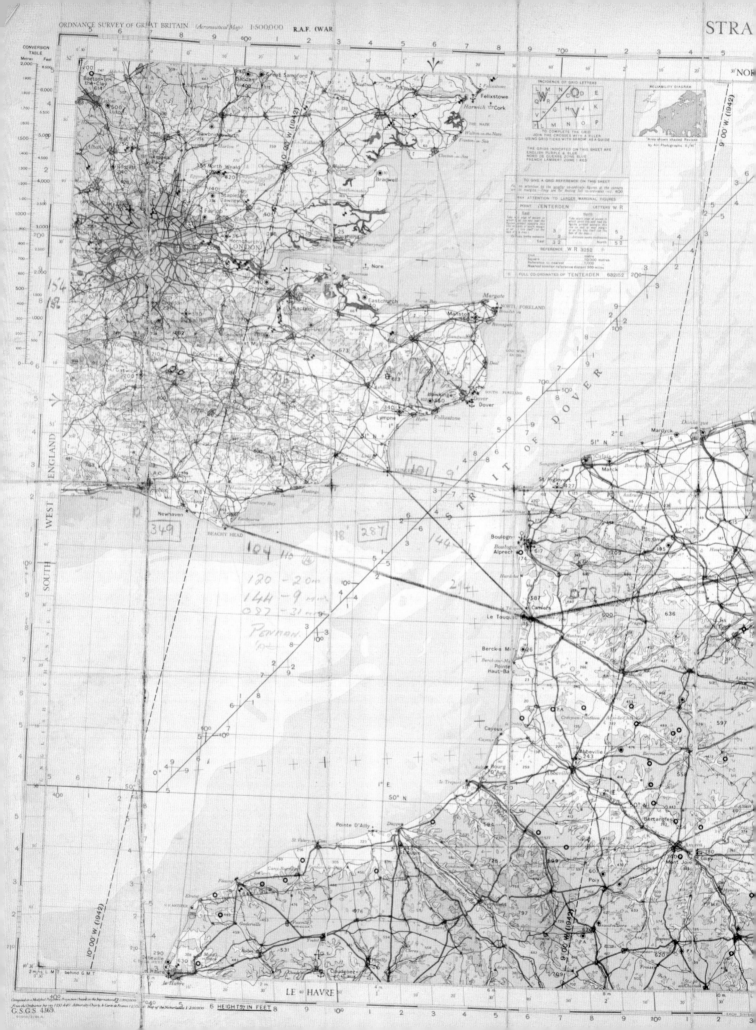

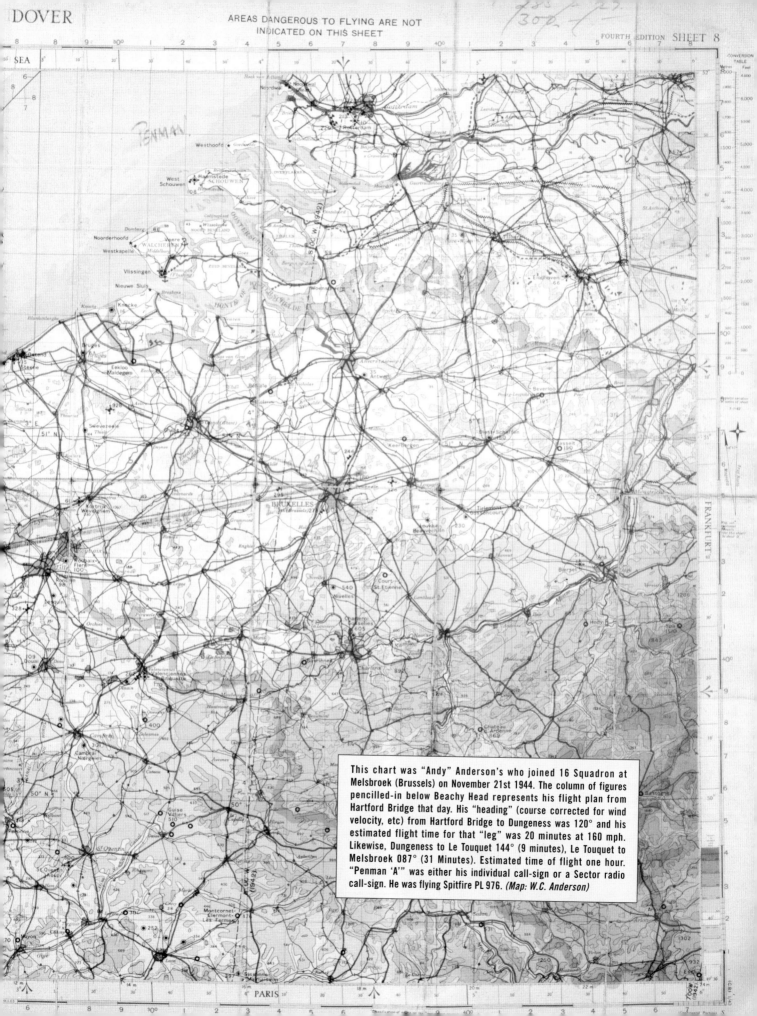

This chart was "Andy" Anderson's who joined 16 Squadron at Melsbroek (Brussels) on November 21st 1944. The column of figures pencilled-in below Beachy Head represents his flight plan from Hartford Bridge that day. His "heading" (course corrected for wind velocity, etc) from Hartford Bridge to Dungeness was 120° and his estimated flight time for that "leg" was 20 minutes at 160 mph. Likewise, Dungeness to Le Touquet 144° (9 minutes), Le Touquet to Melsbroek 087° (31 Minutes). Estimated time of flight one hour. "Penman 'A'" was either his individual call-sign or a Sector radio call-sign. He was flying Spitfire PL 976. (Map: W.C. Anderson)

"For you the war is over" – well, not quite. Amiens-Glisy, September 1944, F/Lt Derek Wales, F/O Jimmy Taylor, P/O Jerry Winter and F/Lt "Tommy" Thompson "capture" F/O Peter Fahy and keep him covered with their Smith & Wesson revolvers. *(Photo: H.J.S. Taylor)*